P9-CRI-280

Plate VIII

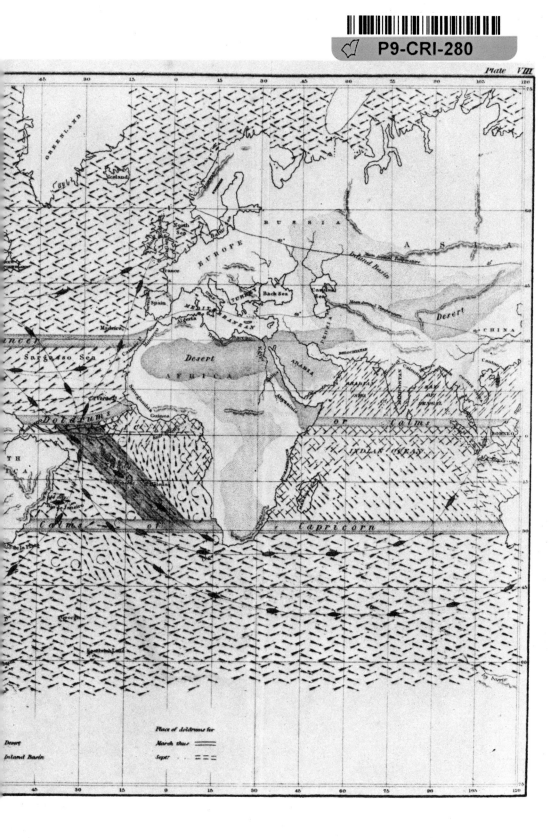

T H E
Challenge

BOOKS BY A.B.C. WHIPPLE

Yankee Whalers in the South Seas
Pirate: Rascals of the Spanish Main
Tall Ships and Great Captains
Tha Fatal Gift of Beauty: The Final Years of Byron and Shelley
Vintage Nantucket

WITH THE EDITORS OF TIME/LIFE BOOKS

Fighting Sail
The Whalers
The Clipper Ships
The Racing Yachts
The Mediterranean
Storm
Restless Oceans

FOR YOUNG READERS

Famous Pirates of the New World
Hero of Trafalgar
The Mysterious Voyage of Captain Kidd

T H E
Challenge

A.B.C. WHIPPLE

WILLIAM MORROW AND COMPANY, INC.
New York

Copyright © 1987 by A.B.C. Whipple

Lines from "So Handy" and "Mainsail Haul" from *Songs of the Sailor and Lumberman,* by William M. Doerflinger, used by permission of the author. © 1951, 1972 by William M. Doerflinger.

All rights reserved. No part of this book may be reproduced or utilized in any form or by any means, electronic or mechanical, including photocopying, recording or by any information storage and retrieval system, without permission in writing from the Publisher. Inquiries should be addressed to Permissions Department, William Morrow and Company, Inc., 105 Madison Ave., New York, N.Y. 10016.

Library of Congress Cataloging-in-Publication Data

Whipple, A.B.C. (Addison Beecher Colvin), 1918–
The Challenge.
Bibliography: p.
Includes index.
1. Voyages to the Pacific Coast.   2. Challenge
(Clipper)   3. Clipper-ships—United States—History—
19th century.   I. Title.
F865.W565   1987   910.4′5   87-1583
ISBN 0-688-07112-0

Printed in the United States of America

First Edition

1 2 3 4 5 6 7 8 9 10

BOOK DESIGN BY BERNARD SCHLEIFER

Author's Note

A CLOUD OF CONTENTION has hung over the maiden voyage of the clipper ship *Challenge* for more than a hundred years. Her logbook has disappeared. Her crew was charged with mutiny and her captain and mate were tried for murder; but the court records also are lost. Waterfront rumor branded Captain Robert Waterman as a sadistic bully; he barely escaped a San Francisco lynch mob. The major maritime historians have tended to blame the *Challenge*'s tragic voyage on a mutinous crew, and have defended Robert Waterman as a captain forced to inflict harsh discipline in order to save his ship.

Meanwhile the details of the voyage lay hidden in the microfilmed issues of three San Francisco newspapers whose court reporters had covered the trials of the captain, mate, and crew after the *Challenge*'s arrival from New York in the autumn of 1851. Two historians who found this newspaper coverage reported some of the details in books that have long since gone out of print. (See Bibliography.)

For nearly a decade I have been researching and writing about the *Challenge*'s controversial voyage and the dramatic period of the American clipper ship that the voyage highlighted. Now, after a more thorough study of those newspapers, of all

Author's Note

the contemporary accounts of the voyage and of the men involved, I have finally been able to piece together the full story of the contest of will and strength aboard that giant clipper ship thundering around Cape Horn—as well as the elements of the glamorous but brutal clipper ship era that led to the inevitable tragedy.

—A.B.C. Whipple

Old Greenwich, Connecticut
1986

Contents

AUTHOR'S NOTE   7

PROLOGUE   13

1. A Radical New Ship Design   23

2. The Cape Horn Sweepstakes   39

3. A Challenge to the *Challenge*   61

4. Tracking the World's Winds   85

5. A Special Breed of Captain   97

6. Trouble in the Forecastle   115

7. *Challenge* vs. *Flying Cloud* I   139

8. *Challenge* vs. *Flying Cloud* II   173

9. Chase, Riot, and a "Waterfront Jury"   191

10. Aftermath   219

11. Survivors   233

CHAPTER NOTES   255

SOURCE NOTES   287

ACKNOWLEDGMENTS   293

BIBLIOGRAPHY   295

INDEX   313

Never in these United States
has the brain of man conceived,
or the hand of man fashioned
so perfect a thing as the
clipper ship.
 —SAMUEL ELIOT MORISON

Prologue

On November 1, 1851, a mob of men stormed up from San Francisco's waterfront, along California Street to the Alsop Building. Many of them were drunk. Some brandished knives; others carried rocks and bricks. One man was swinging a rope with a hangman's noose. Nearly everyone was bellowing. And above the din the men in the Alsop Building could make out shouts of "WATERMAN!" and "MURDERER!"

Charles Griswold, the San Francisco agent for the shipping firm of N. L. & G. Griswold, looked out at the swirling tide of angry faces and turned back to confer with his two clipper captains, John Land and the object of the crowd's wrath, Robert H. Waterman. A window smashed and a brick thudded onto the office floor. Someone started beating on the heavy wooden door. Griswold hastily ordered Captain Waterman to make his escape, and turned to the door to confront the mob. Retreating up the office stairway to search out an ignominious hiding place, Captain Robert Waterman must understandably have wondered how it all had come to this.

The ugly scene on San Francisco's California Street in the autumn of 1851 was a flash point at the end of one of the most dramatic and desperate voyages in the era of the American clipper ship. The voyage and its aftermath epitomized a paradox of midnineteenth-century America. A vibrant, booming young nation, invigorated and united by the Gold Rush and dominating the maritime world, was symbolized by the glorious crea-

13

tion of the clipper ship. Yet beneath the clipper's ethereal white clouds of canvas lay a dark underside of that maritime world, in which derelicts of humanity labored like slaves under the harsh discipline of frustrated skippers and mates. Indeed, in part because of this conflict, the clipper ship itself, the ultimate evolution of the sailing ship,[1] forecast the inevitable decline of American supremacy at sea.

The American clipper ship was a classic example of the aesthetics of utility. For all its graceful majesty, the clipper ship was a freighter—an express freighter but a freighter nonetheless. While her designer and her admirers may have been pleased by her handsome appearance, her prime function was speed. Her beauty was serendipitous; it simply happened that the shape that moved fastest through the water was streamlined and attractive and that the spread of canvas required to move her was a breathtaking expanse of white. But the clipper ship was not just larger, taller, and more beautiful than its predecessors. It also was a new species in the evolution of the sailing vessel, the result of a remarkable convergence of men and circumstances. An urgent demand for speed at sea occurred at the same time that a few brilliant ship designers were eager to create a breakthrough in marine architecture; simultaneously a clan of perceptive shipping merchants persuaded themselves to gamble on a daring new concept; a few shipbuilders were ready to mold the designers' dreams into reality; a band of skilled captains was prepared to drive the new vessels through the oceans' wildest storms at unheard-of speeds; and independently, an ingenious navigator mapped new ocean pathways around the world.

The timing was important. An American preoccupation with speed at sea, originally fostered by smugglers and privateers, was stimulated by a growing market for perishable tea that had to be brought halfway around the world from China. And just when the fast clippers had been perfected, a new impetus came with the discovery of gold in California. The sailing vessel that rose to this challenge had its own unique specifications: a sharp, concave bow; a long, narrow hull; and a towering press of sail. Many sailing vessels were called clippers but were not. During the decade from 1845 to 1855 that has been called the clipper ship era, some 250,000 sailing ships were built in the United

States; not more than three hundred of them were true clipper ships. Even the "Baltimore clippers" that were their progenitors did not have the sharp lines nor the tall masts of the actual clipper ships.[2] Clipper ship builders not only designated them as a particular class of vessel but also gave them names that bespoke their new character. Ordinarily merchantmen were called *Eliza, Commerce, Boston,* and *Pacific.* Clipper owners bragged about their vessels with such names as *Challenge, Peerless, Invincible,* and *Sovereign of the Seas,* or called attention to their fleetness with *Stag Hound, Lightning, Shooting Star, Sweepstakes,* and *Winged Racer;* many of them were fliers: *Eagle, Frigate Bird, Flying Arrow, Flying Cloud, Flying Dragon, Flying Fish,* and even *Flying Scud.*

The clipper ship also was an evocation of an American spirit at the middle of the nineteenth century. After more than two hundred years of colonial struggle and debilitating wars, the twenty-nine United States of America were finally enjoying a prosperity surpassing anything known by their twenty-three million people—or, for that matter, by any people anywhere. With much of the world swept by revolution and counterrevolution, America by contrast was on a clearly posted road to growth and progress. The nation was expanding at an unprecedented rate, its population nearly doubling every two decades, its farms serving as the granary of Europe, its cotton supplying Britain's industrial revolution, its manufactured products attracting global markets. New York had become America's maritime center, handling five times the freight of all the New England cities. New York was the funnel through which most of the nation's production flowed. The cargoes were transshipped by transatlantic packets to Europe, by coastal traders to South America, and by ever faster merchantmen to Asia; these vessels returned with textiles from Britain, coffee and sugar from South America, and tea from China.

America was in a state of exuberant adolescence. The nation itself was still so young that many of its inhabitants were older than the republic. Despite a massive immigration—nearly three million in the decade of 1845 to 1853—nine out of ten Americans were native-born, and their raw pride took a boisterous form. Philip Hone, mayor of New York from 1826 to 1827, commented in his diary in 1850, "The word *world* is in great use with us Americans, when we would assert our superiority and discourage competition. The best in the world, the handsomest in the world, the fastest in the world, unmatchable; there is no use in the world for the world to try to equal us." The United States was a hotbed of invention and self-improvement, of causes and controversies. Midcentury America produced the first sewing machine and safety pin, the first triphammer and ring doughnut, the first evaporated milk and golf ball. By midcentury the telegraph lines ran from New York all the way to Chicago; militant women were holding the first Women's Rights Convention, in Seneca Falls, N.Y.; and Henry David Thoreau was campaigning against dams that threatened to endanger the shad population of New England's rivers. Midcentury America also produced *The House of Seven Gables, Moby Dick, Uncle Tom's Cabin,* and the first edition of *Who's Who in America.* Adolescent America's voice was changing, from imitations of English literature and Old World art to the authoritative American works of Hawthorne, Melville, and Harriet Beecher Stowe and the New World landscapes of George Caleb Bingham and Thomas Cole. But no American expression of native individuality was more spectacular than the clipper ship.

Alexis de Tocqueville had earlier predicted a major promise of America:

Nations, as well as men, almost always betray the most prominent features of their future destiny in their earliest years. When I contemplate the ardor with which the Anglo-Americans prosecute commercial enterprise, the advantages which befriend them, and the success of their undertakings, I cannot refrain from believing that they will one day become the first maritime power of the globe. They are born to rule the seas, as the Romans were to conquer the world.

By midcentury, with the help of the clipper ship, the United States was the premier maritime power of the world. Britain's total tonnage still was a bit larger, but American vessels were so much faster that they carried more goods in a year, and at much higher rates. American vessels, merchantmen as well as clippers, were three times the size their predecessors had been thirty years earlier. More important than size was speed. Horses, river steamers, and railroads were going ever faster; the most dramatic change was that of the sailing ship, which had doubled its speed in less than a decade.

American supremacy at sea resulted from the early United States being predominantly a maritime country, a narrow band of coastal states whose commerce depended on their vessels doing business around the world. But gradually in the forty years after the Louisiana Purchase, a major transformation had been taking place. As early as the beginning of the nineteenth century, Ohio, which had been virtually unsettled fifteen years previously, had a population of more than forty-five thousand. The opening of the Erie Canal speeded westward migration, provided the markets for western agriculture, and stimulated a network of new canals. By 1840 there were 3,326 miles of canals in the United States; a decade later there were 3,600 more. Railroads followed; as early as 1827 the Baltimore & Ohio Railroad was chartered, and by 1850 there were more than nine thousand miles of railway in the United States, double the mileage in Europe. With better transportation than the narrow, rutted roads, Easterners began to pour westward. During the forty-year period before midcentury more people settled in the western states than had come to the original colonies in a century.[3] Still the great mass of settlers was concentrated in the Midwest. Beyond, the Rocky Mountains barred the way "like a Chinese Wall," as one congressman described it. At midcentury the Far West was still thinly settled. But the Gold Rush would swiftly change all that.

During the accelerating westward expansion, eastern shipping remained America's biggest industry. But finally by midcentury U.S. internal commerce exceeded international trade. America had developed a national economy and a national identity. To many midcentury Americans the wave westward was a great crusade summed up in the phrase "manifest destiny," which was coined by John L. O'Sullivan, editor of the *Democratic Review*.[4] O'Sullivan was specifically referring to American agitation to claim the area now comprising the states of Oregon and Washington.[5] But the phrase became a rallying cry for an almost divine right to spread democracy (including, in the view of most Southerners, the democratic institution of slavery) across the continent. Following their self-proclaimed destiny, Americans annexed the Mexican colony of Texas and swarmed on into California.[6] And with the news of the bonanza of gold on the West Coast came the stampede to San Francisco and the gold fields. Even for the majority who stayed home, the Gold Rush focused their attention on the West. The United States of America, they realized, had become a sprawling, continent-wide nation rich in natural resources and seemingly independent of the rest of the world. No longer was the nation a provincial string of seaboard states; now it stretched from ocean to ocean. In the American land of opportunity here was the greatest opportunity of all.

Only partially hidden in this phenomenon was a massive irony. The same westward orientation of America that would transform the nation from the world's preeminent maritime power to a land-based continental colossus at first provided an unprecedented stimulus to the very industry it would inevitably extinguish: shipping. For the eastern merchants the gold miners themselves presented a bonanza. Crowded with a hundred thousand newcomers, many of them suddenly wealthy beyond their dreams, San Francisco provided an irresistible market, with necessities selling at luxury prices. And with that market fifteen thousand miles away by sea, the only competitive vessel was the fast vessel. The tea trade with China had developed the swift sailing ship just in time. With the Gold Rush and the attendant demand for even swifter, sturdier vessels, the sailing ship attained its ultimate perfection in the extreme clipper. Finally the American emphasis on speed had reached the point where a ship with the smaller cargo capacity of a V-bottom could make greater profits than a more capacious round-hulled competitor, not only because the former could command higher rates but also because it could make more passages in a given time.

It was not, however, a proven fact at first. The few merchant shippers who made the necessarily huge investments in the experimental new ships were performing an act of faith. In a sense, also, they were caught up in a compelling fever. Partly because of the gamble inherent in commissioning an expensive, seemingly impractical, perhaps dangerous vessel, partly because of the challenge of the murderous seas off Cape Horn, and not least because of the sheer excitement of those lofty vessels, eastern America developed a clipper ship mania rivaling Gold Rush fever. The press marveled at every new clipper as it came down the ways. Hitherto cautious businessmen offered ridiculous prices to ship their goods aboard a California clipper. Merchant shippers formerly noted for their conservatism wagered fortunes on mammoth racing vessels. It was as if the gods were first making mad those they were about to destroy.

The result was a dramatic decade in which vessels of unprecedented size and sail area were loaded to the gunwales and sent slashing through the world's wildest seas to set speed records that never would be matched. Three quarters of a century later the maritime historian Carl Cutler attempted to describe what it was like:

> The story of the Cape Horn clippers can never be told, or even dimly pictured to a generation that never rounded the Cape. Through the mists of the years and the yellowed salt stained pages of old log books, one catches fleeting glimpses of beautiful, gallant ships urged by relentless masters of the quarterdeck, fighting through incredible conditions for another mile of westing. There are brief sketches of icy infernos, in which are mingled confused impressions of steep decks, cascading water, milky white; of ponderous yardarms slashing through heaving crests; of lofty spars whipping and buckling under an insane spread of rigid canvas that fairly hurled the groaning hull at the seas; of stout shrouds threshing slackly to leeward, while weather stays drum like bars of steel.

"The fact is," wrote Cutler, "that never in the history of the world, before or since, have ships been rigged so heavily or driven so relentlessly as were American clippers in the early California trade."

So great was American exultation during this brief period that many even became convinced that the clipper ship would replace the steamer. The steam-powered vessel had been the last major breakthrough in the evolution of the ship; and mechanical propulsion would eventually supersede sail. But not yet. In the United States, ever since Robert Fulton's *North River Steamboat of Clermont* had swish-thunked her way up and down the Hudson River in 1807, steam-driven vessels had progressed and proliferated. Much of America's rapidly expanding river traffic was by steamer, and sturdier versions were even crossing the Atlantic. But most steamers were driven by paddlewheels, which were useless when heavy seas rolled them out of the water. And a steamship had to carry its fuel, thereby limiting its range. So the heavy-duty oceangoing work remained for the sailing ship.[7] And when larger clipper ships began making record runs around Cape Horn, there were predictions that the sailing ship had actually fought off the challenge of the steamer: One newspaper editorial proclaimed that steam "could never become anything more than an humble auxiliary to the sail." During the early months of 1851, New York shipyards, which had been building more steamers than sailing ships, reversed their priorities, most of them joining the rush to produce clipper ships.

The American clipper ship was also a floating paradox. Historian Samuel Eliot Morison has called it America's finest creation. "The *Flying Cloud* was our Rheims," he wrote, "the *Sovereign of the Seas* our Parthenon, the *Lightning* our Amiens." Yet the lofty sails and the lean, sleek hulls concealed a festering malignancy, an unremitting struggle between the forecastle and the quarterdeck. It had been a generation since eager young Americans had volunteered to ship out around the world for adventure and the opportunity to become captains themselves. Now those who had risen to command found their vessels manned by incompetents and malcontents. The lure of the American West, manifest destiny, and greater opportunity had attracted the new generation of American youth, leaving no one to serve the clippers but those who could not find work elsewhere or who were kidnapped by the crimps who delivered them, drunk and insensible, to the ships. The rigors and increased dangers of the clipper era, aboard driving vessels shipping tons of frigid water across their decks and perched along whipping yardarms in Cape Horn's worst storms, made some of the hardiest seamen decide to retire ashore.[8] Confronted with the fumbling, mutinous landlubbers who replaced them, the clippers' officers resorted to brutal treatment, if only to keep the ship afloat. The inevitable result was a series of tragedies to match the triumphs of the clipper ship era.

Experienced, willing seamen were the only missing factor in the clipper ship equation. The rest of the ingredients were there. What was remarkable was the fact that so few accomplished so much. John Willis Griffiths, a young wizard of the drafting table who fired the imaginations of a few shipowners, and antagonized many an old salt, with his radical conception of a new sailing vessel. William Aspinwall, a conservative merchant prince betting his firm's fortunes on Griffiths' new, untried vessel. Nathaniel Palmer, a salty skipper who whittled out a design that made Griffiths' clippers go even faster. Donald McKay, a self-effacing genius of the mold loft and shipyard who converted Griffiths' and Palmer's ideas into a fleet of record-smashing ships. His friend and competitor William Webb, who outdid him in quantity and strove to match him in quality, especially in his *Challenge,* which was to dare McKay's *Flying Cloud.* Lieutenant Matthew Fontaine Maury, a landlocked naval officer who provided an invaluable map for the navigators of the new clipper ships. Josiah Perkins Creesy, the sure-handed skipper of the *Flying Cloud;* his wife, Eleanor, who navigated the big clipper around Cape Horn. And the most colorful, controversial, and successful clipper captain of them all: Robert Waterman.

Waterman had made more records with his clipper *Sea Witch* than any other captain. But he also foresaw, earlier than most of his fellow captains, that America in midcentury was swiftly becoming a continental instead of a maritime nation. In fact, he himself had become fascinated by California and had bought some farmland near San Francisco. Significantly, he had gone out to California in command of a steamship. The steamer, he told a friend, would shortly replace the sailing ship, and the coup de grâce would come when the railroad crossed the continent, as it inevitably would. The clipper, in Waterman's opinion, was the last futile gesture of the sailing ship.

What he did not comprehend was the full significance of the clipper ship era. He was not alone. Few of his contemporaries recognized that they were living in a time of such important change, an interim between the muscle-flexing adolescence of a young seaboard string of states and the crisis of a Civil War that would produce a mature, united, continental nation. Robert Waterman did understand the paradox of the handsome clipper manned by the vagrants of the waterfront. Yet he became a victim of this paradox when he returned to New York to wind up his business affairs and take his wife back to California. It was at this time that he was approached by George Griswold, whose shipping firm N. L. & G. Griswold was engaged in the biggest gamble of all. On the stocks at William Webb's East River shipyard was the Griswolds' *Challenge,* the largest clipper yet commissioned. If Waterman would come out of retirement just long enough to take the *Challenge* around the Horn, the Griswolds would pay him a bonus of $10,000—a fortune in 1851—for making the passage in 90 days or less. And there was still time for him to supervise her rigging.

Waterman went up to the Webb yard and walked around the huge hull of the *Challenge.* She was a long, lean monster of a vessel, nearly twice the size of his *Sea Witch.* Studying her knife-sharp bow, he could not escape a quiver of anticipation. Certainly he was keenly aware that despite his success in the tea trade he had not faced up to the greater challenge of racing around Cape Horn to San Francisco in a clipper ship the size of the *Challenge.* He returned to the Griswold offices to look at her proposed rigging—and promptly proposed adding more sail. The *Challenge* was an irresistible temptation. And so Robert Waterman made the one big mistake of his career.

1

A Radical New Ship Design

"I HAVE SEEN MANY LAUNCHES," a New Yorker wrote in May 1851, "but never have I witnessed such interest and excitement before." One of the largest crowds that had ever assembled in the city thronged William H. Webb's shipyard at the foot of Fourth Street to stare in wonder at the enormous new clipper ship *Challenge,* poised to slide down her ways into the East River. The participants and guests on the platform seemed like ants alongside the great black hull with its single gold stripe, the gilded eagle figurehead, and the large, eerie eyes painted on the vessel's catheads.

After the obligatory speeches the new masterpiece was christened. The shipyard workers swung their mallets and the chocks fell away. The greased timbers groaned and the big clipper eased stern first down the ways, then gained speed and went thundering into the river. Waves washed sawdust over the feet of the applauding onlookers. Tugs came alongside to take the *Challenge*'s hawsers and tow her to her pier at the foot of Wall Street, where her bowsprit nearly poked out the windows of the N. L. & G. Griswold firm's countinghouse across South Street. By then the Griswolds, Captain Robert Waterman, and friends had adjourned to the Astor House bar to toast the occasion and to make their wagers. The majority were betting that the *Challenge* would easily set a new record for the 1851 season in the race to San Francisco.

It seemed to be the perfect combination. Robert Waterman had come a long way from an apprenticeship on the North Atlantic to success as a record-breaking captain in the China trade. And the *Challenge* was the quintessential clipper ship, the culmination of two centuries of an unremitting American search for speed at sea. The American clipper ship was the logical evolution of the fast little sloops and schooners that had smuggled the many necessities that the British Parliament had taxed beyond the American colonists' ability to pay. Speed at sea had played an important role in winning the colonies' independence. The American Revolution at sea had been won not by the Continental Navy (which lost nearly all of its warships) but by the nimble American privateers running the blockades, preying on British commerce and even taking on the Royal Navy, with the considerable help of the French Navy. Speed had become America's best weapon against the long-established competitors of other nations. Now American merchants favored faster ships for the simple reason that they could make more voyages, deliver more merchandise, and produce greater profits.

But the *Challenge* was something new. Her knife-sharp bow was the emblem of the extreme clipper ship, a phenomenon compounded of opium and slavery, of gold and tea. It is one of the oddities of history that so inert a substance should play a part in fomenting the American Revolution and then be a major cause of a drastic alteration in ship design. Chinese tea had to be shipped halfway around the world, losing flavor every day from the time it was picked and cured. It was tea—its popularity in America and the enormous profits to be made from the first consignment of the season—that set off a headlong burst of radical marine design and produced the first true clipper ships. China's tea would be surpassed, after a decade, only by California's gold as the major incentive to produce the loftiest and largest ships in the history of sail.

By the midnineteenth century the tea trade was half a century old. The first vessel from the new United States to open the trade, the *Empress of China,* had sailed from New York on February 22, 1784, only three months after British troops had returned home at the end of the American Revolution. The 360-ton *Empress* had taken almost fifteen months for the round trip, bringing a return of more than 25 percent of the cost of both ship and cargo.[1] During the half century that followed, hundreds of larger American sailing ships had followed the *Empress's* route down the Atlantic, around the Cape of Good Hope, across the Indian Ocean, and up the South China Sea to Canton. At first their eager American customers had bought not only the tea they brought home but many exotic artifacts of the Orient as well. Porcelain, which had been so common in China that it had been used as ballast in the *Empress's* hold, had been snapped up by wealthy Americans for their parlors and dining rooms. By the 1840s the China trade also included bamboo, silk, nankeen, incense, fans, lacquerware, objets d'art, and firecrackers. At the end of the eighteenth century Chinese merchandise had amounted to one seventh of all U.S. imports. But forty years later the market for Oriental imports was becoming saturated— for all of them, that is, except tea. Americans who had had to suppress their taste for their favorite beverage during prewar years because of Parliament's taxes now consumed it by the gallon. By 1840, tea amounted to 80 percent of China's exports to the United States. More important to the evolution of the clipper ship, American tastes were becoming more sophisticated, preferring the freshest tea, and by midcentury they could afford to pay a huge premium for the first shipment of the season to arrive in the United States.

This was the incentive that led Messrs. William Howland and William Aspinwall, two of the shrewdest shipping merchants in New York, to look for the fastest vessels and the hardest-driving captains. It was why they hired Robert Waterman away from the transatlantic packet service and gave him command of their China packet *Natchez*. What the Howland & Aspinwall company's fleet also needed were faster tea packets. So the partners looked about for the swiftest vessel they could find. They settled on the *Ann McKim*, which had been built in 1832 for the wealthy Baltimore merchant Isaac McKim (who named her after his wife). The *Ann McKim* was the first of the famous "Baltimore clippers" large enough to be ship-rigged.[2] Descended from the privateers that had helped win the Revolution and the War of 1812, the Baltimore clipper was a slim-hulled, fast little craft that had become popular in coastwise and international shipping and even more useful in the opium and slave trades.[3] A schooner upgraded to a ship, the *Ann McKim* promptly proved that the lines of the Baltimore clipper could be translated to a hull large and sturdy enough to support the canvas of a full-sized ship. With a 140-foot V-shaped hull that was only 27½ feet at its widest, and with tall, raked masts, she was the fastest ship afloat. So when Isaac McKim died only four years after her launching and she was put up for sale, Messrs. Howland and Aspinwall snapped her up.

At first she disappointed her new owners: She took 150 days to return to New York on her initial voyage—better time than most of the other tea packets but not as fast as Captain Waterman's voyages in the old *Natchez*. Then, in the spring of 1843, the *Ann McKim* came romping home from Canton in only 96 days, a new record. She thereupon played her part in transforming ship design by transforming Messrs. Howland and Aspinwall. Heretofore they had been known for their caution, usually purchasing secondhand vessels that had proved themselves (like the *Ann McKim*). Now, basking in the glory and profits of their fast China trader, they decided to make their bid for a new vessel to take further advantage of speed in the tea trade. The *Ann McKim* was ten years old; her 494-ton capacity was less than the current demand for the first pick of the season. What was needed, clearly, was a ship with her speed and more cargo space. So the two partners looked about for an imaginative designer. Their attention was attracted to a young man who was the most promising marine architect of the early 1840s. He was also the most controversial.

John Willis Griffiths was the first of a new breed of ship designers. An ebullient little man with a round face and pug nose, he had been born in New York in 1809. For one who became so famous, little is known about his upbringing, although he probably was taught the rudiments of ship design by his father, who was a shipwright in one of New York's East River yards. By the time he was nineteen, the young Griffiths was a draftsman in the Gosport Navy Yard in Portsmouth, Va. In his early twenties he produced the plans for the *Macedonian,* which became the fastest frigate in the Navy. In 1836, at twenty-seven, he published in the *Portsmouth Advocate* a series of radical proposals for changing marine architecture, which evidently intrigued the partners of the prestigious New York firm of Smith

& Dimon, who hired him as a designer. New York provided the perfect stage for John Griffiths. In February 1841 he exhibited at the American Institute a model of a hull unlike anything built before. Three years later he delivered, to an audience of mostly skeptical shipbuilders and merchants, the first formal lecture ever given in the United States on marine architecture.

A brilliant mathematician and physicist and a wizard at the drafting table, Griffiths was an outspoken advocate of a wholly new concept of ship design. Unlike most of his contemporaries who gradually improved on the performance of a ship's hull, refining it largely through observation and experience, Griffiths used hydrostatic equations to work out the relative efficiencies of different forms as they moved through the water.

He did not endear himself to his fellow shipwrights with such charges as "The science of ship building has long been shackled with deep-rooted prejudices" and references to "the miserable failures in ship building." His colleagues who still preferred to work from whittled models of time-tested shapes were offended by such pronouncements as "The man who builds one hundred ships by the same model, contracted or expanded, has had no more real experience than the man who has built but one. It is impossible to model vessels by eye, having no reference to known laws that govern the elements." Griffiths could be precise and straightforward, but he could also lapse into ornate prose: "The hoary head of prejudice, mantled with a guise of experience, dams up the stream of knowledge, and hurls defiance at the man who dares to assert that the fields of science are open alike to all." Griffiths was eager to put his theories into practice at the same time that Messrs. Howland and Aspinwall were looking for someone who could produce a more commodious *Ann McKim*. William Aspinwall, it happened, had been one of the merchants in Griffiths' lecture audience and one of the few who had taken him seriously. Aspinwall asked the young man to draw up a set of plans for a fast new tea clipper. Griffiths was particularly pleased because he was fascinated by Howland & Aspinwall's *Ann McKim,* whose design pointed in the direction of his ideal sailing vessel. And not only the *Ann McKim:* Griffiths believed that some of his drawing board concepts had been confirmed in, of all places, a brewer's vat.

Ten years earlier he had happened upon an obscure British

publication entitled *Nautical and Hydraulic Experiments, with numerous scientific miscellanies,* written by Colonel Mark Beaufoy, a Fellow of England's Royal Society. Mark Beaufoy was a brewer's son who at fourteen had listened with disbelief to a lecture in which an English mathematician claimed that a cone would offer the least resistance if pulled through the water blunt end first. The lecturer was actually quoting Isaac Newton, who in the seventeenth century had worked out on paper a set of equations that he translated into what he called "the solid of least resistance": a fat cone whose length was only three times its breadth. For many years, in fact, European shipbuilders had copied this bulbous form in their hulls.

Young Mark Beaufoy, however, instantly suspected that Newton's mathematical model made no practical sense, and he devised a simple test. Floating a cone-shaped piece of wood in one of his father's beer vats, he ran a line over a pulley to a bunch of keys that served as a counterweight. As he thought, the weight of the keys pulled the cone through the water more slowly blunt end first and faster when the cone was turned around. After a series of more complicated tests in specially designed tanks, Beaufoy reported his findings in his *Nautical and Hydraulic Experiments.* In laymen's terms, he had found that the hull that offers the least resistance to the water is long with a V-bottom and has its widest breadth nearly amidships.[4]

Beaufoy's tests had been conducted more than thirty-five years before Griffiths read about them. Characteristically, although Beaufoy had lectured to his fellow Royal Society members on his findings, conservative British ship designers had ignored them. John Griffiths did not.

Tank tests were a novelty in America. But Griffiths conducted his own and performed some further experiments. What he discovered in the tank and refined on the drafting table at Smith & Dimon carried Mark Beaufoy's findings a long step further. Griffiths' conclusions overturned most of the accepted principles of ship design throughout the world, and they naturally caused a sensation in New York.

Not only should a longer, slimmer, V-bottomed hull move through the water at maximum speed, Griffiths argued, but also the sailing ships of the time were designed stern-end-to. Even the fast little *Ann McKim* had a rounded bow and a tapered bottom under her stern. Griffiths' tank tests convinced him that what gave the famous Baltimore clipper her speed was her leanness—her greater length in relation to her width. Similar ships in Griffiths' tank, slim but with narrower bows, moved even faster through the water. And hulls with longer bows—with the maximum width farther aft—were faster yet.

If Griffiths' conclusions were correct, the conventional wisdom concerning a ship's stern was wrong. Most sailing vessels of the 1830s and early 1840s had relatively sharp sterns like the *Ann McKim*'s, the logical theory being that this shape permitted the water to flow aft cleanly and with a minimum of drag; as proof most mariners pointed to the clear, comparatively undisturbed wake of such ships. What Griffiths' experiments indicated was a hidden underwater drag, undetectable at the surface but a hindrance nonetheless. The tank test models that had the least resistance were those with a flatter, rounder stern. Accordingly, Griffiths decided, the most effective way to increase the speed of a hull through the water was to sharpen its rounded bow and round out its sharper stern.

It is no wonder that most of the old salts scoffed at such theories. Virtually since the beginnings of the sailing ship, the accepted hull conformation had been what Americans called the "cod's head and mackerel tail," a rounded bow that rose up over the waves and a thin stern to let the water run past. Sharpen the bow, Griffiths' critics argued, and the ship would dive for the bottom; flatten the stern and the wake's suction would slow her down.[5] So it is all the more remarkable that in the face of almost universal opposition, the previously penny-wise Messrs. Howland and Aspinwall took the gamble they did.

In fact, not all of the Howland & Aspinwall partners accepted John Griffiths' theories at first. On a mid-July morning in 1843, after Griffiths had delivered his plans, Aspinwall met with his partners, among them the elder Howland brothers, in the boardroom of their granite countinghouse at 54–55 South Street. One after another expressed his concern over the ship's bow lines, her tall masts, and the narrow freeboard between deck and waterline. Aspinwall responded by suggesting that they ask Griffiths himself to answer their questions.

Later the same day Griffiths and his boss, William Smith of the Smith & Dimon shipyard, joined the partners in the Howland & Aspinwall boardroom. Smith let Griffiths do the talking, and the young designer's confidence was reassuring. The sharp bow was compensated for by the buoyancy of the outward flare at deck level, he explained. This new clipper would be faster than the *Ann McKim,* he argued, and just as safe. Griffiths was so persuasive in his straightforward manner and in the authority with which he defended his plans that when he had finished, the partners simply nodded to one another, and Aspinwall told Griffiths and Smith to go ahead. She was to be a 750-tonner, 250 tons larger than the *Ann McKim;* and she would be called the *Rainbow*.

As the *Rainbow* took shape in the Smith & Dimon yard on the East River, the controversy swelled. Not only did her bow curve inward, but it also flared out as it reached deck level. This was the first "clipper bow," described by maritime historian Alexander Laing as "about as much an innovation as can be claimed for any shape in the gradual evolution of shipping." Griffiths' reasoning was that when the concave bow sliced into a wave, instead of riding up and over it as the rounder bow did, the flared top would provide the necessary buoyancy to keep her from diving into the seas. And the *Rainbow*'s sharp bow extended farther aft than any of her predecessors'. The conventional sailing ship of the 1840s was nearly as wide at the bow as amidships. Not the *Rainbow;* her forward section was leaner, and her greatest width came almost at her midsection. Overall she was slimmer than any merchant ship yet built.

Conservative shipwrights and skippers argued that Griffiths' new ship was "inside out": sharp-ended where she should be bluff-bowed to shoulder the seas aside, and fat-sterned where she should be thin. Griffiths ignored their criticism—which surprised no one; he was generally regarded as an impractical dreamer, anyway. Messrs. Howland and Aspinwall kept their faith in him nonetheless. But the master shipwrights at Smith & Dimon, recognizing their critical role in proving out a new design, meticulously took their time. Meanwhile William Aspinwall also slowed progress of the *Rainbow*'s construction by enlisting a second opinion on the vessel's rigging.

Perhaps he had been stung by the waterfront critics who were referring to the new ship as "Aspinwall's folly." And he may have had second thoughts about Griffiths' plans for the *Rainbow*'s masts, which seemed extremely tall for so slim a hull. Aspinwall had a high opinion of British marine architects, and he decided to ask some of them what they thought of the *Rainbow*'s spar plan. Either because they disagreed with Griffiths' plans or because they felt obliged to earn their commission, they responded with a number of proposed alterations. But by the time their spar plans were received in New York, the *Rainbow*'s mast steps and spars had been completed. Aspinwall studied the British plans, approved of them, and sent them along to Smith & Simon, where Griffiths quietly put them away. The *Rainbow*'s rigging remained as he had planned it; and Aspinwall, none the wiser, later credited the vessel's performance partly to the rigging plans he had had the foresight to solicit from England. The *Rainbow* sailed for China early in 1845—and promptly was dismasted.

Howland & Aspinwall had given the *Rainbow*'s command to the white-haired veteran of their captains, John Land; Robert Waterman at the time was en route home from China (and setting another record) in the *Natchez*. The *Rainbow* was only four days out on the North Atlantic when a winter gale brought all three of her lofty topgallant masts crashing down around her hull. Captain Land managed to salvage her maze of tangled rigging while continuing south under reduced sail. Once the *Rainbow*'s topmasts were restored and her rigging readjusted, she made a fast run for the rest of the voyage. Despite the fact that she reached the China Sea during an unfavorable monsoon, she made the voyage in 102 days. By the time she had loaded her tea, the monsoon had changed against her again. One near-typhoon blew out a complete set of sails and she was delayed while spares were made. Yet her time to New York was the same 102 days. During one breathtaking day while reaching up the Atlantic under a northeast trade wind, she logged the unheard-of speed of 14 knots.[6] And she set a new record for the round trip, earning Howland & Aspinwall a profit of $45,000, more than it had cost to build her. Then, on her second voyage, again against the monsoon, the *Rainbow* made Hong Kong in

99 days and came home in 84, even before the ships that had left China ahead of her could bring home the news of her arrival in Hong Kong.

The *Rainbow* was not, as she has often been called, the first true clipper ship. Her sharp bow and lean lines would be made even sharper and leaner in succeeding vessels. Every designer and builder would add his own modifications, especially in size: Clipper ships would reach half again the length and twice the tonnage of the *Rainbow*. Still, although the later, larger clippers would reach greater speeds, she remained the breakthrough. The clipper ship represented an evolution rather than a revolution. And in fact, John Griffiths was at work on the next stage in this evolution when Howland & Aspinwall came to him again. Flushed with success—and cash—after the fast voyages of their *Ann McKim* and *Rainbow,* as well as those of the *Natchez* under the command of Robert Waterman, the Howland & Aspinwall partners were ready for another gamble. This time they planned to combine the fastest ship with their most successful captain. If Robert Waterman could set records with an old hooker like the *Natchez,* what might he do with a new ship designed by Griffiths? So Messrs. Howland and Aspinwall turned to Griffiths for another vessel, and they asked Waterman to supervise her rigging and prepare to take her quarterdeck.

In drawing up his plans for this new ship, Griffiths followed the same general lines of his *Rainbow*—with one significant exception. At the heart of his theory of the faster sailing ship was the hull with the V-bottom. But while the *Rainbow* had been built, Griffiths' V-bottom theory had been challenged, not by another marine architect but by a salty sailor who had scarcely seen a shipyard since his boyhood.

Nathaniel Brown Palmer was a shipbuilder's son who had made his mark as a skipper, especially in the cotton trade, where he had made an intriguing discovery. A bale of cotton, some four hundred pounds compressed into a burlap-covered rectangle, fitted more efficiently into a flat-bottomed hull, which also happened to slide more easily over the silted mudbanks at the mouth of the Mississippi River, which was only 14 feet deep at high tide. What Captain Palmer discovered was that a flat-floored sailing vessel, when properly rigged and handled, could make excellent time. Palmer's *Huntsville* made the usual 18-day passage from New Orleans to New York in two weeks; one record-breaker was ten days. So "Captain Nat," as he was generally known, persuaded the *Huntsville*'s owner, E. K. Collins, to commission a few flatter-bottomed packets for the highly competitive transatlantic trade.[7] Palmer commanded three of them, and they confirmed his prediction: On a dozen westward voyages during 1839, they averaged nearly two weeks faster than most of their competitors.

Palmer thereupon applied his flat-floor theory to the China run. Given command of the slow tea packet *Paul Jones,* he spent 111 long days slogging out to Canton and 118 days coming home. He vented his frustration, however, in whittling out his conception of the ideal hull for a China trader. It combined John Griffiths' sharp bow with a fuller bottom. By chance one of his passengers on the homeward voyage was William Low, a partner in New York's A. A. Low & Bros., returning with his pregnant wife, Ann, from a stint as Low's Canton representative so Ann could have her baby in the United States. Impressed by Palmer and his whittled model, Low took both to his brother Abiel, head of the firm, as soon as the *Paul Jones* docked. And in less than a week, New York's Brown & Bell shipyard had started construction on a new China packet based on Palmer's design.[8]

The Lows named her the *Houqua,* after a popular Canton merchant who was a friend of the firm's partners. She was launched on May 3, 1844, only four months after her keel-laying (and one month after the birth of William and Ann's son); in fact, she was completed more than eight months ahead of John Griffiths' *Rainbow,* whose plodding construction took more than a year. The *Houqua* was a 600-tonner, 143 feet long and only 32 feet wide. The Lows took on Palmer as well as his model, and under his command the *Houqua* raced to China in only 95 days; with the combination of speed and the greater capacity of her rounder hull, she paid for her initial cost ($45,000) in her first few voyages.

Like the *Rainbow,* the *Houqua* was more a prototype than a true clipper ship. And she posed a dilemma for John Griffiths as he prepared his plans for his newest vessel. He had argued—and seemingly proved with the *Rainbow*—that the V-shaped hull was faster than the U-shaped one. Should he stick to his theory, sacrificing cargo space for speed? Had the *Houqua*'s combination of capacity and speed proved his theory false, or was she a fluke? Griffiths and Palmer were acquainted, and perhaps they discussed (or argued about) their conflicting theories.[9] Griffiths could be stubborn. But this time he compromised. And the result was his masterpiece.

The *Sea Witch* could claim the title, if any vessel could, of being the first true American clipper ship. Sharper-bowed, longer, larger, slimmer extreme clippers would follow her. But she was the first. Her bow was narrower than the *Rainbow*'s, with a wider flare at deck level to keep her from shipping too much water. She was almost ten feet longer and 150 tons larger than the *Rainbow*. Her stern, like the afterbodies of the *Rainbow* and the *Houqua,* was clean and narrow, permitting a relatively unobstructed wake. Her greatest breadth was a few feet farther aft than in previous vessels. She was leaner than her predecessors.[10] But her major innovation was a combination of both the V- and the U-shaped hulls. The *Sea Witch* had a sharp keel and above it a rounder hull; a cross section of her hull resembled the top of a fat wineglass. In short, the *Sea Witch*'s hull had both the *Rainbow*'s sharp keel and the *Houqua*'s fuller-bodied bottom just above it. This modification of two designs, this compromise between theory and experience, proved to be faster as well as more commodious and became a pattern for most of the clipper ships that followed.

The *Sea Witch*'s hull was the combined product of John Griffiths and Nathaniel Palmer. But her soaring masts and acres of canvas came straight from Robert Waterman. Her mainmast, nearly 150 feet tall, topped that of any other ship at the time. Aboard the *Natchez* Waterman had had to rig studding sails on the run; the *Sea Witch* had studding sails in her original spar plan. Above her royal topgallants Waterman called for skysails. Fore-and-aft sails—staysails, ringtails, water sails—were rigged between the *Sea Witch*'s masts and at bow and stern. Nearly half a dozen jibs and flying jibs reached out along her bowsprit.

Overall the *Sea Witch* had more sail area than U.S. Navy warships three times her size.

Her launching, at Smith & Dimon's yard at the foot of Eighth Street, was a major New York event. She was the handsomest ship in New York Harbor, a gleaming black hull with a gold stripe above the waterline that directed the eye to her black dragon figurehead. The launching had been planned for December 7, 1846. But it was postponed until December 8, because December 7 was Robert Waterman's wedding day.[11]

The thirty-eight-year-old captain and Cordelia Sterling, thirty-four, were married in Bridgeport, Conn., the wedding reception ending with the bride and groom being escorted to the train to New York. Next day Cordelia Waterman stood under the dragon figurehead, called out, "I christen thee *Sea Witch;* may you always bring your captain and crew safely home," smashed a bottle of champagne against the clipper's bow, and burst into tears. Robert and Cordelia Waterman took a short honeymoon trip to Canada, returning in time for him to fine-tune the last of the *Sea Witch*'s rigging. He did not wait to have a first Christmas with his bride. So anxious was he—not to mention Messrs. Howland and Aspinwall—to test the new clipper's speed that the *Sea Witch* sailed from New York on December 23, in the midst of a blustery northwester that sent her roaring down the North Atlantic.

Thus started what historian Carl Cutler describes as "by all odds the most remarkable ten years of sail in the history of the world. Before her brief life had ended, the *Sea Witch* had broken more records than a ship of her inches had ever broken and in company with other clippers had established the majority of sailing records that still survive." The *Sea Witch*'s launching, in short, could be said also to be the launching of the clipper ship era.

During the three years that she was under Waterman's command, the combination of sharp clipper and driving captain fanned New Yorkers' clipper fever to a white heat. Of all the fastest passages home from China, Waterman and the *Sea Witch* made the first two (his 78-day *Natchez* voyage remained the third fastest), and three of the first six. In her greatest burst of speed the *Sea Witch* reached 16 knots, faster than any contemporary sailing vessel. Later, bigger, more extreme clippers would surpass this speed. But what made the *Sea Witch* so consistently successful was her ability, particularly under Waterman's command, to keep moving in all weather. The lofty rigging he had designed for her never gave way. And in light airs all those studding sails and ringtails seemed to reach out and catch every bit of breeze. The *Sea Witch*'s best ten-day average was a then-astonishing 12½ knots, nearly that of her predecessor *Rainbow*'s top speed in a short dash. And under Waterman the *Sea Witch* improved with each voyage. Her first cargo of tea reached New York in 81 days from Canton. That was only three days longer than his 78-day record abroad the *Natchez,* and it was against the monsoon. Waterman announced that he was "just getting her shaken down for the next scamper." On the second voyage—with his wife Cordelia aboard—he came home from Canton in 77 days. This broke the *Natchez*'s record, which Waterman proceeded to lower the next year. On March 25, 1849, the *Sea Witch* came scudding up the northeast coast with everything aloft and straining before a fresh southeasterly: 74 days, 14 hours from Hong Kong.[12]

At first the semaphore operator on Navesink Highlands did not believe that the arriving vessel could be a tea clipper because it seemed impossible to reach New York this soon with the January crop. The *Sea Witch* was the heroine and Waterman the hero of the hour. John Griffiths, never burdened with false modesty, wrote of the ship he had designed: "The model of the *Sea Witch* had more influence upon the subsequent configuration of fast vessels than any other ship ever built in the United States." As for Waterman, he decided to rest on his laurels. He retired and handed over the command of the *Sea Witch* to George Fraser, his first mate and almost as much of a driver as he had been. Waterman was only forty-three. Perhaps he believed that even he could not surpass the passages he had made with the *Sea Witch*. Moreover, he had amassed a great deal of money on her record-breaking runs. And Cordelia Waterman made no secret of her resentment over his long absences at sea.

As for the *Rainbow,* she was the first of the new China clippers to be lost at sea. One day after the *Sea Witch*'s return from her second voyage, on March 17, 1848, the *Rainbow,* with

Captain William Hayes replacing John Land, sailed again for China. Her route was around Cape Horn, but she never reached Valparaiso, her first port of call. Somewhere between the North Atlantic and the South Pacific she disappeared with all hands. She had been under sail almost continuously and had crowded four voyages into three years.

There were a few clucking sounds from some of the old salts who had predicted that Griffiths' sharp-bowed creation would dive to the bottom. But most of the doubters had been converted by now, with half a dozen tea clippers cutting weeks off the China run. And there were clippers abuilding in nearly every East River yard. A. A. Low & Bros., the *Houqua*'s owners, ordered two more. One, the *Samuel Russell* (named after the Lows' Canton agent), was planned to rival Howland & Aspinwall's *Sea Witch* but could not match her. The other, the *Oriental,* played a role in stimulating what would later be the British clipper ship era.

By the time the *Oriental* reached Hong Kong in October 1850, Britain had repealed her venerable Navigation Acts, which had prohibited American vessels from carrying tea from China to England. The long-range effect was to stimulate the very competition whose absence had stultified the British merchant marine. English shippers, most of whom had fought bitterly against repeal, accepted the inevitable and commissioned American shipyards to build fast vessels for them; and shipbuilders along the Channel and the Clyde suddenly woke up to the modern clipper design.

In the short run, however, the repeal of the Navigation Acts[13] turned the most lucrative part of the tea trade over to the fast American ships. The *Oriental* was the first, taking aboard a cargo of tea at a price nearly twice the normal rate and rushing it to London in 97 days—a passage that took the slower British packets almost half a year. For nearly a decade the China-to-England route became a maritime racecourse for the new American tea clippers. More and more of them took off from New York, ran down around the Cape of Good Hope and across the Indian Ocean to the China Sea, adding another leg from China to England before returning to New York. It was then, with the impetus of the American tea trade reaching its peak, that the news spread of what would become the single most important stimulus to the clipper ship in the United States. The California Gold Rush would offer the newly developed American clipper its greatest opportunity and its sternest test. It would introduce a new stage in the evolution of the sailing ship. Now the trim tea packets of the China run would give way to the mammoth racing machines of the Cape Horn passage. And of these majestic new clipper ships the latest and largest was the *Challenge*.

2

The Cape Horn Sweepstakes

IN THE MIDNINETEENTH CENTURY, no two American cities were at once so similar and dissimilar as New York and San Francisco. Both were favored with large, protected harbors. Both still had low skylines dominated by the masts of hundreds of ships. Each in its way was a bustling, even frenetic, boomtown. Each offered countless opportunities to amass considerable wealth. Neither city offered much organized police protection, and the citizens of both cities were plagued by marauding gangs. In both cities the gulf between rich and poor was wide. And in both cities foreigners were discriminated against and physically harassed. Most of all, in both cities the major preoccupation was money.

The dissimilarities, of course, were what stood out. The ships dominating New York's skyline were hives of activity as they loaded for the voyage around Cape Horn; most of the ships in San Francisco were deserted hulks abandoned by gold-hungry crews and swinging silently at their anchors off Rincon Point. San Francisco's counterparts of New York's new rich were instant rich. While the number of New Yorkers was increasing, nothing could match the population explosion in San Francisco, more than a hundredfold since the discovery of gold. San Francisco's police protection consisted largely of a volunteer Committee of Vigilance that also influenced the city's politics. And San Francisco's racism took a more violent form, including mass physical assaults.

In the last analysis, San Francisco in the midnineteenth century was like no other city in the world. Certainly it was the newest city in the world; it had exploded from a hamlet to a metropolis almost overnight. For centuries this part of the American West Coast had slept under the soft Pacific sun. Fifteenth-century Spanish explorers, concluding that there were few precious metals on this coast, had turned their attention back to the richer fields of Central America. Despite its magnificent harbor, San Francisco remained a backwater visited only by passing whalers and merchantmen for wood and water.

California was still a Mexican colony and San Francisco was a tiny settlement called Yerba Buena (Green Herb, after a local mint) when Richard Henry Dana, Jr., aboard the hide drogher *Alert,* visited the port in the winter of 1835–36. Its appearance contrasted sharply with what the gold-seekers would find only a decade and a half later. In his *Two Years Before the Mast,* Dana described the arcadian simplicity of the area, which was inhabited by "hundreds and hundreds of red deer." During a month's stay "not a sail came or went." But Dana recognized that "this magnificent bay" was the best anchorage along the entire West Coast of America, and prophesied: "If California ever becomes a prosperous country, this bay will be the centre of its prosperity."

That was what Captain Robert Waterman found fourteen years later. Yerba Buena, however, had become San Francisco and quite a different town. Custom House records listed a total of 91,405 newcomers during 1849 from U.S. Atlantic ports alone. By year's end the ships were arriving at the rate of one a day, and the rate increased through 1850. The *Pacific News* reported on a particularly busy period in November: "The number of vessels entering our harbor is really a matter of wonder. Within forty-eight hours ending on Sunday night, nearly sixty sail entered the Golden Gate. The history of the world presents no comparison." The flood of immigrants came from nearly everywhere in the world. A hundred bedraggled British argonauts arrived after crossing the Atlantic and the Isthmus of Panama and sailing up the West Coast. During one eleven-week period in the spring of 1849, nearly sixty-five hundred immigrants arrived from Mexico and three thousand from Panama, Peru, and Chile. Even that Pacific paradise Tahiti lost 120 residents to the Gold Rush. Australia sent off shiploads of men, many of them exiled British convicts. From France came 3,885 lucky winners of a grand lottery held by Emperor Louis Napoleon. Perhaps the greatest wave of immigrants came from China, where desperate Pearl River farmers fleeing famine were packed aboard vessels by shipping agents who advanced the $40 steerage fare for "contracts" that amounted to virtual slavery in California. In 1849, forty-five such ships sailed from Hong Kong, followed by nearly a hundred during the next two years. More than twenty-five countries (excluding Japan and Russia, whose governments forbade emigration) sent prospectors to California. It was estimated that nearly 25 percent of California's newcomers were from foreign lands. They joined an even larger flood of Americans from all thirty-one states, and California became America's greatest melting pot.

San Francisco was the way station for those who rushed on to the gold fields. But many newcomers, finding jobs plentiful at salaries unheard of at home, swelled the new city's population. By day San Francisco was aptly described by a resident as "one of the most heterogeneous masses that ever existed since the building of the Tower of Babel." By night it was a glowing tent city. "The houses are mostly of canvas," a visitor reported, "which is made transparent by the lamps within, and transforms them, in the darkness, to dwellings of solid light. Seated on the slopes of its hills, the tents pitched among the chaparral to the very summits, the city gleams like an ampitheatre of fire."

As Robert Waterman had expected, the exploding population meant a rapidly rising demand and increasingly higher prices. The safest, surest, and easiest way to make money was not from the gold fields but from the gold diggers. Already the law of supply and demand had raised San Francisco's prices astronomically. A barrel of flour (worth $6 in New York) sold for $200. A bushel of potatoes cost $16, a pound of sugar $4, one egg $1, a pair of boots $100. The price for one wooden plank was $10. Whiskey was $40 a quart, a pack of playing cards $5. Even a five-month-old penny newspaper from New York brought 50 cents to $1. Wages had risen proportionately. A Massachusetts man was surprised to find so many of his former neighbors working at menial jobs for five times what they had earned at home. Another Easterner remarked, "A graduate of Yale considers it no disgrace to sell peanuts on the Plaza, a disciple of Coke and Blackstone to drive a mule team, nor a New York poet to sell the New York *Tribune* at fifty cents a copy." San Francisco's inflation was vividly demonstrated to one arriving argonaut who stepped ashore, approached a waterfront idler, and offered him half a dollar to carry his suitcase to the nearest hotel. The San Franciscan tossed two half-dollars at the man's feet and snarled, "Carry it yourself."

The miners flocking back from the gold fields were eager to spend their newfound wealth, and an army of predators stood ready to oblige them. "What is considered a fortune at home," a newcomer wrote to his relatives back East, "is here mere pocket money." San Francisco in the early 1850s had nearly a thousand gambling halls, which were licensed by the city and were open twenty-four hours a day, seven days a week. One affluent prospector wagered—and lost—a poke of gold worth $60,000 on the turn of a single card. Another won $89,000 in a faro game and a few days later lost $100,000. And what the professional gamblers did not get, the prostitutes did.

The first wave came from South America.[1] Competition shortly arrived in the form of two hundred courtesans from Marseilles, and part of Commercial Street became known as French Town because of the many bordellos that sprang up in the area. The South Americans and the French were soon followed by girls from the eastern United States, Australia, and China. So well did they profit from the eager argonauts that one Chinese madam retired home with a fortune, as did a particularly popular *fille de joie* who amassed a reported $50,000 in one year. Others married their patrons and settled into comparative respectability.

But for those with any money to invest, the most promising prospects were in real estate. Captain Waterman's hankering for a California ranch was not a little stimulated by the transactions he saw in San Francisco and environs. A legendary character in a city of many was James Lick, who arrived two weeks before James Marshall's discovery at Sutter's Mill. Lick set out to buy land in San Francisco. His first lots cost him about $16 each; by March 1849 he was paying $22; by September the average cost of a lot had soared to $3,000; and Lick started selling. By the time Waterman arrived in San Francisco, James Lick was already the richest man in the city.

So valuable was land becoming that the city's waterfront started inching out into the bay, with the landfill immediately sprouting more buildings. Montgomery Street, on the waterfront in 1849, was nearly in the city's center by 1850. A dozen piers, one of them nearly half a mile long, reached out to accommodate the ever-increasing fleet of ships. The tents ringing the bay were gradually giving way to wooden shacks, which were being built at the rate of twenty a day. One man claimed to have seen a prefabricated home unloaded from a ship in the morning and occupied that evening. The sprawling ranks of wooden shacks were periodically swept by fire; between December 1849 and September 1850, large sections of the central city were reduced to cinders and quickly rebuilt. Partly because of the fire hazard, the wealthier San Franciscans began to build more substantial structures of adobe, stone, and precious brick on the hills back of the waterfront.

Fortunes were meanwhile being made in all sorts of real estate. A one-story building occupying only 20 feet of frontage on a busy street sold for $50,000. Rents were proportionately high: A cigar shop, more a booth than a store, rented for $4,000 a month. One of the city's few two-story buildings, the Parker House, which had cost $30,000 to build, rented for $120,000 a year. Such immediate profits stimulated a heady flow of money, at interest rates as high as 180 percent a year.

What attracted Robert Waterman was a longer-term, potentially more rewarding investment. The inflation in real estate, he calculated, would inevitably spread from the city to the surrounding countryside. In the meantime San Francisco offered a rapidly expanding market for the vegetables, fruits, and beef he could raise on a ranch. The problem was to select the right area. Many a hasty real-estate investor had been tricked into buying land at an unlikely building site. A typical example was a much-touted New York, California, which made a tentative appearance with a few shacks before succumbing to the voracious local mosquitoes.

Waterman was fortunate in having a friend, a fellow sea captain named Archibald Ritchie, who had scouted out and bought a 12-mile-square stretch of fertile land in the Suisun Valley, part of Solano County and on the Sacramento River about thirty miles northeast of San Francisco. Ritchie offered Waterman a half interest in the property, and on August 29, 1850, the two captains became partners, with Waterman paying $17,000 for his half share. Waterman looked forward eagerly to retirement from the sea and the life and rewards of a farmer. To his partner Ritchie he confided his belief that "the days of the sailing ship are numbered," adding, "I just don't warm to these newfangled steam ships." He was convinced that the steamer, too, would soon be eclipsed. As he explained it to Ritchie, "it will be about ten years or so till the railroad pushes on to this coast." Then, he predicted, "away will go most water shipping."

Clearly, in Waterman's view, it was time to change careers from sea captain to farmer. He boasted to one of his new neighbors that "the gold diggers of the Mother Lode are begging for more fruit and vegetables from the Suisin Valley." Waterman and Ritchie turned for advice to a nearby agricultural expert named Joseph Allison, who rode over their property with them and helped survey the boundary lines, lay out the roadways, and decide where to plant which vegetables and fruit and which areas to set aside for pastureland. Now it remained only for Waterman to return to New York, settle his business affairs, and bring his wife back with him to the ranch.

Midnineteenth-century New York, like San Francisco, was still primarily a seaport. The lithographs of Manhattan produced at the time by Nathaniel Currier and his partner-to-be James Merritt Ives show a skyline not of buildings but of masts. By midcentury New York was the preeminent port of the new United States. Half a century earlier it had ranked fourth, surpassed by Philadelphia, Boston, and Charleston. But the combination of the transatlantic packets, the Erie Canal, the tea trade, and the city's hard-driving merchants had made New York the busiest port, universally recognized as "the great commercial emporium of America."

From the start, New York had many natural advantages over most of its eastern rivals. It did not appear so at first; Sandy Hook, a bar built up by centuries of shifting sands, nearly blocked the entrance to the harbor. But there were deep-water passages through this barrier; and, in fact, Sandy Hook presented a less formidable obstruction than the shoals of Chesapeake Bay or the islands clotting the entrance to Boston Harbor. Among New York Harbor's natural advantages were the Navesink Highlands, the highest point on the northeastern coast south of Mount Desert, Maine; atop the Highlands' 266-foot-high hill in the 1840s were twin lighthouses that marked New York Harbor far to sea. And inside Sandy Hook the harbor provided protection from storms, a large anchorage area, and minimal danger of freezing up, as Boston Harbor frequently did. New York Harbor often remained open when others to the south, with slower-moving waters than the Hudson and East rivers, were shut off by ice.

In the midnineteenth century New York Harbor presented a busy spectacle of sloops, ships, ferries, and steamers rushing to and from the crowded piers lining the Hudson and East rivers. To Captain Waterman it was a more familiar scene than that of San Francisco Bay. New York Harbor was where he had taken so many dramatic departures and where he had been welcomed after his record-breaking passages. No doubt he wasted little time before dropping into the clipper captains' rendezvous, the Astor Bar, to greet old friends and hear the latest gossip about clipper launchings and sailings. The Astor, on Broadway between Vesey and Barclay streets, was also the gathering place for the merchant shippers, most of whom met daily at the bar's marble-topped tables to whet their appetites with Michael the bartender's famous rum punches before moving on to Delmonico's for a two-hour dinner. More business was done and more maritime news was exchanged amid the smoky commotion of the Astor Bar than at the 'Change itself, the porticoed, bulbous-domed Exchange Building at the corner of Wall and William streets, where the merchants gathered later in the afternoon.

New York's signs of shipping wealth were everywhere. Stores, shops, hotels, restaurants, and office buildings were rising all through lower Manhattan. The Astor House was rivaled by two more hotels on Broadway, the pretentious St. Nicholas at the corner of Broome Street and the luxurious Metropolitan at the corner of Prince Street. By day, downtown New York presented a tableau of private carriages awaiting the wealthy shipowners' wives while they shopped in the department stores along Broadway, notably A. T. Stewart's "marble palace," the majestic six-story establishment that occupied the entire block on the east side of Broadway between Chambers and Reade streets. So distinctive was the white marble façade with its fifteen plate-glass show windows that its owner did not even bother to put his name on the building. Inside the store some two hundred clerks sold more than $10,000 worth of Brussels carpets, Lyon silks, Paris gowns, Irish linens, English woolens, and cashmere shawls every day. By night the carriages lined the curbs in front of the Metropolitan and St. Nicholas hotels while the merchant shippers and their wives danced the waltz, the polka, and the gavotte. A disapproving observer of New York's spendthrift scene, James Fenimore Cooper, occasionally came down from his Hudson River estate to view what he described as the city of the "hundred dollar handkerchiefs." In a letter to his wife he complained that the metropolis had become one "great arena for the women to show off their fine feathers in." Indeed, he reported, Mrs. William Wetmore had made a particularly ostentatious appearance "in a dress that cost, including jewels, thirty thousand dollars."

Diarist George Templeton Strong referred to New York as a "Jack the Giant-killer's beanstalk" of a city, and grumbled, "You often have to wait ten minutes before you are able to cross the street." Broadway's more expensive stores and shops were generally on the west side of the avenue; and so dense and heedless was the traffic that it was often dangerous to cross from the "dollar side," as it was known, to the more modest establishments of the "shilling side" to the east. New York's shipping and mercantile explosion drove the more affluent Manhattanites north to build their mansions. Imposing residences were rising along Fifth Avenue, which was paved with Belgian blocks and cobblestones only as far as 18th Street. Beyond that the avenue was a dirt road on a good day and a rutted quagmire when it rained. But lower Fifth Avenue presented a grand façade of porticoed brownstones with Palladian windows and polished brass kept gleaming by armies of servants, impressive testimony to the wealth that shipping had brought to the city.

The environment in which the merchant princes flourished, midcentury New York was a rich stew of sophistication and superstition, of luxury and disease. New York had more than its share of theaters and mansions, as well as clairvoyants and quacks. It was a city that supported opera houses and lavish department stores but whose populace was ravaged every summer by incurable cholera. The city was characterized by a unique blend of lingering taste for the classics of the Old World and an attraction to the novelties of the New. New York's wealthy filled their libraries with leather-bound, gold-stamped sets of Tennyson, Dickens, Scott, and Byron. But what they were reading were the works of the new American authors: James Fenimore Cooper's Indian stories, Henry David Thoreau's *Walden,* Ralph Waldo Emerson's essays, and Herman Melville's South Seas romances. (Melville's more ambitious *Moby Dick* was far less popular.) New Yorkers' taste in art was also being weaned away from Europe and Britain by such painters of Americana as George Caleb Bingham and the landscape artists of the Hudson River School. By the time John James Audubon died in the fall of 1851, his *Birds of America,* despite their relatively high prices, had decorated hundreds of New York parlors. Nathaniel Currier and James Ives were pioneering the mass production of lithographs covering everything from disasters to sentimental rural scenes. Currier and Ives shrewdly exploited New York's clipper ship fever with a series of lithographs of these vessels. But they also reflected the growing American preoccupation with the West by marketing hundreds of depictions of explorers, homesteaders, and the steamships and railroads that were opening up the land beyond the Appalachians.

One measure of New Yorkers' taste, particularly that of the merchants, was the popularity of the city's newspapers. With a population of half a million, New York had 50 newspapers, 14 of them dailies. The proprietors of the most successful journals were as conspicuous as their products. Henry J. Raymond, the squat, dapper founder of the highly literate *Times,* was a familiar man about town behind his handsome span of thoroughbreds. Ebullient, white-whiskered Horace Greeley made a reputation for not just embracing causes in his *Tribune;* he smothered them. But the most notorious newspaper publisher was the *Herald*'s James Gordon Bennett. In contrast to Greeley and Raymond, Bennett had no interest whatever in swaying public opinion; he viewed his mission simply as peddling news— and newspapers. Nothing was unfit to print in the *Herald*. If, as frequently happened, the target of a slanted editorial physically attacked Bennett, the *Herald* gleefully reported the episode. And New Yorkers responded to Bennett's mass appeal. The *Herald,* which had been launched in 1835 from a rented cellar room with a packing case desk, was by the late 1840s published in its own marble building on Printing House Square at the corner of Broadway and Park Row; and James Gordon Bennett was one of New York's millionaires.[2]

Bennett's *Herald* was especially popular with New York's shipping merchants because of his "Marine Intelligence" column, which reported the important arrivals and sailings and the launching of every new clipper ship. The *Herald* covered the shipping business because that was where the money was, and Bennett personally reported most of the news along South Street.

Like most New Yorkers, Bennett recognized that the business heart of the city was South Street, the epicenter of the merchant shipping hierarchy. Popularly known as the "Street of Ships," South Street was the busiest, noisiest, smelliest, and most exciting area of Manhattan. Long piers projected into the river, all of them jammed with tall ships, some two or three deep on each side. Walking down South Street under the ships' bowsprits was like strolling through a cathedral forest. Along the piers the masts, thick as tree trunks, rose into a sky nearly obscured by the thick foliage of their rigging.

A forest above and a bustling swarm of humanity below. Wagons and barrows clattered over the cobblestones. Shouting drivers and fishmongers competed with screaming gulls around the fish market at the corner of Fulton and South streets. A constant tide of people flowed through the clutter of barrels and boxes stacked everywhere along the piers. Across South Street from the long piers, squat under the soaring masts and with bowsprits poking at their windows, were the brick and granite countinghouses. Most were three- to five-story structures that provided warehouse space as well as offices. Just inside the entrance was the firm's showroom, where its goods could be inspected by potential wholesale purchasers. Behind it was the office, where rows of clerks sat on their stools adding up their accounts, making out bills of lading, keeping inventory, and copying orders and letters. Every copy was done by hand; carbon paper had not been invented, nor had the typewriter. Here in the back office the din of South Street was muffled, and usually the loudest sound was the scratch of the quill pen.

This inner sanctuary was an all-male preserve. The lowest-ranking clerks were the "boys" who served mainly as messengers. For a working day that usually ran from 7 A.M. to 8 P.M., the junior clerk was paid $1 or $2 per week; some were apprentices who were merely given room and board. Most of them knew that if they worked hard, they would get ahead. An ambitious clerk could look forward to a steady if slow procession up the ladder to copying, then to such special jobs as dealing with customers, then to bookkeeper, and finally perhaps to confidential chief clerk, the partners' right-hand man. The promotions also brought higher, if still meager, salaries. And the most ambitious clerks put aside money from their pay packets until after a few years they could do a bit of investing on their own. Often a merchant would let some of his clerks purchase merchandise and ship it on their own account aboard one of the firm's vessels. And the smarter the clerk, the sooner he had accumulated sufficient capital to start his own firm.

At the rear of the counting room were the desks of the partners. Some sat on a dais overseeing every move of the clerks. Others had private offices and even conference rooms. (One furnished his office with a single chair behind his desk so that visitors, unable to sit down, would state their business and get out.) The upper floors of the countinghouse generally served for storage of goods about to be exported or just unloaded and awaiting auction or purchase.

One of the most imposing countinghouses on South Street was that of N. L. & G. Griswold, a large granite structure at 71–72 South Street. Captain Waterman knew it well; it was only a couple of blocks north of the headquarters of Howland & Aspinwall, his last employer. Waterman may well have encountered George Griswold in the Astor Bar; but that would have been no place to talk business, so Griswold undoubtedly invited him to come around to the office.

Nathaniel L. and George Griswold had come to New York from East Lyme, Conn., before the turn of the century, to ship flour to the West Indies and bring back sugar and rum, and were veteran shipping merchants when they entered the tea trade. By the 1840s, N. L. & G. Griswold had forty-three ships flying their distinctive house flag checkered with thirteen blue and twelve white squares. Their most famous ship was the *Panama,* whose name became a hallmark of the firm when they printed it on the labels of their tea chests and cartons. One New York merchant wrote, "I do not suppose there is a country store however insignificant, in the whole United States, that has not seen a large or small package of tea marked 'Ship *Panama*' and 'N. L. & G. Griswold.' " In fact, the Griswolds named three of their vessels in succession *Panama.*

The Griswold brothers were conspicuous for their size; both stood more than six feet tall, and "Old Nat," as he was known, was one of the rare South Street merchants who wore a slouch hat instead of the customary merchant's silk topper. Nat was the shipping expert and his brother George was a wizard of the balance sheet. The Griswolds drove their captains hard, and their clerks were frustrated by both brothers' maddening penmanship. George's scrawl was so indecipherable that he often could not read it himself; in fact, one Griswold clerk was indispensable to the firm because he alone had mastered George's hieroglyphics.

The Griswold brothers found time to branch out into other profitable endeavors, George into banking and real estate and Nat into dredging. Nat's greatest coup came when he convinced the New York State legislature that New York Harbor needed to be deepened; as a result, he won a dredging contract that netted him $100,000. The Griswolds were noted for their conservatism. They did little chartering or selling on commission; they owned all their ships and held their own tea auctions, realizing from $400,000 to $700,000 per cargo. So the other South

Street merchants were astonished to hear that the staid old Griswold brothers had reacted to the news from California by commissioning the largest, sharpest new clipper of them all, to be named the *Challenge*.

This was George Griswold's reason for approaching Robert Waterman. The *Challenge,* he boasted, would be the pride of the U.S. merchant marine. No one doubted that she would set a record on the California passage, probably one to stand for all time. Here was the perfect opportunity for the recordholder of the tea trade to add to his glory as the champion of the much more glamorous Cape Horn sweepstakes. This sort of talk was known to appeal to Robert Waterman even more than the $10,000 bonus that Griswold offered. Waterman's mind probably was made up even before he went to William Webb's East River yard to look at the huge streamlined hull crouched at the water's edge awaiting her masts, her spars, and her skipper.

With their offer to Captain Waterman, as with their commissioning of the *Challenge,* the firm of N. L. & G. Griswold was making its bid for supremacy in an intensely competitive struggle to dominate the lucrative new California trade. New York's merchant shippers were a tightly knit group of hard-headed businessmen who made New York a center of wealth. The word "millionaire" was being heard for the first time in America. Already there were at least fourteen New Yorkers who had amassed this hitherto unheard-of fortune, nearly all of them in shipping and related businesses. And the merchant shippers wielded power beyond their wealth. While there were some retailers, middlemen, and jobbers who made even more money than the men who owned New York's ships, it was this little clan of not more than a couple dozen men who precipitated a revolution in ship design.

Most of them were transplanted New Englanders. As their own cities had become eclipsed by New York, they had migrated to Manhattan, where they proceeded to dominate the city's shipping business and infiltrate the boards of directors of the city's banks and insurance companies. They were a hard-working, ambitious group. Some of them brought their New England firms to New York; others started out as clerks in South

Street countinghouses and rose to partnership. Few had been educated beyond primary school. A New York contemporary provided a glimpse of these laconic, granitic Northeasterners in his description of one of them as "the personification of a Yankee—if there is such a race—long legs, hatchet face, skin and bones, slight, pokey, and keen as a brier." Clannish and self-confident, they formed their own New England Society in the City of New York to promote Yankee solidarity. The society's annual dinners were highlighted by toasts to "New England habits—industry, enterprise, and shrewdness" and "Yankee capital—the real wealth of nations." And when they gambled and won in the tea trade, it was the same small group of successful, influential South Street merchant shippers who thereupon made the all-important contribution to the development of the clipper ship: They paid for it.

Besides the Griswolds, the New Englanders managing New York's shipping business included the Low brothers from Salem, Massachusetts. Their firm was founded by Seth Low, who had spotted the potential profits in the tea trade as early as 1833 and had sent his son Abiel off to Canton. By midcentury Abiel had returned and was the chief partner of the firm of A. A. Low & Bros., which included eleven brothers. The Lows, with their *Houqua, Samuel Russell,* and *Oriental*—not to mention the canny Captain Nat Palmer as a Low consultant—were major contenders in the tea trade.

Prominent among the transplanted New Englanders was the firm of Howland & Aspinwall, which had commissioned the *Sea Witch.* By the late 1840s, William Aspinwall was turning his restless energy to a grandiose project that one day would help sound the death knell for the clipper ship. His new venture reflected a farsighted conviction in the rich promise of a continental nation. The plan was for a steamship line along the West Coast from Central America to California, a risky proposition if only because of the difficulty in getting a steamer to the Pacific. Moreover, in these pre-Gold Rush days there was little evidence of enough business to support a ship line along the sparsely populated, undeveloped West Coast of America. Nonetheless, Aspinwall persisted and, with the help of a government mail contract, finally convinced his partners. On October 6, 1848, the firm dispatched to California the 1,050-ton sidewheel steamer *Pacific* on a voyage that would turn out to be miraculously well timed.

When the *Pacific* departed, there had been rumors of a gold strike in California, but few, including Messrs. Howland and Aspinwall, were taking them seriously. Only seven passengers occupied the *Pacific*'s new staterooms. But on December 5, two months after she had sailed, President James Polk made the electrifying announcement of California's gold strike: "The accounts of the abundance of gold in that territory are of such extraordinary character as would scarcely command belief. . . ."

By the time the *Pacific* had worked her way through the Strait of Magellan and up the West Coast of South America to Panama, 106 days out of New York and two weeks behind schedule,[3] she was met by a clamoring crowd of nearly seven hundred gold-seekers who had steamed to the eastern side of the Isthmus and raced across. With 375 passengers, 100 more than her intended capacity, crowded aboard, the *Pacific* steamed on to San Francisco. And the New York merchants who had scoffed at a West Coast shipping line now were asking if Aspinwall had had some advance knowledge of President Polk's announcement.

In fact what Aspinwall had been planning was control of the shortcut across the Isthmus, where he now set out to build a railroad. To devote all his time to this project, he resigned his active partnership in the shipping firm. With a new group of partners he established the Panama Railroad, and in a magnificent feat of engineering he built one of the most extraordinary railroads in the world. It burrowed through man-made ravines and spanned valleys with high trestles for 47½ miles from Manzanillo to Panama City. Its eventual cost of $8 million was six times the original estimate, and the project took five years, 2½ times what had been planned. In the process the pestilential jungle killed some ten thousand of the Chinese, Irishmen, and blacks imported to build the line. (The railroad's hospital was partly supported by the sale of corpses, which were pickled, packed in barrels, and shipped to medical schools in the United States and Europe.)

The Panama Railroad also nearly ruined Aspinwall and the firm of Howland & Aspinwall with him. While it was under construction, the lure of an Isthmus crossing attracted the attention of another shrewd New Yorker, "Commodore" Cornelius Vanderbilt, already one of America's wealthiest men largely through his monopoly of the ferry business in New York Harbor. Vanderbilt chose a route across Nicaragua, which was more than a hundred miles wider between the two oceans but five hundred miles closer to the United States. And the crossing was mostly by water: The hundred-mile-wide Lake Nicaragua could be reached from the Caribbean via the San Juan River. The two New York titans of commerce shortly were locked in a bitter battle of the Isthmus, with Vanderbilt's contractors offering higher pay to Aspinwall's workers and with the promise of competition—plus the construction costs and delays—lowering the price of Aspinwall's Panama Railroad stock. Some of his partners dropped out. His former Howland & Aspinwall partners loyally came to his aid with further backing.

By 1851, Vanderbilt's American Atlantic and Pacific Ship Canal Company was offering service from New York to San Francisco via Nicaragua in direct competition with Aspinwall's Panama route. But Aspinwall fought back, transporting his passengers by train to the end of the Panama Railroad's track and on muleback from the terminus to Panama City. Not until 1855 was the final link completed and the trans-Isthmus line formally opened (at Aspinwall, the new name for Manzanillo). By that time there was traffic in both directions, with successful gold-diggers returning home, and there were enough passengers to support both lines. Aspinwall's Panama Railroad paid off its enormous cost in only six years; and its stock, which had been nearly worthless during the railway's difficult days of construction, paid dividends as high as 44 percent. Aspinwall's biggest gamble had won. And in the process, the now-efficient Isthmus crossing replaced the clipper ship for merchandise as well as passengers to San Francisco.

A particularly colorful firm of New Englanders in New York was that of Grinnell, Minturn. Their countinghouse was at the corner of Fletcher and South streets, right across from that of A. A. Low & Bros. Grinnell, Minturn & Co. had been founded by Joseph Grinnell of New Bedford, Massachusetts, and his eccentric cousin Preserved Fish.[4] The original firm of Fish & Grinnell, started in 1815 to market New Bedford's whale oil, expanded into the transatlantic packet trade and became Grinnell, Minturn & Co. when Robert Minturn, Joseph Grinnell's brother-in-law, joined as a partner. Soon, like their fellow shipping merchants, Grinnell and Minturn had plunged into the tea trade.

That was where the fortunes were being made.[5] Not only could a shipping merchant double his money in a year, especially if he brought home the first crop of the season; he also discovered a profit center in, of all places, U.S. Customs. A major part of the investment in a shipment of tea was the customs duty, which could amount to as much as 200 percent. A typical cargo of tea that cost $200,000 in China, for example, was charged $400,000 in duty in the United States. But it sold at auction in New York for as much as $700,000, bringing the merchant shipper a profit of $100,000 on one voyage alone. Some of the shrewder tea shippers shortly discovered that some customs agents leniently allowed a shipper up to 18 months to pay the duty, without interest, thus permitting him to use the pre-tax profits from one voyage to finance the next one. A customs duty that could amount to as much as $400,000 thus became an interest-free "loan" large enough to permit the shipper to invest in two cargoes of tea, and a fast tea clipper could make two round-trip voyages in that time. So, again, speed helped the merchant pyramid his earnings.

One New York firm that took an ingenious advantage of the China trade was F. & N. G. Carnes. Frank Carnes, stationed in Paris, purchased samples of the finest French merchandise that was selling at premium prices to wealthy Americans. His brother Nathaniel in New York sent the samples to China, where they were copied in perfect detail and mass-produced at a fraction of French prices. Soon the artisans and workshops in Canton were churning out imitation French ivory chessmen and fans, peacock feathers, backgammon boards, jewelry, and silk goods to be shipped to New York, where the Carnes firm sold them at one tenth the cost of the French originals. Some of the dress goods even bore imitation Paris labels. Within a few years the New York market was flooded with Chinese imitations, by which time the firm of F. & N. G. Carnes had made a fortune.

The China trade required huge investments, and only a few of the wealthiest shipping merchants had or could call on such large sums. Because of the inherent dangers of ocean shipping, especially in the hard-driven clippers, it was a high-risk business. So these conservative businessman learned to gamble. And when the Gold Rush offered its own high-stakes wager, the South Street merchants were ready. They reacted with the same assumption that had motivated Robert Waterman to buy his ranch in California: Their richest prospects lay in taking advantage of San Francisco's rapidly rising demand. The money was to be made not by transporting impoverished would-be gold diggers but by shipping them the necessities they would need and would shortly be able to pay for at extravagant prices. So the New York merchants became engaged in a double race. While rushing their tea clippers home for the San Francisco trade, they meanwhile hurried to commission larger, sturdier vessels. Clearly the Cape Horn passage required something more than a tea clipper. The seas off Cape Horn were generally stormier than those off the Cape of Good Hope. Moreover, the cargoes for California—tools and machinery, building materials and canned goods—were a lot heavier than tea. New York's shipping merchants needed big, strong vessels that could carry more cargo and battle to windward through the punishing westerlies off Cape Horn.

And faster vessels. Rarely had there been such a sudden market as that in San Francisco; but it was a highly volatile market. A cargo of any scarce merchandise would bring a huge profit only to the merchant who got it there first. This simple law of economics was elementary to the canny Yankees in South Street's countinghouses, who also were not unaware that a bigger, faster clipper could perform equally well in the tea trade, outsailing the current tea clippers with the first cargo of the season. In fact, the shrewd Abiel Low instructed this captains to let other skippers take the most expensive first pick of the crop and wait a week or two for the second offering, which was cheaper. One of the fast Low tea clippers still could beat the other vessels home, thereby making money at both ends of the voyage. And because California had nothing to export—except gold dust, which could be sent across the Isthmus—New York shipping merchants could send their clippers on to China to load for London or New York in an around-the-world trade.

The New York merchants, scrambling to turn their tea clippers around as soon as they came home, were somewhat embarrassed to be beaten by a transatlantic packetowner who was a stay-at-home Yankee in Boston. Warren Delano was a rarity among Boston's merchant shippers, most of whom still were unconvinced that greater speed was worth sacrificing capacity with the narrow-hulled clipper ship. Delano owned the clipper *Memnon,* a near-sister ship of the *Sea Witch,* also designed by John Griffiths, who had hoped to match her performance. The *Memnon* rarely did (possibly because she never had Robert Waterman on her quarterdeck), although she performed well in the transatlantic packet trade. Delano took her off the Atlantic run and sent her to New York to load for San Francisco in April 1849, while his New York competitors still were bringing their tea clippers home. The *Memnon* sailed from New York on April 11. Forty-five days later she put into Montevideo with a mutinous crew, most of whom Captain George Gordon replaced with local sailors. The *Memnon* finally reached San Francisco in 130 days (123 sailing days), a record for the voyage and a full 20 days better than the 150-day passages of the fastest previous vessels. Her record stood for nine months, until the best of the New York tea clippers got into the race.

The first of them was the Low brothers' *Samuel Russell,* with a Low brother, Captain Charles, as skipper. He had almost missed out, arriving home with the *Houqua* just in time to assume command of the *Russell.* She sailed for San Francisco on January 15, 1850, only six days after Low's arrival home. She was so crammed with 1,200 tons of merchandise for the gold-diggers that Captain Low had to make room in his cabin for her sails because the forepeak was full of cargo. He later claimed that "her scuppers were not more than a foot out of the water." One boarding sea swept away the *Russell*'s binnacle and her two compasses, and Low had to navigate with an unreliable six-inch boat's compass until he could borrow a couple of ship's compasses from a vessel the *Russell* overtook; Low promised to return them in San Francisco and roared on. Off Cape Horn, he recalled, "the ship's decks were flooded day after day. Sometimes she would go under water and it seemed as though she would never come up." But Captain Low brought her charging through the Golden Gate (without benefit of pilot because he considered their rates too high) in only 109 days from New York, cutting the record time by a full three weeks. Low was in San Francisco six weeks recruiting a crew to sail on to China; and still he had to leave the borrowed compasses with his benefactor's shipping agent because the ship had not yet arrived.

The Lows' *Houqua* did not do as well as the *Samuel Russell*; the *Houqua* took 130 days for the voyage, arriving on July 23, 1850. But on the next day Howland & Aspinwall's *Sea Witch*, with Robert Waterman's former first mate George Fraser in command, proved that she still was the clipper to beat, storming into San Francisco Bay only 97 days after leaving New York. She was the first vessel to make the passage in under 100 days, and she did it against the Antarctic's winter westerlies. Within less than a year the record for the Cape Horn run had been cut by more than a month. No sailing ship of the *Sea Witch*'s 170-foot size would ever match this passage.

But larger, faster ships were now being rushed to completion by the frantic shipbuilders. A few New Yorkers spoke out to deplore the mad rush to deplete eastern warehouses of goods at the risk of causing shortages at home in order to make quick profits at the other side of the continent. When word of this attitude reached San Francisco, one newspaper editor had a sardonic and perceptive reply:

> If our merchants on the Atlantic coast may complain that they have been injured by sending out to California the useless trash, that they could sell nowhere else, they may well be proud that the discovery of golden sands has done more in four years toward improvement in the style of shipbuilding than would have occurred from other general causes in half a century. The antiquated hulks which, like huge washing tubs, have been floating about the seas, sailing about as fast sideways as in any other

direction, have been forced by the rapid spirit of trade with California to give place to entirely new models, graceful in their motions as swans on a summer lake and fleet as a cloud that is blown before the gale.

Graceful, fleet—and huge—ships were indeed splashing into New York's East River at an increasing rate. Manhattan's yards produced thirteen clippers in 1850; fifty-four were built in 1851. They were being launched so fast that frequently New Yorkers could watch a new one proceeding down the harbor with riggers still in her yards fine-tuning her shrouds and stays. With the East River yards working at capacity, some New York shipping merchants turned to New England. For their first new California clipper the Low brothers selected a brilliant young ship designer named Samuel Hartt Pook, who had a knack for marine architecture in his genes; his father was a prominent ship designer for the U.S. Navy. Young Samuel Pook had become an observant student of the theories of John Griffiths and had adopted them so successfully that his reputation had reached New York. Because Pook was a free-lance designer, the Lows picked Samuel Hall's shipyard for the construction of the clipper. They had some trouble persuading the conservative Hall to follow Pook's extreme design, but Hall grumblingly consented and built the *Surprise*.

Pook's creation resembled the *Sea Witch,* but at 1,261 tons was more than two hundred tons larger. And she created a sensation, partly because Hall, finally converted to the clipper, completed all of her rigging while she was still on the ways. Even her skysail yards were sent up atop her masts, and all her flags were flogging in a brisk autumn breeze when she splashed into the Charles River on October 5, 1850, less than three months after the *Sea Witch's* dramatic arrival in San Francisco.

Abiel Low presented Hall with a $2,500 bonus at the launching. His confidence was not misplaced. Under the command of the salty down-east Captain Philip Dumaresq (pronounced "Demerrick") and with a crew of 50, the *Surprise* loaded in Boston and New York and sailed for California in December. Driving her hard all the way (he reefed her topsails only twice during the entire voyage), Dumaresq brought her into

San Francisco Bay in 96 days, 15 hours, cutting nearly half a day off the *Sea Witch*'s record. He then took her on to Hong Kong (in 46 days) and to London (in 107), paying for her cost of construction and making a $50,000 profit on her first voyage. Samuel Hartt Pook's fame has not lasted as it should have. Such Pook-designed clipper ships as *Red Jacket, Game Cock, Northern Light,* and *Herald of the Morning* would establish him among the top few marine architects of the clipper ship era.

With most of their competitors commissioning new clippers in New York and New England, Messrs. Grinnell and Minturn now made a shrewder move: They sent their agents scouting the shipyards for a clipper already under construction whose owner might be interested in selling her for a quick profit. Their scouts found one in East Boston, Massachusetts, in the shipyard of a builder whose name had just begun to be heard in South Street's countinghouses. He was Donald McKay; and his newest clipper was to be called the *Flying Cloud.*

3

A Challenge to the *Challenge*

AMONG THE MANY SHIPBUILDERS at work on fast new vessels for the Cape Horn passage, two of the most skillful were William Webb in New York, who was rushing completion of the *Challenge,* and Donald McKay in East Boston, who was putting the finishing touches to the *Flying Cloud.* The two men had been apprentices together; both had studied and adapted the theories of John Griffiths; now they were simultaneously producing clipper ships that would compete with each other in the race around Cape Horn. Other clippers were taking to the water and loading for San Francisco at the same time. But these two were the largest, and both were expected to set new records for the passage to California.

Captain Robert Waterman, conferring with William Webb on the rigging of the *Challenge,* was unaware of the threat from East Boston; the *Flying Cloud* had only just caught the eye of the scouts from Grinnell, Minturn. And the name of Donald McKay had not yet become one to reckon with. New York's captains and merchants considered the New York shipyards as unrivaled. The East River yards were where the biggest, fastest new clippers were being built. Indeed, the earliest clippers were known worldwide as "sharp ships on the New York model." John Griffiths testified that the East River yards' workmanship was "the standard for nearly all parts of the commercial world." But the New York shipyards were expensive. For one thing, the demand was high; as the *Herald* reported, there was "a perfect mania for shipbuilding," and the East River yards were swamped with orders. Moreover, lumber costs were greater in New York than in New England. The forests of oak trees that supplied ships' frames were farther away from New York than from Boston, Portsmouth, New Hampshire, or Bath, Maine. The tall white pine that made the best masts and spars also had to be shipped down to New York from New England. And the demand was so great, the *Herald* reported, that "every farmer who has a tree for sale refuses to part with it except at an enormous price."

As a result, more New York–registered vessels were being built outside the city. But the East River yards built the big ones, and in actual tonnage New York led the rest of the nation by a large margin. Concentrated in a one-mile stretch along the East River from Corlears Hook to 13th Street, the New York shipyards presented a skyline of looming superstructures surrounded by their latticed scaffolding. The big ships in various stages of completion lined the river, their sterns at the water's edge, poised to slide down the ways as soon as they were completed. The wide ramp alongside each hull was crowded with workmen carrying timbers and fittings to deck level. Others swarmed over the scaffolding finishing the hull planking. Back from the water's edge the area resembled a lumberyard, with planks and beams of every size and shape stacked row on row, some seasoning in the sun and others ready for use. The shipyards seemed even noisier than South Street, with steam hoists chunking and hissing, saws shrieking and whining, and men shouting to one another over the din. The air everywhere was permeated by the pungent scent of new sawdust and the acrid smell of bubbling tar.

The East River yards were the beneficiaries of the mid-nineteenth-century wave of immigration; but the sudden supply of labor included few skilled shipwrights, and it took more than a year of apprenticeship to train them. This scarcity had led in the early nineteenth century to the formation of unions to agitate against the shipyards' traditional dawn-to-dusk work hours (4:30 A.M. to 7:30 P.M. during the summer) for wages as low as $1.25 per day. In 1833, the two unions representing the most sought-after workers united under the imposing banner of The New York Journeymen Shipwrights' and Caulkers' Benevolent Society and threatened to strike for a ten-hour day at better pay.

The shipyard owners resisted at first, especially those who had signed contracts at prices estimated on the basis of the traditional work rules. But after a year of sporadic strikes, the NYJSCBS finally won a ten-hour working day from 6 A.M. to 6 P.M. with an hour off for breakfast and dinner and brief interruptions for a tot of morning and afternoon grog. At the same time the pay was raised to $1.50 per day.

Life in the East River shipyard was punctuated by a Mechanics' Bell, paid for by the union and mounted on a metal tower atop a shed on Lewis Street between Fourth and Fifth streets in the center of the shipyard area. A local workman was paid $50 a year to ring the bell at 6 A.M. to start the shipyard day, at 8 A.M. for breakfast and at 9 A.M. to resume work, at noon for dinner and at 1 P.M. for the afternoon work period, and at 6 P.M. for closing time. By 1840 the pay for a ten-hour day had risen to $2. Spurred by rising wages, New York's shipbuilders adopted a number of labor-saving devices. The two-man teams that worked in a sawpit, one man in the pit and one on the plank, were replaced by a steam sawmill. New derricks hoisted the heaviest frames; before their introduction, all other work in the yard had paused while everyone joined a frame-lifting gang. And a lathe now punched out treenails—the wooden fasteners for the ship's planking—that skilled carpenters hitherto had chopped out of oak blocks with a hatchet. Still, the shipyard was so labor-intensive that when the rush of clipper orders forced the builders to expand and the number of workers swelled to ten thousand, the wage was driven up to the unbelievable sum of $2.50 per day. Shortly the big vessels, the clippers and the packets, had taken over the East River yards. Only their owners could afford the mounting costs.[1]

Of all the East River shipyards, perhaps the busiest was that of William Webb, which stretched along the East River from Fifth to Seventh streets. He was the remarkable son of a remarkable father. Isaac Webb had been famous for the quality of his ships—one of them was Waterman's *Natchez*. But by the 1840s he had become even more renowned as "the father of shipbuilders," because so many of his apprentices, including his son as well as Donald McKay, went on to build the most successful vessels of the clipper ship era. Isaac Webb died at forty-six. William was only twenty-four when he inherited the shipyard. He soon became known for his swift packets; one of them, the *Yorkshire,* was called "the fastest packet of her time." A stocky, steady man, his balding head fringed with curly hair, Webb had an innate feel for the proper dimensions of a ship's hull; he devoted as much attention to his painstakingly whittled models as to the drawings on the drafting tables. He cherished and preserved his father's devotion to quality. And when the Gold Rush precipitated the demand for big, fast, strong ships for the Cape Horn passage, most of New York's shippers turned to him. So busy was the Webb shipyard that N. L. & G. Griswold, even with their influence, were lucky to get him for their ambitious venture.

Perhaps one reason—and a sure sign of the clipper fever sweeping South Street—was that N. L. & G. Griswold instructed William Webb to take no account of the expense so long as the finished vessel was the finest and fastest clipper of them all. Her timbers were to be selected carefully and ordered specially if necessary. Only Webb's best shipwrights were to be assigned to her. And her lines were to be the sharpest yet designed.

As he did with every new vessel, William Webb first made a meticulous model of the clipper-to-be. The midnineteenth-century shipbuilder's model was a work of art in itself. Prospective vessels had been carved in miniature for centuries. But the Americans had perfected the "lift model," so called because it was carved not from a solid block of wood but from separate horizontal layers, or "lifts," usually alternating between cedar and pine and held together by dowels. Moreover, it was a vertical half model—that is, it represented one side of the vessel. Since both sides would be identical, there was no need for a full model. This breakaway miniature permitted the marine architect to test various alterations in the shape of the hull simply by changing the layers. Carl Cutler called the lift model "the most important invention in the history of wooden shipbuilding" and claimed, "It is doubtful whether the clipper ship would have attained anything like the degree of perfection it eventually did, without the assistance of this invention."

William Webb whittled, shaped, sanded, and smoothed the *Challenge* model until he had precisely what he wanted. It was his refinement of the hulls that John Griffiths had given the *Rainbow* and the *Sea Witch*. The *Challenge* would have an even sharper bow and a less rounded stern than her predecessors. Once his layered lift model had achieved the perfect shape, Webb pulled out the dowels, separated the layers of wood, and outlined them on graph paper so that the relative differences could be measured. This was what the marine architects called the "sheer plan." Since the model had been made to exact scale, simple multiplication provided the dimensions of each "layer" of the actual hull-to-be. These dimensions were then laid off on the floor of the shipyard's mold loft. The usual scale was one-quarter inch on the sheer plan for each foot of the ship, so a ruler indicating 48 times the length of a line on the drawing automatically provided the full size as it was transferred to the loft floor.

The mold loft was a marvel of the midcentury shipyard. The size of a ship, the barnlike structure featured a shiny black floor on which a full side of the vessel was charted in chalk. And since there could not be a separate mold loft for every layer, each was drawn over the other. To distinguish one from another, the layers were drawn in different colors. The mold loft's floor thus became a kaleidoscopic pattern of intersecting curves. Indeed, learning to "read" the outline of each layer by following the line of one color and ignoring the others was one of the first and most difficult lessons to task the apprentice shipwright—not to mention the art of visualizing the one-dimensional lines as a three-dimensional ship's hull.

It was here, while translating the varicolored maze of chalk lines into a full-bodied vessel, that Webb made his final adjustments, thinning the upper layers at the forward end for a sharper bow and widening the lower layers at the middle for less dead rise (V-shape) to give the vessel a flatter bottom. The patterns on the mold loft floor were in turn used to make wooden molds, which were to the shipbuilder what paper patterns are to the dressmaker. The molds were handed over to the foreman in charge of shaping the timbers. In a large yard like Webb's, hundreds of timbers were already stockpiled and carefully stacked according to size, shape, and, most important, type of wood. For the *Challenge*'s keel Webb chose the best and thickest white oak, with somewhat thinner white oak for her framing timbers and planking, and white pine for her decks. A favorite wood for all clipper ship builders was live oak, which not only stood up under great stress but also grew in distorted shapes that could be used for such curved supports as the ship's knees, the angled pieces of wood used to buttress the deck timbers against the sides of the hull. Live oak grew in the swampy forests along the southeastern coast, where gangs of workmen felled the trees and floated them out to lumber schooners to be taken to New York and New England. Live oak brought premium prices—as much as $1.50 a cubic foot, compared to 65 cents for white oak. It was half again as heavy, and so tough that it was difficult to carve and shape without splitting. But its great tensile strength made it worth the extra work and expense. Webb set aside the best pieces in his yard for the *Challenge*'s knees, keelson, and bow and stern planking.

The wood for the *Challenge*'s timbers and planks had been harvested during the winter, when the sap had descended into the base and roots. (Sap tends to induce rot when the tree is cut.) The trunks and branches, selected for straight supports and spars, curved ribs and knees, were floated down rivers to waiting vessels, dozens of which could be seen sailing along the East Coast during the midnineteenth century. Unloaded at the shipyard, the trees were stripped of their bark and sawed into timbers or slabs. Then they were stacked in the yard to dry and season, in the course of which the wood shrank as much as 8 percent. To protect against later dry rot, they were soaked in salt solutions or chloride of zinc.

While the proper timbers were being selected, other workmen were laying down the slipway, the bed on which the *Challenge* would be born. Strong, square blocks of wood were laid in a line leading to the water's edge. These blocks, stationed so they could be knocked away at launch time, formed the base on which the keel would be laid. The keel was the ship's backbone, and William Webb was particularly careful in selecting the best white oak for it. No single tree trunk was large and sturdy enough for the *Challenge*'s 224-foot keel; separate sections of oak were fitted together with a diagonal tongue-and-groove and secured with long iron pins, called driftbolts, to fashion the centerpiece on which every other timber would depend. A longitudinal space between the keelblocks was left so that another, lighter "false keel" could be attached below it. This gave the ship a deeper, sharper keel; and it was attached lightly so as to break away if the vessel should run aground.

Above the *Challenge*'s heavy keel Webb's workers laid down her keelson, the inner keel to which the framing timbers would be secured. The *Challenge*'s keelson was doubled to give the huge hull extra strength. Both keelsons were bolted with iron to the keel; the combination of keel and double keelson formed a massive base 11 feet thick. From this sturdy base rose the *Challenge*'s tall ribs, each matching its wooden pattern from the mold loft and the original model. The timbers were bolted to the keelson and supported by knees of white oak. It was a tedious and painstaking procedure for the *Challenge* because Webb insisted on using tough live oak for her side timbers forward of the foremast and astern of the mizzen, where she would be pounded by the seas. Moreover, he introduced an innovation designed to make the clipper's hull even stronger: iron braces strung diagonally across the insides of the timbers and riveted to them wherever they crossed. The braces, four inches wide, three-quarters inch thick, and only four feet apart, rose from the keelson to the upper deck to form a rigid latticework of support. An early U.S. version of the iron frames that would be used in what the British would call a composite construction,[2] this iron skeleton made the *Challenge*'s hull almost indestructible.

The hard pine deck beams were now hoisted in place and the side timbers and their iron braces were made fast, with more white oak knees supporting the beams. At Webb's insistence, as many as 18 bolts were driven through the beams to the knees and side timbers. Meanwhile, the scaffolding was rising alongside the great hull as it took shape, and a gang of specialists working along the stages of the scaffolding bent the planking into place over the side timbers. This planking, the *Challenge*'s skin, was carefully culled from the shipyard's stacks of hard pine and live oak. The long planks were half a foot thick. Some were selected because they already curved, but most of them had to be steamed in order to be bent to the proper shape. Each of the steamed planks was secured to its side timbers by a clamp that was tightened day by day to bend it gradually.

Another gang marched steadily up the long gangway outside the scaffolding, carrying the loads of white pine for the *Challenge*'s 240-foot deck; it was 3½ inches thick, and Webb rejected every piece that had a knot. Yet another gang concentrated on drilling holes in the side planking and the deck boards for that ingenious fastener called the treenail (pronounced "trunnel"), a hardwood bolt that was pounded into each hole and expanded and clinched on the inside by driving a wedge into it. The outside end of this wooden bolt would swell when the hull was in the water, forming an impervious, immovable fastening. Thousands of holes were drilled into the *Challenge*'s hull and decks, to be filled with treenails of tough locust wood. As the scaffolding stages mounted higher, the planking crew left long rows of treenails projecting from the hull; and for a while the *Challenge* bristled like a porcupine until another crew followed the first, sawing off the projecting treenails so they were flush with the planking. Here, too, Webb added a safety measure for the *Challenge,* insisting that wedges be driven into the outside as well as inside ends of the treenails to make them doubly secure.

William Webb's shipyard was run on the principle of an early assembly line, in this case with separate teams of specialists moving over the stationary hull. The *Challenge*'s plankers, carpenters, and caulkers were followed by sheathers, who covered her bottom with metal to protect it from barnacles, weed, and boring worms. More carpenters littered her decks with their lumber and tools as they built her deckhouses, companionways, rails, and hatches. The *Challenge*'s hatch framings and the fife rails for her running rigging were carved from imported East India teak, and the combings of her companionways were of mahogany. Then came the cabinetmakers to panel the clipper's great cabin and her six staterooms with wainscoted oak and rosewood and to decorate her passageways with elaborately carved oak pilasters and cornices. Although clipper ships were designed primarily for cargo, their owners believed in the finest accommodations for the rare passengers who would pay the premium fare for the trip around Cape Horn.

More specialists installed the *Challenge*'s galley and copper pumps, her water tanks and cleats, her five boats, and her three anchors, which weighed a total of more than seven tons. The scaffolding now supported hundreds of men painting her hull black, with a single gold stripe from bow to stern and two round eyes at the catheads where her anchor lines passed from the deck. At her stern more painters embellished the counter with gilded branches; her name, CHALLENGE; and below it, NEW YORK. Another specialist worked under her bowsprit, installing her figurehead: a gilded eagle with widespread wings. And while Webb's workmen swarmed over the *Challenge*'s hull, Captain Waterman was supervising her all-important rigging.

The clipper ship's radical hull was of little use if it did not support enough sail to drive it through the water at the fastest possible speed. But the ship could be equally crippled by too much sail: She could dive too deeply into the head seas and reduce her speed, or lose her balance and heel over at angles that nullified the precise, trim design worked out on William Webb's drawing tables. Or she could simply lose her top-hamper, as so many clippers had.

Waterman prided himself on his expertise with a ship's rigging. His successful voyages had resulted to a large extent from his ability to shift the balance of his vessel until it was precisely right, to adjust the rake of her masts, to add spars and sails without making her top-heavy. And while so many other captains had lost their topmasts, Waterman had yet to lose a spar.

He was the acknowledged expert on the most efficient use of the ultimate refinement of the oceangoing sailing vessel: the square-rigged ship. Schooners with their fore-and-aft sails were more efficient for constant tacking alongshore in the coastwise trade. But for the long haul over the open sea there was nothing like a square-rigger.[3] The view from astern made it clear: Spreading all her sail, a square-rigged vessel presented an almost solid blanket before the wind so that scarcely a stray breeze could slip past. The clipper ships carried more square sails than any of their predecessors. Besides the studdingsails reaching out beyond the yardarms, most clippers carried five instead of the normal four yards atop one another. The sails were generally called, from lower to upper, the main, the topsail, the topgallant, and the royal topgallant, to which the clipper designers added a skysail. Waterfront wags claimed that some clippers also carried a cloud-cleaner, a star-gazer, a skyscraper, and even an angel's footstool, the latter so sensitive to the slightest breeze that no sneezing was permitted on deck while this sail was set. What the sailors were mocking was the clipper captain's attempt to put up clouds of canvas in light airs to catch every bit of breeze and thus keep her moving ahead. That was the fundamental mission of the clipper: to keep moving. Good time over an extended voyage depended as much on the ability to ghost along in near-calms as to reach the highest speed in a gale.

Although it may look picturesque today, the midnineteenth-century square-rigger was the ultimate modern refinement. The earlier huge, nearly unmanageable sails had been divided into smaller sections of canvas[4] mounted on separate yards one above the other, providing the skipper with a vast variety of sail plans. He could shorten or add sail in any number of increments. He could also reef (roll up) part of each sail to reduce its area of exposure to the wind and thus the overall wind pressure on the vessel's rigging. Few designers and even fewer captains had perfected the delicate balance of all this canvas. Waterman was one of the rare captains. The trick was to take every advantage of the stability of the *Challenge*'s enormous hull. At more than two thousand tons, she was a great brute of a ship, 224 feet long, the longest sailing vessel in the world—27½ feet longer than the biggest man-of-war in the U.S. Navy, the *Pennsylvania*. What Waterman had to do was design a sail plan that would drive this enormous hull right up to but not beyond the precise point of equilibrium.

Two rigging plans for the *Challenge* survive, the one proposed by Webb and the expanded one proposed by Waterman. There must have been some lively discussions between the Griswold partners and William Webb; shipbuilders disliked having a skipper tell them how to rig their vessels.[5] But the Griswolds backed Waterman, as George Griswold had promised. The *Challenge*'s final rig may have been refined by Webb's experts, but its daring loftiness came from Waterman. Her mainmast rose 230 feet to the gilded ball at the tip of the main-truck, almost four times the height of the tallest buildings in New York. To support this superstructure, the mainmast was three feet in diameter at its base, the width of a large oak tree. The *Challenge*'s foremast, only slightly shorter at 219 feet, was taller than the mainmasts of most ships. And her mizzenmast rose 190 feet. Her main yardarm was the size of the mast of a medium-size ship: 90 feet long and two feet wide. With studding-sails reaching out over the water from their yards, the *Challenge*'s main yard stretched 160 feet. Her three masts raked slightly, a little more than an inch to the foot in length. This towering array of masts and spars was designed to carry an unheard-of amount of sail: With everything set—fore, main, and mizzen, mainsails to skysails plus staysails between the masts and studdingsails reaching outboard—the *Challenge* spread 12,780 yards, more than seven miles, of Colt's best cotton duck. That was one suit of sails; her full complement, including spares, was more than twice that amount. The rigging to support the *Challenge*'s masts and spars, at Waterman's insistence, was made of the finest four-strand Russian hemp. And the running rigging to move the yards and hoist the sails was handspun Manila hemp.

To this orchestration of rigging Waterman added his own variations. The *Challenge*'s foremast stays, for example, were not made fast to the ship's bowsprit, as was the normal case. Waterman knew that too many foremasts had crashed to the deck when the bowsprit, battered by the waves of a storm, weakened or gave way. So the *Challenge*'s foremast was held in place by heavy shrouds anchored to the forepart of the hull itself. And the *Challenge*'s bowsprit, which supported as many as half a dozen jibs and other sails, was sturdier than the bowsprits of other ships. Another Waterman innovation was securing the mainmast stays to special bitts near the foremast on the main deck instead of to the anchor windlass on the foredeck, at once providing greater security and a clearer working area forward. In fact, all but a few lines from the *Challenge*'s rigging were led to her main deck, so her sailors would not have to work on the raised foredeck in the spray and boarding seas off Cape Horn. A ship's reporter who inspected the clipper after her rigging had been completed, claimed, "Of all the vessels which we have seen, not even excepting ships of war, we do not recollect one whose deck room for working ship is so spacious and well arranged as that of the *Challenge*."

Besides being the largest clipper[6] with the greatest sail area, the *Challenge* set another record before her launch: She cost $150,000, more than double that of the other clippers built in 1851. Still, the Griswold brothers could take pride in their selections of William Webb and Robert Waterman. Just as designer John Griffiths and Captain Waterman had combined to produce the record-breaking *Sea Witch,* so Webb and Waterman were about to launch the most promising clipper of them all. At the same time, however, another big, fast clipper was taking form in a shipyard in East Boston, one that would challenge the *Challenge* for the record on the Cape Horn passage to San Francisco.

The *Flying Cloud*'s designer and builder would later be acclaimed as the Leonardo of the clipper ship. But he called himself "a mechanic." His rise to prominence as a midcentury shipbuilder was a classic example of the talent, industry—and luck—that made the clipper ship era possible.

Donald McKay built his first vessel as a youngster when he and his younger brother Lauchlan constructed a sailing dory on the banks of the Jordan River near their farm outside Shelburne, Nova Scotia. In 1826 the McKay family pooled its savings to pay for Donald's stormy passage aboard a lumber coaster from Halifax to New York. He was sixteen years old and he brought with him little besides the homespun suit, made by his mother, that he wore when he stepped ashore in New York.

Young McKay went straight to the best-known shipyard along the East River, Webb & Allen, where he landed a job as a laborer. It was not long before he caught the eye of Isaac Webb, then thirty-two years old and already known for the solid training he gave his apprentices. They earned it. The indenture agreement that McKay signed on March 24, 1827, bound him as an apprentice to work from sunrise to sunset six days a week for $2.50 per week plus $40 a year for clothing.[7] In return Isaac Webb agreed to "use the utmost in his endeavors to teach, or cause to be taught or instructed, the said apprentice in the trade or mystery of a ship-carpenter."

McKay's contract was for the four years, six months until he reached twenty-one. For nearly all of that time he worked at most of the jobs in the Webb shipyard while learning the "mystery" of being a ship's carpenter. He later referred to his restrictive contract as "slavocratic." Yet he always remained grateful to Isaac Webb for the education he received—and for Webb's understanding when McKay asked to be relieved of the contract a few months before he had served his time. He had received an attractive offer from the shipyard next door. Isaac Webb agreed to release him, and in 1832 McKay went to work as a full-fledged shipwright at Brown & Bell. At this point he made another move that would result in advancing his career even more: He got married.

Albenia Martha Boole was the perfect bride for a young farmer's son aspiring to be a shipwright. She was the daughter of a shipbuilder, John Boole; two of her brothers were shipbuilders; and she had learned enough about the business so that she could design and lay off a ship's plans herself. She brought her husband a dowry sufficient for them to buy a small house on East Broadway. Even more important, Albenia's progressive father had seen to it that she had a much better education than most young women in the nineteenth century; so she was able to fill the many gaps in her husband's schooling, especially the elements of mathematics and engineering that became essential to his career as a shipbuilder.[8]

Second only to McKay's fortunate choice of a wife was a friendship he struck up with John Griffiths in the Smith & Dimon yard near Webb's. Griffiths was one year older than McKay and already beginning to formulate the theories that would lead to his controversial clipper *Rainbow*. Donald McKay's formative years could scarcely have been better planned. His days were spent working on the details of the transatlantic packets being built by Brown & Bell; his evenings were devoted to lessons in mathematics from his wife and lengthy discussions with John Griffiths over the comparative merits of the sharper bow, the longer hull, and the narrower afterbody of the fast sailing ship of the future. And it is likely that another Isaac Webb apprentice, his son William, sometimes joined them. It is not difficult to imagine these evenings in the parlor of McKay's East Broadway house, nor an exaggeration to suggest that the discussions, no doubt punctuated by lively arguments, contributed mightily to the development of the clipper ship.

By 1840 William Webb had inherited his father's shipyard; John Griffiths was lecturing and writing about his radical new designs; and Donald McKay had suffered a setback. On the recommendation of Jacob Bell, he had been hired by the Brooklyn Navy Yard, where he had become a foreman—and had met an unexpected obstacle. It was a time of violent reaction by New Yorkers to the flood of immigrants threatening to take their jobs, and the native Americans in the Navy Yard had refused to work for a "foreign" Nova Scotian. Again Jacob Bell came to McKay's rescue by sending him to Wiscasset, Maine, to supervise the design of some packets being built for New Yorkers. McKay soon discovered what Bell already knew: The conservative New England shipbuilders were not keeping up with the advances being made in the East River yards. It was the opportunity the ambitious young shipwright had been looking for. Within a year he had become a partner of the Newburyport, Massachusetts, shipbuilder William Currier. Two years later McKay formed another partnership, this time with Newburyport's William Pickett. Of the ships launched from the yard of McKay & Pickett, one, the 620-ton *Joshua Bates,* was the most important for McKay's fast-rising career, mainly because of the brilliant, eccentric, chauvinistic Bostonian for whom the *Joshua Bates* was built.

Enoch Train was a New Englander who enjoyed competing with his New York counterparts. He had taken them on successfully in the South American trade; now he was planning to go head to head with them in the hotly competitive transatlantic packet business. Train was aboard a Cunard packet to Liverpool to set up a terminal for his proposed White Diamond Line when he fell into a conversation with a fellow passenger, a New York merchant named Dennis Condry. It was one of those coincidences that kept occurring during the evolution of the clipper ship—William Aspinwall dropping in on John Griffiths' lecture, Nat Palmer finding William Low aboard his China tea trader when he was whittling out his new hull design. Dennis Condry, it happened, owned a merchantman, the *Delia Walker,* whose construction had been supervised by Donald

McKay, and the ship's performance had made Condry an ardent McKay booster. Over the brandy and cigars in the mid-Atlantic, Condry listened to Enoch Train complain that much as he would prefer to commission a New England shipyard to build his new packets, he would probably have to turn to the superior yards in New York. Condry asked Train if he had ever heard of Donald McKay. Train had not. Condry persuaded him not to make a commitment until he had at least talked to McKay. Bemused and intrigued, Train agreed, and on his return to Boston went up to Newburyport.

It was a meeting that clipper ship historian Arthur Clark characterized as "the swift contact of flint and steel." Within an hour Train had commissioned McKay to build the *Joshua Bates*. At 620 tons she was small by transatlantic standards; but Enoch Train was captivated by her lines. At her launching in 1844, without waiting to see how well she performed, he grasped McKay's hand and dramatically announced: "You must come to Boston; we need you; if you wish financial assistance to establish a shipyard, let me know the amount and you shall have it."

McKay may or may not have known how thinly stretched Train's finances actually were at the time. Evidently Train needed McKay's expertise as much as McKay needed Train's backing. But Train's encouragement was enough for McKay. The following year he and Pickett dissolved their partnership and McKay moved to East Boston, setting up his own shipyard at the foot of Border Street. Again his family moved with him, this time to a house he rented on Prince Street while he started the construction of a larger house on White Street, a few blocks from his shipyard. Over the next decade McKay's East Boston yard launched nine vessels for Train, most of them for his White Diamond Line. Increasingly larger and capable of carrying more passengers at ever greater speeds, the McKay packets, with Train's gigantic "T" emblazoned on their foretopsails, made the difference between success and failure for their owner. And for Donald McKay, the business provided by Enoch Train launched him at the age of thirty-four on a career that would make him the best-remembered shipbuilder of nineteenth-century America.

Not until he had built seventeen ships did McKay design and construct his first true clipper. The *Stag Hound,* as he called her, out-Griffithed the early Griffiths. Her 226-foot-long, 40-foot-wide hull was sharp-bowed and V-bottomed—four years after Griffiths had adapted Captain Nat Palmer's flat-floored design. Although the normal time for building a ship was half a year, McKay rushed the *Stag Hound* to completion in only one hundred days.[9] At 1,500 tons with a towering cloud of 11,000 yards of canvas, she was the largest U.S. merchant ship at the time. But not for long: Within a year after her December 7, 1850, launching, so feverish was the race to build ever-larger ships that a dozen bigger clipper ships went down the ways.[10] An early entry in the Cape Horn sweepstakes, the *Stag Hound* was, like many a McKay clipper, "overhatted," with rigging so lofty that the first good gale took her top-hamper away. But she went on to pay off her owners, Boston's Sampson & Tappan, for her $70,000 cost with her first cargo, which she rushed to San Francisco in 108 sailing days. In a little over ten months from the time of her departure from New York, she was back after circumnavigating the globe to bring home a cargo of tea. Besides paying for her construction, the *Stag Hound* earned a profit of $80,000 on her first voyage.

Donald McKay's backer Enoch Train had an ambitious young cousin[11] who had joined the firm as a junior clerk and worked his way up to a partnership. In his later years George Francis Train wrote a volume of memoirs in which he took credit for many of Enoch Train's dealings. Among the vessels Donald McKay had built for Train's White Diamond Line was the *Ocean Monarch,* which at 1,300 tons was in 1846 one of the largest ships in the packet trade. As George Francis Train remembered it half a century later, he went to McKay in 1850 and said, "I want a big ship, one that will be larger than the *Ocean Monarch.*" McKay's response was, "Two hundred tons bigger?" "No," Train recalled saying, "I want a ship of 2,000 tons," and added, "I shall call her the *Flying Cloud.*" Whether or not it was George Francis Train who first proposed the name still remains a question; his recollections of her tonnage and her first voyage, for example, are incorrect. In any case, what made the *Flying Cloud* immortal was the ship herself and her builder. And whether it was George Francis or Enoch Train who ordered the new clipper (or, more likely, George Francis acting on Enoch's orders), it was Enoch Train's firm that set on course a contest between the two most successful shipbuilders in mid-nineteenth-century America.

A frequent visitor to Donald McKay's shipyard during the winter and early spring of 1851 was Henry Wadsworth Long-fellow, who was fascinated by the wooden skeletons rising along the harbor's edge and who enjoyed the smell of fresh sawdust and the racketing sounds of saw and adze. He was particularly captivated by the craftsman's hull model and by the intricate details in which the bewildering patterns on the mold loft floor gradually became a graceful vessel, and he was understandably impressed by the spectacle of the *Flying Cloud* rising above all the other hulls in McKay's shipyard. When Longfellow returned to his house in Cambridge after his visits to East Boston, he began composing a poem:

> A little model the Master wrought,
> Which should be to the larger plan
> What the child is to the man,
> Its counterpart in miniature . . .

With an ear as true as his eye, Longfellow built his poetic ship from anchor to each "tall and tapering mast" and gave his poem the title "The Building of a Ship"; it was published a year after the launching of the *Flying Cloud*. "The Master," as Longfellow called McKay, had no pretensions to being a literary critic and was unlikely to comment on it as poetry. What he did know was that Longfellow's poem was very nearly a technically accurate manual on how to build a clipper ship.

Longfellow knew his ship's timbers, and he had surveyed McKay's yard with an observant eye:

> Timber of chestnut, and elm, and oak,
> And scattered here and there, with these,
> The knarred and crooked cedar knees,
> Brought from regions far away,
> From Pascagoula's sunny bay,

> And the banks of roaring Roanoke. . . .
> Choose the timbers with greatest care;
> Of all that is unsound beware;
> For only what is sound and strong
> To this vessel shall belong.
> Cedar of Maine and Georgia pine
> Here together shall combine. . . .

Unlike William Webb, who chose white oak for the keel of the *Challenge,* Donald McKay chose rock maple for the keel of the *Flying Cloud.* As with the *Challenge,* the *Cloud*'s keel was too long (208 feet) for one tree trunk, so separate sections were fitted together by the same tongue-and-groove method and secured with iron driftbolts. Above the *Flying Cloud*'s keel Donald McKay provided an ingenious addition; it had been used in British shipyards and had been introduced to Americans by Robert Bennet Forbes (who also perfected the Forbes double topsail). McKay drilled circular grooves along the length of the keelson and filled them with salt pickle to protect the wood further against rot.

Longfellow's poem meticulously followed the construction of the *Flying Cloud* as she took form on her slipway.

> Day by day the vessel grew,
> With timbers fashioned strong and true,
> Sternson and keelson and sternson-knee,
> Till, framed with perfect symmetry,
> A skeleton ship rose up to view!

And it was at this point in the *Cloud*'s construction that a marine architect could detect that she would not be merely a larger version of McKay's *Stag Hound.*

Since his move to New England, McKay had kept in touch with John Griffiths. Moreover, Griffiths was continuing to publish his theories on the proper design of a clipper ship. His most influential book, *A Treatise on Marine and Naval Architecture,* came out only a few months before the launching of the *Flying Cloud.* But McKay already knew that in the *Sea Witch* Griffiths had adapted Nat Palmer's flat floor into a compromise hull that had a sharp keel and a fuller body. McKay had given his *Stag Hound* the sharp V-bottom of Griffiths' earlier models. Now, with the *Flying Cloud,* McKay altered the design to a comparatively flat-floored hull.

The ribs of the *Cloud* rose gradually but impressively from her keel and keelson. Describing the phenomenon, Longfellow wrote:

> And around the bows and along the side
> The heavy hammers and mallets plied,
> Till after many a week, at length,
> Wonderful for form and strength,
> Sublime in its enormous bulk,
> Loomed aloft the shadowy hulk!

The workers' "heavy hammers and mallets" resounded through the shipyard. But McKay had also been quick to adopt most of the newest machinery from the New York yards. Chuffing steam engines hoisted the heaviest timbers, and screaming steam saws cut the planking to the correct lengths. McKay had devised his own version of the mechanical saw, one that could be swiveled to cut in any direction, saving thousands of man-hours formerly devoted to hand-carving the intricate curves of a ship's knees and ornaments.

McKay's ideas and refinements were everywhere; so was McKay. Workers on the scaffolding would discover him standing alongside them chalking the side of a rib that needed to be shaved, testing a row of treenails for fit, rejecting a slab of planking that was an inch or two out of line. McKay rarely raised his voice, but the firm line of his stubborn jaw was unmistakable. His bushy brown hair, usually sawdust-spotted, was held in place with a hat; McKay never appeared in the yard in workman's clothes. It was the custom of the time for the boss to wear a business suit, so it was impossible to miss McKay as he climbed about a ship or picked through the stacks of timber. A photograph of him shows the high brow, the leathery skin, the piercing eyes, and the spare figure conditioned by years on his feet in the open. McKay spent very little time behind a desk.

He had no pretensions. "My speech is rude and uncultivated," he said at one launching, "but my feelings, I trust, are warm and true." He was a workman, less the "mechanic" that he called himself than a devoted craftsman, nursing along and worrying over every detail in each of his ships. Night watchmen at his yard claimed often to have seen McKay materialize alone in the dark standing beside one of his ships in her slipway and caressing her hull.

McKay expected excellence from his workmen, dealt firmly with those who failed him, and rewarded those who met his strict standards. He kept men on the payroll when there was not enough work for them during lean years. He often helped a worker's family with a gift or a loan. His generosity would hurt him in later years, but during this period of clipper prosperity he could afford to treat his employees well. It was their boast that the McKay yard was like a huge family. McKay himself by this time had reason to devote himself almost entirely to his shipyard. His wife, Albenia, had died in December 1848, and he turned to his ships for solace. By then he had kept a promise made twenty-two years earlier on his departure from Halifax. Five of his brothers, with their families, had moved to East Boston to work in the McKay yard. Later his mother and father also would settle in Boston. So there were relatives on hand to help bring up his motherless children. But throughout their marriage Albenia McKay had also served as a silent business partner, balancing the shipyard's books; reviewing ships' plans with her husband; and keeping track, largely through her shipbuilding brothers, of the latest clipper designs in New York.

Within a year McKay had taken another wife. Mary Cressy Litchfield of East Boston had come to work as his secretary and had become his invaluable assistant after Albenia's death. Mary continued to help at the shipyard after their marriage, and one of her major contributions was suggesting the names of some of his later clippers—*Westward Ho, Sovereign of the Seas, Romance of the Seas.* But she could not replace Albenia McKay in casting a balance sheet, and it is probable that McKay's later reputation as a better shipbuilder than businessman reflected the loss of Albenia's sure managerial sense.

Donald McKay was not a revolutionary theorist like his friend Griffiths. McKay's contribution to the clipper ship was

his unerring ability to synthesize the contributions of his contemporaries, to reject and select and in the process produce a
near-perfect combination in ship after ship. He made no design
breakthroughs like Griffiths or Palmer. His friend and competitor William Webb built more clippers. But McKay remains the
most famous clipper ship designer, largely because he combined
the ideas and expertise of all the shipbuilders to produce a fleet
of sailing vessels unmatched by any in history.

In the *Flying Cloud* McKay made another change. Although she was 250 tons larger than the *Stag Hound,* her sail
plan was smaller.[12] No doubt the *Stag Hound*'s near-dismasting
explained this alteration. McKay was forever learning from his
own experience as well as others' examples. "I never yet built a
vessel that came up to my ideal," he once said. "I saw something in each ship which I desired to improve on." So he planned
fewer yards of sail for the *Flying Cloud.* And he made the *Cloud*'s
masts extra-thick.

Now the work went with a rush. The *Cloud*'s figurehead,
a white and gold angel with a trumpet, was joined to her bow.
The cabinetmakers paneled her cabins in rosewood and mahogany. The latest in winches and windlasses, pumps and capstans,
cranes and ventilators were installed on her 235-foot deck. The
nearby sail loft became a sea of white as acres of Colt's cotton
duck were cut and sewn for the *Cloud*'s three sets of sails, the
lightest for calms and the heaviest for the storms off Cape Horn.[13]
It was while the *Flying Cloud* neared completion that the scouts
from Grinnell, Minturn studied her and made their recommendation to the firm's headquarters in New York. George Francis
Train gave his version of what happened next:

> No sooner was the *Flying Cloud* built than many ship-
> owners wanted to buy her. Among others the house of
> Grinnell, Minturn & Co., of the Swallowtail Line, of
> Liverpool, asked what we would take for her. I replied
> that I wanted $90,000, which meant a handsome profit.
> The answer came back immediately, "We will take her."
> We sent the vessel to New York under Captain Cressy
> while I went on by railway. There I closed the sale, and
> the proudest moment of my life, up to that time, was

when I received a check from Moses H. Grinnell, the New
York head of the house, for $90,000.

George Francis Train's recollection half a century after the
event is almost certainly in error. Surely Enoch Train, the un-
disputed boss of the firm, would have been the one to make the
decision to sell the *Flying Cloud*. What is true is that nearly all
of the Grinnell, Minturn vessels were busy on the firm's Swallowtail transatlantic packet line, that Grinnell and Minturn wanted
to get into the California trade, and that there was no better
way to make a dramatic comeback than by sending out the biggest new clipper of them all. No doubt they were keeping a
wary eye on their competitor N. L. & G. Griswold's even larger
clipper rising on her stocks in William Webb's yard; perhaps the
sight of the *Challenge* alone was enough to induce them to put
up $90,000, which was considerably more than Donald McKay
was charging Enoch Train to build the *Cloud*.[14]

As for Train, presumably he set his high asking price on
the assumption that no one would pay that much—and if they
did, why not make a big profit on the ship without the risk of
a single voyage? His White Diamond packet line was a drain on
his finances at the time. McKay's *Stag Hound* was still unre-
ported en route to San Francisco. Whatever Enoch Train's reasoning, he later admitted that selling the *Flying Cloud* was a
mistake he regretted for the rest of his life.

The *Flying Cloud*'s ownership was of little concern to the
crowds that gathered around McKay's East Boston yard on the
morning of April 15, 1851. Among the special guests under the
tent McKay usually provided for such an occasion must have
been his friend Longfellow, who described the climactic scene
in his "The Building of the Ship":

> Then the Master,
> With a gesture of command,
> Waved his hand;
> And at the word,
> Loud and sudden there was heard,
> All around them and below,
> The sound of hammers, blow on blow,

Knocking away the shores and spurs.
And see! She stirs!
She starts,—she moves,—she seems to feel
The thrill of life along her keel,
And spurning with her foot the ground,
With one exulting, joyous bound,
She leaps into the ocean's arms!

McKay is said to have disapproved of the excessive festivity of most ship launchings; when his packet *Daniel Webster* had been launched the previous year, the honored statesman had had to cut short his speech because a prominent Boston merchant toppled drunkenly into the harbor and had to be fished out with a boathook. The *Flying Cloud*'s launching was unmarred by such incidents, however, and as soon as her topmasts were in place, she was towed to New York by the steam tug *Ajax*. Her captain was already aboard, tuning and testing her stays and running gear, studying her response to the helm, and checking out every detail so she would be ready to go to sea the moment her cargo was aboard. Josiah Perkins Creesy[15] evidently had been Enoch Train's choice for command of the *Cloud;* and presumably no one at Grinnell, Minturn, her new owners, preferred another candidate. Creesy, a native of Marblehead, Mass., was a veteran of the China trade with a record for fast passages nearly as impressive as that of Robert Waterman.

The *Flying Cloud* had beaten the *Challenge* into the water; the latter was still on her slipway at William Webb's yard when on April 28 the *Cloud* came into New York Harbor on her towline and was warped into Pier 20 nearly a mile down the East River, where Grinnell, Minturn's Swallowtail packets docked. Throughout the month of May, Pier 20 swarmed with arriving carts, drays, and wagons; longshoremen loading the ship's hull; and thousands of sightseers admiring the new clipper. Her foretopsail yards were adorned with a rippling banner proclaiming "FOR CALIFORNIA!" Her maintop, taller than any nearby building, and her huge hull lorded over the Swallowtail packets around her. For the moment the *Flying Cloud* was the largest merchantman afloat.

But only for the moment. She was still taking on cargo

when on May 24 the *Challenge,* nearly two hundred tons larger, thundered into the East River before a record audience at William Webb's shipyard. For a fortnight the two clippers, at their piers a few blocks apart, vied for New Yorkers' attention. Messrs. Grinnell and Minturn contributed to the drama by inviting special guests, including the press, to inspections and dinners aboard the *Flying Cloud.*[16] Similar receptions aboard the *Challenge* were presided over with greater flamboyance by Robert Waterman, who delighted in playing to his audience. Meanwhile, New York's shipping merchants rushed their goods aboard the *Challenge* as well as the *Flying Cloud.* One of them, Joseph Brewster, went aboard the *Challenge* on the morning of July 12, 1851, to check on the goods he had sent aboard. The *Challenge*'s deck hatches were closed and it was dark belowdecks where Brewster was walking along a passageway. He stepped into an open 'tweendeck hatchway, fell fourteen feet into the hold, and died of a fractured skull.[17] With a month's head start, the *Flying Cloud* filled her hold before the *Challenge* could. The *Cloud*'s hatches were closed and she was made ready to sail. Josiah Perkins Creesy and his wife unpacked their belongings in the captain's cabin. Eleanor Creesy was nearly as essential to the future of the *Flying Cloud* as her husband: She served as his navigator. And among her effects were two volumes titled *Wind and Current Charts* and *Sailing Directions.* Both were compiled by Matthew Fontaine Maury, a man who would contribute nearly as much to the successes of the clipper ship era as all the merchants, shipbuilders, and captains combined.

4

Tracking the World's Winds

EVERY GOOD NAVIGATOR knew that the shortest distance between two ports was not a straight line but the way of the wind. More than most clipper captains, Robert Waterman was famous for his knack of finding the wind. His 78-day run home from Canton in 1845 without once tacking had become a South Street legend. Like most captains, however, Waterman recognized that his knack was a combination of luck and expertise. By the mid-nineteenth century most skippers were familiar with the trade winds; but their global patterns, their seasonal fluctuations, and, equally important, the infinite variety of ocean currents still remained mysteries. So when a comprehensive new analysis of the oceans' wind and current patterns became available, Captain Waterman was one of the first to seize on it.

So was Eleanor Creesy. Her husband, however, was somewhat less enthusiastic; Josiah Perkins Creesy liked to play his hunches. But his commonsensical wife-navigator made sure that this enormously useful new aid to navigation was aboard the *Flying Cloud*. Thus both the *Cloud* and the *Challenge* had the advantage of Matthew Maury's *Wind and Current Charts*. And Maury's *Charts* had become available through another of those fortuitous coincidences of the clipper ship era, in this case when a landlocked naval officer stumbled onto a collection of cast-off ships' logs and recognized their hidden value.

The officer was Matthew Fontaine Maury. He had been born on a Virginia farm and had followed an older brother into the U.S. Navy, where he became particularly interested in navigation. His first sea duty was as a midshipman aboard the newly launched 44-gun frigate *Brandywine* in the autumn of 1825, on a glamorous cruise, as it happened: The *Brandywine* had been selected for the honor of returning the Marquis de Lafayette to Paris after a triumphal year-long tour of the new nation in whose war for independence he had played an important role. Then nineteen, Midshipman Maury was suitably impressed by the commanding figure of General Lafayette. He was even more impressed by the North Atlantic, which made him and nearly everyone else aboard the *Brandywine* seasick. But his chief discovery on this first voyage was a more dismaying one: Nathaniel Bowditch's *New American Practical Navigator,* the bible of the Navy that every midshipman was required to purchase along with his uniform, did not answer all of Maury's questions.

On his first shore leave, in Cowes on the Isle of Wight, where the *Brandywine* put in after disembarking Lafayette at LeHavre, Maury searched the bookstores for more useful works on navigation, without success. By the summer of 1826 the *Brandywine* had returned to the United States and set out again, this time around Cape Horn to relieve the frigate *United States* on her Pacific station; there Maury was transferred to the sloop-of-war *Vincennes.* The *Vincennes* was popularly known as "the fastest sailer in the Navy," but Maury was more pleased to discover that her library included many books on navigation, mathematics, and trigonometry; and he spent much of his off-watch time immersed in these books and chalking equations of spherical trigonometry on the round shot in the *Vincennes'* gun racks.

In 1829 the *Vincennes* was ordered westward across the Pacific for home, the first U.S. Navy vessel to circumnavigate the globe. Maury was fascinated by the variety of winds and currents in the Pacific, the China seas, the Indian Ocean, the Cape of Good Hope, and the South Atlantic. The long voyage also gave him time for more studying. Thus, during his first four-year tour of duty, the young midshipman was provided with an unparalleled opportunity to train himself as a navigator while studying firsthand most of the oceans of the world. He was not yet twenty-five.

And, it turned out, he had already become a bit overconfident. On March 3, 1831, appearing before an examining board of venerable naval officers, the young midshipman audaciously worked out the answer to a lunar navigation problem by spherical trigonometry instead of simply parroting Bowditch's rule; striding confidently to the blackboard, he chalked out his computation to prove it. The examiner questioning him could not follow his complicated solution and declared it incorrect. Maury insisted that he was right. The other board members, equally baffled, muttered to one another and agreed to support the examiner. The brash young midshipman was told to read his Bowditch more carefully and was listed as twenty-seventh in the class of forty, a low rating that had the effect of stalling his promotion for at least two years.

Three months later Maury was off to sea again, as sailing master of the sloop-of-war *Falmouth,* bound down around Cape Horn. His duty was to direct the officer of the watch on the vessel's course and how much sail to carry; more important, he was also the captain's navigator. Accordingly, before sailing he searched New York's bookstores for information on the winds, currents, and weather conditions of the North and South Atlantic and Cape Horn, and was disappointed to find virtually none. Sailing down the Atlantic, he kept a meticulous log of the winds and the weather, the currents and the stars, as well as records of the distance covered every 24 hours, the changing tides, and any errors in the *Falmouth*'s charts. By October 1831 the *Falmouth* was attempting to round the Horn against one of the cape's infamous westerly gales. As navigator, Maury took her farther and farther south, to 62° 5'S, near Antarctica's Palmer Archipelago, where he suddenly found more favorable winds. Meanwhile, wedging himself into his tiny, lunging stateroom, he compared his readings of Cape Horn's winds and currents with the reports he had assembled from published accounts by previous navigators of the cape, and composed his own recommendations for rounding the treacherous bottom of the continent.

He had guessed, and then proved by observation, that the prevailing winds south of the cape revolve in a clockwise circle around a low-pressure center. There are rare intervals when the flow reverses and a sailing ship can ride a favorable easterly past the Horn. But most of the time the cape's westerlies come screeching head-on against the ship's course, and the sailing skipper would cover as much distance tacking against them as by going south to find the easterlies at the bottom of the circle.

Maury took the *Falmouth* south of the storm she had encountered and around the Horn to Valparaiso in 24 days. (Another sailing ship entered the passage at the same time, stayed north, fought the westerlies for 38 days, and had to put into Talcahuano, south of Valparaiso, for repairs.) Summing up his findings in a scientific report to which he gave the title *On the Navigation of Cape Horn*, Maury mailed it to the *American Journal of Science and Arts* in New Haven, Conn. The *Journal*'s editor, Benjamin Silliman, received it some months later. He had never heard of Midshipman Matthew Fontaine Maury, but he was impressed enough to publish the report. Thus Maury made his first contribution to the clipper ship captains who a decade and a half later would be following him around Cape Horn.[1]

By May 1834 Maury was back in the United States; in July he married Ann Herndon, a distant cousin. And he started writing a book on navigation. He had plenty of time for it. The U.S. Navy, in the view of some of its old-line officers, was cursed by peace, which brought a reduced budget and put most of its officers on the beach at half pay. Maury was not to receive orders for sea duty for another four years. But his enforced idleness gave him the time he needed to complete his book.

His main complaint with Bowditch's *New American Practical Navigator*, besides its omissions and errors, was that it had been written for veteran captains and assumed too much knowledge to be useful for neophyte midshipmen. So Maury set out to simplify the principles of navigation. In April 1835, he sent off to Key & Biddle, a publishing firm in Philadelphia, the manuscript of *A New Theoretical and Practical Treatise on Navigation*. Key & Biddle accepted it and took a year to publish it.

The book's reception was almost universally favorable. The ultimate accolade came from Nathaniel Bowditch, who recommended that Maury's book replace his own as the required text for U.S. Navy midshipmen.[2] (It took the Navy eight years to follow Bowditch's suggestion.) Not the least of the rewards to Maury and his wife, who by now had given birth to a daughter, was a brisk sale of the *Treatise on Navigation*. And to cap his good fortune, Maury finally received in June 1836 his promotion to lieutenant. He seemed at last to be launched on a distinguished naval career.

His family had grown to a son and two daughters when finally Maury received orders to report to the brig *Consort* in New York. But the *Consort* would not be ready for sea for a few months. And because it had been nine years since he had seen his parents, who were now living in Tennessee, Maury decided to visit them on his way to New York. It was a decision that would forever alter Maury's career and incidentally be a major boon to the clipper ship era.

On the night of October 17, 1839, on his way to New York to report aboard the *Consort,* Maury was riding atop a stagecoach. The local agent at Lancaster, Ohio, had overbooked the coach, and Maury had relinquished his inside seat to a lady and joined two other passengers alongside the driver. Outside Somerset, Ohio, the driver let the stagecoach wander off the narrow road. Its right wheels sank into a soft shoulder and the coach toppled down a slope, throwing Maury clear. As he hit the ground he felt his right leg break.

Almost miraculously the others were unhurt. Maury lay on the slope for more than an hour while a fellow passenger rode one of the horses for help, returning with another coach and a local doctor. Maury was taken to a tavern in Somerset, since there was no hospital in the town. The fall had broken his right leg above and below the knee and had dislocated his kneecap. The doctor wrenched his knee joint back in place but did such a poor job of setting the fractures that another doctor was sent for. He rebroke and reset the leg—like the previous operation, without anesthetic.

It was early January 1840 before Maury, with a cast on his leg, was able to leave Somerset, going by sleigh to the nearest railhead and by train to New York. There he found that the *Consort* had sailed without him. In any case, he was in no condition to walk a pitching deck. He made his way home to Fredericksburg, Virginia, to recuperate and to confront the probability that he would always limp, that he would never be able to go to sea again, and that at age thirty-three his naval career apparently was at an end.

The best therapy, besides constant and still-painful exercise, was writing. The *Southern Literary Messenger*'s editor, Thomas W. White, agreed to a series of articles proposing reforms in the U.S. Navy. Assuming the pen name "Harry Bluff," Maury accused the Navy of deteriorating and offered some suggestions for remedying the situation. He called his series "Scraps from the lucky bag," Navy parlance for a ship's lost-and-found. Among his proposals was a Naval Academy similar to the Army's Military Academy at West Point. He also accused the Navy of graft in its ship-repairing procedures; twice as much was spent on repairs, he claimed, as on a ship's original cost. Hundreds of naval officers wrote—most of them anonymously to avoid reprisals from their seniors—to agree with Maury's criticisms and suggestions for reform. To Maury's dismay, the editor of Washington's *National Intelligencer* nominated "Harry Bluff" for Secretary of the Navy.

Not all of the readers were so approving. The Navy's commodores were perhaps understandably incensed. And when the true identity of "Harry Bluff" was inevitably revealed, Maury had reason to fear for his career once more. So he was surprised when in 1842 he was assigned to what seemed to him a challenging new post. The Navy's Depot of Charts and Instruments needed a principal. To the crusty top command the Depot of Charts and Instruments obviously looked like a perfect backwater in which to get rid of their troublesome lieutenant. But to Maury it was a godsent opportunity to remain in the service at a time when shore duty billets were scarce, and he was in no mood to inquire into the reasons for his good fortune.

The depot was a fusty, dusty warren of archives and scientific instruments; its major function in 1842 was to provide the correct time for the Navy's chronometers. The depot also was the repository for its sextants, barometers, thermometers, quadrants, and other navigational instruments. But its most important possession, Maury shortly realized, was a collection of ships' logs.

They had gathered in an ever-growing collection since the

early days of the U.S. Navy, one of those forlorn and embarrassing residues that nobody wanted but nobody could dispose of. By Navy regulations every ship's log was sent to the depot at the end of each voyage. There they sat, unread, regarded as historical records that might be needed sometime but never were. A few years before Maury's appointment, a predecessor had tried unsuccessfully to sell them as waste paper. It remained for Maury to realize that these shelves of neglected logbooks provided an invaluable aid to navigation.

A ship's logbook is a diary of her voyage, a chronicle of events, a daily record of the vessel's position, and—what was important to Maury—of the weather. The simple, brilliant realization that struck him when he surveyed the shelves of logbooks was that here was a running record of wind, weather, and current conditions along every route traveled by every vessel in the U.S. Navy. Not the general wind patterns across the oceans; not the vague maps of currents like the Gulf Stream; but specific observations of the precise wind direction and velocity along the major tracks of every ocean for every day of every ship's voyage. All that was needed, Maury realized, was to collate this information in a different way: by area.

Maury's discovery was rendered all the more important by a finding he had already made at the depot: The U.S. Navy had little navigation information of its own and few charts even of the waters off America's own coast. He had earlier pointed out to the Secretary of the Navy that U.S. ship captains were "dependent upon foreigners for the information by which we determine latitude and longitude at sea. The charts used by an American man of war when she enters the Chesapeake Bay," he wrote, "are English and we are dependent upon the English Admiralty for them"—an Admiralty against which the new United States had gone to war twice in the previous sixty-five years.

But the possibilities presented by the dusty Navy logbooks were greater than anything provided by foreigners. All Maury and his staff had to do was select an area of the ocean, go through the logs of Navy vessels that had traversed the area, and collate their observations. The result would be a compilation of information on the average weather, winds, and currents along the route. During all the centuries of seafaring and log-keeping this simple reorganization of vital information had never been systematically applied. Mariners had recorded overall observations and recommendations for the best tracks over various routes, though many a successful skipper had kept his most useful findings to himself. Such phenomena as the trade winds and the major gyres, the patterns of circulating ocean currents, were imperfectly understood. What Matthew Maury had come upon was a simple method of presenting the findings of hundreds of previous navigators to those who followed them. Maury explained it in a letter to Congressman and former President John Quincy Adams, who retained an abiding interest in the depot (and, Maury knew, a powerful influence in Congress and the Navy): Maury's plan was to organize the information in charts for navigators "in such a manner that each may have before him, at a glance, the experience of all."

Adams, it happened, was more interested in building a naval observatory; ever since he had been president he had campaigned for his "lighthouse of the skies." And shortly after Maury's appointment to the depot, Congress authorized $25,000 for an observatory that would also house the depot. The structure, which was built on a rise between D and E streets at 23rd Street in Washington in 1844, was welcomed by Maury, who became the first superintendent of the U.S. Naval Observatory. Even more welcome was the authorization to build a superintendent's house; Maury's family had grown to four children, with another on the way. But despite his increased responsibilities, he was determined to concentrate on his grand plan to aid the navigators of the midcentury world.

Under his direction the depot's fourteen staff members began assembling the logbook information by area. Maury then converted the written comments into pictorial charts, recording the logbooks' observations on maps of the oceans. Winds were represented by symbols that looked like shuttlecocks, each radiating lines whose length indicated the reported velocities; the head of the shuttlecock pointed in the observed direction of the wind, and its width represented the variations in the wind's direction. Ocean currents were indicated by arrow-shaped symbols; their length represented the current's strength, and figures alongside showed its speed.[3] The charts included such additional information as compass variations, differing water temperatures, and, in the earliest versions, the names of the Navy vessels whose logs had supplied the information.

Maury's superiors for once agreed with him wholeheartedly. They not only encouraged him in his project but also, at his urging, directed all Navy captains to fill out and send in special abstract logs that Maury designed to elicit specific information he needed for further charts. To supplement the logs he also persuaded some naval officers to record their ships' positions periodically, seal the information in drift bottles, and toss them over the side. All of this information was understandably slow in coming, but Maury and his staff found enough in the Navy's logbooks to produce the first pamphlet of charts in 1847. He gave them the workmanlike title *Wind and Current Charts,* and appended a slim volume titled *Explanations and Sailing Directions to Accompany Wind and Current Charts* (later simplified to *Sailing Directions*) in which he highlighted some of the lessons learned from the *Charts.* Both pamphlets were offered to Navy captains and navigators, but a few of the more alert civilian skippers, including some clipper captains, heard of them and asked the Navy for copies. Maury encouraged their use by clipper captains. Like nearly every other American he had marveled at the radical new tea clippers, the *Houqua,* the *Rainbow,* and the *Sea Witch,* and he realized how important it would be to the skippers of these racing vessels to have at hand his observations of the winds and currents of all the oceans. But it was an obscure captain of an ordinary trading vessel in the Atlantic who proceeded to make Matthew Maury famous in the commercial maritime world.

His name was Jackson and he was a veteran of the Rio trade. Early in 1848, he was about to take his usual cargo of flour to Brazil and return with coffee when he heard of the Navy's new *Wind and Current Charts* and *Sailing Directions.* Captain Jackson obtained copies of the pamphlets and took them aboard his bark *W.H.D.C. Wright* before sailing from Baltimore.

The first edition of *Wind and Current Charts* was especially detailed for the North and South Atlantic oceans. And one of

Maury's major discoveries in the Navy logbooks was that there were, in effect, shortcuts through the Atlantic's doldrums on both sides of the equator. Most navigators, accepting these frustrating windless areas as inevitable, resigned themselves to being slowed down and assumed that only the lucky skipper got through with a minimum of delay. But the pattern revealed by the hundreds of Navy observations was one of varying widths. "The calm belts of the sea," Maury explained, "like mountains on the land, stand mightily in the way of the voyager." But, he added, "like the mountains on the land, they have their passes and their gaps." Not only are some Atlantic doldrums narrower than others, but they also fluctuate with the seasons. So Maury was able to point out where the narrowest calm belts should be at different times of the year. Thus a navigator could plot his course to meet the doldrums where they presented the thinnest band of windless weather and get through the area with a minimum loss of time.

Moreover, *Wind and Current Charts* and *Sailing Directions* offered another vital discovery, particularly for a captain on his way to Rio. The normal route, which virtually all navigators followed and which was recommended by contemporary navigation manuals, went far out across the Atlantic on a slant toward the continent of Africa. A look at the map will explain why. Jutting halfway across the South Atlantic is Brazil's Cape de São Roque. It was an article of faith among Atlantic skippers that the worst mistake one could make was to get in under this cape on its north side, where contrary currents and trade winds blowing from the southeast would make it almost impossible to round the headland and proceed down the coast. In trying to avoid the cape, some Rio-bound captains went so far east that they sailed the equivalent of two transatlantic crossings, meanwhile wallowing along inside the doldrums instead of going straight through them.

But among the Navy's logs were some observations by navigators who, by accident or design, had sailed close to the coast above the cape. Instead of countercurrents, some had found "the current in their favor," Maury reported. And instead of head-on southeasterlies, there was a strong band of offshore winds that helped rather than hindered a sailing vessel rounding the cape. Maury's *Charts* showed these winds on the north side of the cape, and his *Sailing Directions* urged its readers not to go haring off into the Atlantic but to "Stand boldly on, and if need be, tack, and work by under the land." Maury was rarely equivocal about his recommendations. Here, he announced triumphantly, was a "Fair way to Rio."

That is exactly what Captain Jackson found. Following Maury's *Charts* and *Directions,* he went breezing down to Rio in 38 days from the Virginia capes, a passage that had usually taken him 55 days. Unloading his flour and taking on his coffee, Captain Jackson returned in 37 days. When he came into Baltimore Harbor more than a month ahead of schedule, the waterfront bars and countinghouses erupted with the news, which promptly spread up the coast to New York and New England, aided by a glowing editorial in the Baltimore *American*. Suddenly every skipper wanted copies of Matthew Maury's *Wind and Current Charts* and *Sailing Directions*.

Maury seized on the new demand by asking every commercial skipper to whom he gave his pamphlets to return the favor by filling out one of his abstract logs on the next voyage. Thus in a stroke he expanded what had been a compilation of old logbooks into a self-perpetuating supply of new information. Eager navigators snapped up five thousand copies of the first edition of *Charts* and *Directions;* and a revolutionary new service, a mutual exchange of information from all the oceans of the world, was under way.

In the decade that followed, as the abstract logs poured in, Maury annually updated and expanded his *Charts*. To the charts of the Atlantic and Pacific oceans he added similar observations on the Indian Ocean, as well as pilot charts that listed the average winds for each month and indicated the number of days the winds could be expected to blow at what velocities and from what directions, thus indicating the different routes that were best at different times of the year. In a steady flow of publications he presented charts of the trade winds and the monsoons, thermal charts, storm charts, and even a chart for whalers showing the best hunting grounds for their quarry.[4]

By 1851 a thousand American captains were using Maury's *Charts* and *Sailing Directions* and sending in his abstract logs.

Captain Phinney of the clipper *Gertrude* spoke for many others when he accompanied his abstract log with the note: "I am happy to contribute my mite towards furnishing you with material to work out still farther towards perfection your great and glorious task. . . . For myself, I am free to confess that for [the] many years I commanded a ship . . . I yet feel that until I took up your work I had been traversing the ocean blindfold."

Maury was especially gratified by the clipper captains' reception of his *Charts* and *Sailing Directions;* in his view the clipper ship was "the noblest work that has ever come from the hands of man." And it was not surprising that his *Wind and Current Charts* and *Sailing Directions* were the most important volumes in Eleanor Creesy's chart table aboard the new *Flying Cloud.* On the stormy fifteen-hundred-mile racecourse to the bottom of the world and back, a navigator needed all the help he—or she—could get.

5

A Special Breed
of Captain

In his book *Democracy in America,* Alexis de Tocqueville contrasted the American skipper with his Old World counterpart:

> The European sailor navigates with prudence; he sets sail only when the weather is favorable; if an unfortunate accident befalls him, he puts into port; at night he furls a portion of his canvas, and when the whitening billows intimate the vicinity of land, he checks his course and takes an observation of the sun. The American neglects these precautions and braves these dangers. He weighs anchor before the tempest is over; by night and day he spreads his sails to the wind; such damage as his vessel may have sustained from the storm he repairs as he goes along; and when at last he approaches the end of his voyage, he darts onward to the shore as if he already descried a port. The Americans are often shipwrecked, but no trader crosses the seas more rapidly.

De Tocqueville, writing in 1834, was describing American captains in general. But his characterization was particularly apt for the clipper captain, who had these qualities in the extreme. Like the clipper ship, he was a special breed and a valuable commodity. Like the clipper ship, he was the product of naval wars and smuggling, of races across the Atlantic and around the world to China. And like the clipper ship, he was the result of perfect timing: a maturing generation of American boys to whom the natural thing had been to go to sea in hopes of becoming a mate or a captain. A famous example was Joseph Peabody's East Indiaman *George,* known as the "Salem frigate"; over the years forty-five of her sailors rose to captain, twenty to first mate, and six to second mate.

Most young Americans learned the hard way, as Robert Waterman did, on the windy North Atlantic. The success of a transatlantic packet depended on her speed, regardless of calm and storm. An ambitious young man in the packet trade, one who turned out with a will to climb the ice-coated rigging and loose or furl the frozen sails, could count on rapid promotion. And the mate who could get the best performance out of the transatlantic trade's infamous "packet rats" was well on his way to becoming captain. The North Atlantic was the perfect proving ground for anyone aspiring to the quarterdeck. It is one of the world's most trying oceans, especially in winter on the westward passage against the prevailing winds. Packets regularly arrived in New York or Liverpool with their decks and yards encased in ice and one third of the crew in sick bay with frostbite or broken bones. The North Atlantic tested ships' officers as well as providing opportunities for them. On a stormy transatlantic run the skipper would spend a week or more on his quarterdeck, lashed to a chair for an occasional catnap. Those who survived were capable of handling almost anything. Yet even some skippers who had been successful in the packets were defeated by the hurricane-strength winds and heavy seas off Cape Horn or the typhoons of the Indian Ocean and the South China Sea.

The clipper captain had to be a formidable combination of technician, meteorologist, shipwright, skipper, and authoritarian. The calculations required to fix his ship's position could cover two or three pages. He had to tell from the color of the sky, the slant of the wind, and the shape of the clouds what sort of weather lay over the horizon. He had to know precisely how much wind each of his sails could take up to the last second when they would be blown to tatters. He had to be capable of rerigging on the run: shifting spars, adding studdingsails, raking the masts to get a little more speed out of the vessel. And because of the clipper ship's propensity for losing her high-strung top-hamper, he had to be capable of repairing the ship after a dismasting while losing as little of her speed as possible in the process. He was required to assert constant authority over a sullen crew often on the point of rebellion, and he had to be able to face down the toughest forecastle troublemaker in any situation. He was also the ship's doctor, frequently called on to set broken bones, stanch arterial bleeding, and diagnose the many illnesses that could affect the crew in all latitudes and weather conditions.[1]

Most of all, the clipper captain had to be one with his ship. To a greater extent than his contemporaries in the rest of the merchant marine, he had to have a sixth sense. His ship talked to him even when he was in his bunk, her creaking timbers or groaning masts telling him whether she was moving well down her plotted course or straining to the point of damage. A change in the heel of the vessel could wake him from a sound sleep; he usually had an extra compass swinging on gimbals above his bunk so he could check the course immediately on waking. By the thrumming of the rigging he could tell without going on deck when it was time to shorten sail—or, more important, when to loose more sail. (If, for example, the reef lines were tapping instead of drumming against the sail, that meant the canvas was not taut enough and it was time to add more.) Always he had to keep his vessel driving forward at top speed and at the knife edge of disaster. Most merchant skippers shortened sail when the winds became dangerous. Not the clipper captain: Gale winds provided his opportunity to achieve the speed necessary to get there before his competitors. His hard-driving style was a hallmark known around the world as "carrying sail New York fashion." He fought the storms off Cape Horn not just to get through them but also to do it in record time.

The unremitting pressure, day and night for two to three months, wore most captains out; they became ill or went berserk or simply gave up and eased the ship to her destination under reduced sail. The few who stuck it out, who kept her racing through storms and moving in calms, became the elite. They knew it, and they played up to it. The typical New York clipper captain dressed the part in a tall beaver hat, a long pearl-buttoned coat (custom-made by Brooks Brothers), trim, sharply creased trousers, and elastic-sided boots. Some carried gold-topped canes. The clipper captains made the popular City Hotel their headquarters, and while their ships were loading for San Francisco, they met daily at the Astor Bar for a noon drink and a wager or two on the next voyage. When a clipper ship returned to New York, his fellow captains congregated at the Battery to greet him and escort him to a homecoming dinner. There were a few salty New Englanders who disdained such display; but to New Yorkers the top-hatted, swaggering clipper captain was the hero of the hour.

He was rewarded well. To lure the best captains into the rich San Francisco trade, merchant shippers offered up to $3,000 for a single voyage around Cape Horn, with a $2,000 bonus for an especially fast passage. Many clipper captains were permitted to ship merchandise of their own, which could net them three or four times their pay and bonus; others were given part ownership of the entire cargo, sharing in the huge profits with the shipowner.

That was why Captain Robert Waterman was a wealthy man in his early forties. But he was more than a highly successful clipper captain; he was also the most colorful and the most controversial. Seamanship was in his blood. His father, Thaddeus Waterman, was a whaling captain; his mother was a Nantucket Coffin. Thaddeus had been among the group of Nantucket whalemen who had left home during the American Revolution. On their island thirty miles at sea they had been caught in the crossfire between Tories and Patriots; so they sailed to New York and 120 miles up the Hudson River to a settlement on the eastern shore called Claverack Landing, a shipping point for farmers of the Hudson River Valley. In 1784 they renamed the town Hudson.

On March 4, 1808, Thaddeus and Eliza Waterman's son Robert Henry was born. He was their third child and second son; his sister, Emma, was five, and his brother, Edward, was two; a fourth child, Elizabeth, was born three years later. In 1816 Thaddeus Waterman, after twenty-five years as a whaleman, was lost at sea. Eliza Waterman, unable to support her four children, left Hudson and moved in with relatives in Fairfield, Conn. Four years later, twelve-year-old Robert Waterman went to sea.

He had caught the eye of Captain John Sterling in nearby Stratford. Sterling had noticed the young man hanging about the wharves of Fairfield and Bridgeport and offered him a berth as a cabin boy on a voyage to India. Waterman quickly learned the way of the ship and signed on for Captain Sterling's next voyage, aboard the packet *Splendid* to South America. Reminiscing later, Waterman recalled that he nearly killed himself by trying an old sailors' trick. While repairing the running rigging, he decided to shinny down the edge of a sail to avoid the normal, longer route across the yardarm and down the shrouds. The wind was light; the sail flapped loosely and almost flipped him into the sea. He slid dizzily down the sail's edge, "tearing my fingernails out and skinning my shins," and at the last moment caught a bolt rope just in time to avoid plunging over the side. He not only survived but also earned another berth under Captain Sterling, this time aboard the *Nimrod* to China. Soon Waterman had graduated to the rough school of the transatlantic run and was advancing rapidly. By twenty-one he was the youngest first mate in the transatlantic packet trade and a protégé of Captain Charles Marshall, the salty skipper of the Black Ball Line's *Britannia*. On one voyage to Liverpool Waterman dived overboard to rescue a seaman who had fallen from a yardarm, holding the man's head above water until a ship's boat reached them. Next day he was upbraiding the same man for malingering.

The North Atlantic quickly separated the landlubbers from the seamen, and it was up to the mate to convert the former into the latter, by example when possible and by brute force if necessary. Confronted with the snow squalls, sleet storms, and towering waves of the North Atlantic, many a foremast hand understandably tried to avoid coming on deck with his watch. Even more men quailed at the prospect of climbing out on the icy footrope of a yardarm in such weather. Robert Waterman dealt with these men equitably but summarily. He expected no more than he would do himself, but he was ruthless with those who could not meet his standards. Anyone who tried to duck his duty was quickly beaten into submission. The nickname "Bully Waterman" began to spread through the waterfront saloons on both sides of the Atlantic. But however objectionable Waterman's methods—and he was not the only "bucko mate" in the transatlantic trade—a Waterman crew was an efficient one. The result was that when Captain Marshall, after a record of 94 transatlantic passages, retired from the quarterdeck at 42 and bought into the Black Ball Line,[2] he promptly signed on Waterman as captain of one of the newest and largest Black Ball packets, the *South America*. Waterman was twenty-eight.

For four years he relentlessly drove the *South America* back and forth across the Atlantic. Then Howland & Aspinwall lured him into the South American trade, giving him the *Natchez,* which he took to Rio and around Cape Horn to Valparaiso, bringing home copper and hides on some near-record voyages. Thus began his love affair with the *Natchez;* and it was when Howland & Aspinwall transferred her to the China trade that Waterman set new speed records on the China passage.

By this time Robert Waterman was the talk of New York shipping circles.[3] More than any other clipper captain of the time, he seemed to have an innate wind sense: Wherever the wind was along his route, he found it. And despite his reputation as a driver of men as well as of ships, there were several veteran seamen who regularly signed on aboard whatever vessel Waterman commanded.

Between voyages Waterman also became a popular man about town. He worked at it, strutting up Fifth Avenue to join his fellow captains at the Astor Bar and preening himself in the Metropolitan Hotel ballroom, where the belles of the city waited for him to ask them for a waltz. He was five feet, eight inches tall but looked taller, with a slim build tapering from a barrel chest. His curly black hair already receded slightly at the temple, accentuating his high forehead. He was one of the few clean-shaven captains. His aquiline nose, sensuous, full lips, and jutting jaw gave a Byronic cast to his profile. And he dressed the part in his beaver topper and frock coat of wool or Canton silk—"a strutting dude of sail," a contemporary called him. One Manhattan debutante whom he favored was Cynthia Jones, daughter of Judge Samuel Jones. But during a visit to his family home in Fairfield, Cordelia Sterling made Waterman forget Cynthia Jones.

Cordelia was a belle of Bridgeport, an accomplished equestrienne and the baby sister of Waterman's first captain, John

Sterling. No doubt Cordelia and Robert had met as children, but since she had grown up in Bridgeport and he in Fairfield, they probably had not been childhood playmates. Now their courtship was interrupted by Waterman's voyages to China in the *Natchez*. And after their wedding in 1846, their honeymoon was cut short so Waterman could take command of the *Sea Witch* on her maiden voyage. Cordelia accompanied him in the *Sea Witch* only once. Undoubtedly she played a part in her husband's decision to retire from the sea, even though the Gold Rush had precipitated the most exciting period of the clipper ship, the races around Cape Horn. The record-smashing voyages of the *Sea Witch* had been enough to provide for Waterman's comfortable retirement. He was attracted by the rich prospects in California—not, however, to grub for gold but to make some shrewd investments of his earnings in California's promising real estate.

The Pacific Mail Company steamer *Northerner* was leaving New York for San Francisco by way of the Strait of Magellan, and Waterman took over her quarterdeck. The *Northerner's* owner was also aboard. When she put into Valparaiso for coal, someone asked why she needed two masters. Waterman pointed to her owner, laughed, and said, "Hell, he cleans the knives. *I* navigate the ship." (He recognized that all a steamer skipper could do was navigate.) As soon as the *Northerner* dropped anchor in San Francisco Bay, Waterman headed for the Suisun Valley in Solano County, where he formed his partnership with fellow Captain Archibald Ritchie.

Cordelia Waterman obviously was pleased—only to be disappointed when on her husband's return to New York George Griswold talked him into taking command of the *Challenge*. Suddenly their plans were to be postponed for nearly a year. Not only that; Waterman also was devoting all his time to his new clipper, supervising her rigging and preparing to make one last bid for glory before the clipper ship era, as he saw it, came to an end.

There was no confusing Robert Waterman with Josiah Perkins Creesy. Unlike Waterman the dandy, Creesy paid little attention to his appearance. He was six years younger than

Waterman. But by 1851, as the two were taking command of their rival vessels, Creesy looked ten years older, with a creased, salt-stained face, grizzled gray whiskers, and eyes with a permanent squint from the sun. Creesy had a reputation for "sharpening his pencil" and recording every fast passage he made, from port to port and from landfall to landfall along the route. He was a stern disciplinarian, but nobody gave him the nickname "Bully." He paid more attention than Waterman or most captains did to selecting his crews; usually this was the first mate's job, under supervision of the ship's owners. But Creesy took part in the recruiting; and during his voyages he frequently disdained the accepted practice of giving orders through his first mate, preferring to bellow at his men through a weather-beaten brass trumpet that could be heard in the highest maintop.

Born in 1814 in Marblehead, Massachusetts, Creesy had learned the rudiments of seamanship aboard a friend's thirteen-foot Cape Ann dory, which he borrowed to sail to the nearby harbors of Salem and Boston to study the local East Indiamen and talk to their sailors. At an early age he shipped out aboard one of these vessels. And he quickly worked his way aft from the forecastle until, still in his twenties, he was given command of a China packet.[4] By 1851 he had established a reputation as a driver, and Grinnell, Minturn had high hopes for him as skipper of their new *Flying Cloud*.

The popular distinction in the 1840s and 1850s was between the captain who had "come in through the hawsehole" (near the forecastle) and the one who had "come in through the cabin door" (aft in officers' quarters). Waterman and Creesy were hawsehole skippers, as were many of the most successful clipper captains, including that father figure of them all, Nathaniel Palmer. Born in 1799, he was a decade older than most of his fellow captains and already had had half a dozen careers at the beginning of the clipper ship era. As a teenager he had smuggled goods to his hometown of Stonington, Conn., during the War of 1812. A sealing captain at twenty-one, he had made seven voyages to the islands off the bottom of South America; during one of which he had discovered the Antarctic archipelago that bears his name. He had run guns and troops to

Simón Bolívar in South America and carried cotton north from New Orleans. He was still in his thirties when he helped design the flat-floored transatlantic packet, and forty-three when he whittled out the model of what became the celebrated *Houqua.* He commanded as well as supervised A. A. Low & Bros.' fleet of clippers, meanwhile playing an important role in their highly successful round-the-world trade from New York to San Francisco to China to London and/or New York.

Captain Nat was a popular and influential member of the Lows' firm; the brothers depended on his approval of the plans for each new vessel and his sage advice concerning most of their far-flung trade. The youngest Low brother, Captain Charles, acknowledged Palmer's avuncular supervision in Low's training for the quarterdeck. He was Palmer's third mate aboard the *Houqua,* and he recalled that Captain Nat "was a believer in good food, not alone for the cabin; he believed in giving the sailors the very best of salt beef and pork and plenty of it; and everything else they had to eat was of the very best." Unlike many of his fellow clipper captains, Palmer never took out his disappointments or frustration on his crew. His most violent expression of disgust was to throw his white beaver hat on the deck and stamp on it. But the kindly old captain could be less ingratiating to his fellow skippers than to his crew. Palmer had a habit of taking a new clipper on her maiden voyage, bringing her thrashing home with her spars and lines weather-beaten, and handing her over to another captain in the Low fleet. When the new captain ordered her spars and lines replaced, Palmer the supervisor would complain at the extra expense.

Two of the Lows' captains were Nat's brothers; and the Lows were treated to the spectacle of the three Palmer captains feuding with one another. The youngest, Captain Theodore Palmer, had a hot temper and fought with Captain Nat nearly every day he was ashore. Captain Ted had worked his way aft in the transatlantic trade and because of his experience with the Liverpool packet rats considered most foremast hands, according to Low, as "mere brutes, to be dealt with as such"—an attitude that was not appreciated by his oldest brother. Captain Alexander, the middle brother, wrote Low, was an expert navigator, one of the few capable of taking lunar as well as solar observations. But Captain Alexander was an unusually suspicious type; he "could not bear to see two or three men talking together," Low recalled; "he was apt to imagine they were talking against him."

A hawsehole skipper who could easily have come in through the cabin door was the youngest of the Low brothers and the only one of the clan who wanted to go to sea. Charles Low also was the most articulate of the clipper captains, writing his colorful, anecdotal memoirs, apparently with total recall, at seventy-nine.[5] Charles's parents and older brothers tried to keep him ashore, knowing that the real money was to be made in their countinghouse if not in a hong at Canton. At fourteen, while learning the business in a dry-goods store, Low sneaked away from work to climb the rigging of the ships along the South Street waterfront. At fifteen he was working in one of his father's stores, which happened to be on Fletcher Street just across from a sailors' boardinghouse, where he spent all his spare time listening to tall tales of life at sea and learning how to tie knots, splice a line, and box the compass. By the time he was sixteen he was fretting to go to sea, still against the better judgment of the rest of the family. When he tried to stow away in the bread locker of his brother Abbot's schooner *Mazeppa,* the Lows finally were convinced that he would never be happy ashore. He was sent to navigation school, and in November 1842 he signed on as a cabin boy (at no pay) aboard the Lows' China packet *Horatio*.

Young Charles learned fast and rose rapidly through the ranks to third mate aboard his family's *Houqua*[6] and on to second and first. After only five years at sea, he was promoted to the *Houqua*'s quarterdeck. It was during his first command that his budding career as a clipper captain almost came to a sudden end. The *Houqua* had rounded the Cape of Good Hope en route to China when she ran afoul of one of the Indian Ocean's worst typhoons. The *Houqua*'s sails were torn to tatters, her hull was rolled onto its beam ends, and Low was swept overboard, being saved at the last moment when a line whipped against him and he caught it to pull himself back aboard. He managed to right the ship by slashing her rigging and letting her masts go by the board. Then, with all hands manning the pumps, he took the jury-rigged *Houqua* three thousand miles on to Hong Kong, where he even managed to sell his water-damaged cargo at a profit.

It was remarkable how many clipper captains had come in through the cabin door. William Howland made a series of fast passages to China in the tea clipper *Horatio* and to California in the *Sea Serpent*. But he never overcame the stigma of not having been a foremast hand, perhaps partly because of his punctilious, not to say pompous, bearing on the quarterdeck. He wore kid gloves and spoke to no one aboard except the first mate. Howland, however, was a captain of contradictions. He dyed his moustache black but left his hair and beard gray. Though aloof from the crew, he wept openly when a man fell overboard and drowned despite Howland's desperate attempts to find him. Howland rarely went forward of the quarterdeck except to distribute Bibles to the crew; yet his ships were among the few where grog (a daily tot of rum) was served to all hands. And Howland was known to get drunk at the end of the voyage even before his ship had reached her anchorage or pier.

Captain Lauchlan McKay did not come in through the hawsehole, but he knew his ships better than most captains because he built them: He was a shipwright before becoming a skipper. One year younger than his famous brother Donald, Lauchlan had followed him to Isaac Webb's East River yard and had undergone the same apprenticeship that turned out so many successful shipbuilders. At first the two brothers set out on parallel careers. While Donald was establishing himself in East Boston, Lauchlan stayed in New York to become a shipwright at the Brown & Bell and Smith & Dimon yards. Then he went to sea for the first time, as a carpenter in the U.S. Navy. After a voyage aboard the frigate U.S.S. *Constitution,* Lauchlan took a leave of absence from the Navy and joined his brother at his East Boston yard. There, with help from Donald, he wrote the first comprehensive U.S. book on ship design, *The Practical Shipbuilder,* which became the bible of many U.S. shipyards. He returned to New York for a stint as a master shipwright and foreman at Brown & Bell, then went back to Boston and opened his own shipyard with yet another McKay brother, Hugh. In

1849, Lauchlan was in the transatlantic trade in command of his brother Donald's fast and popular packet *Jenny Lind*.

Anyone who might have belittled Lauchlan McKay for coming in though the cabin door was silenced after his voyages as skipper of his brother's celebrated clipper *Sovereign of the Seas*. Lauchlan McKay was forty-one when he took command of the huge new 258-foot *Sovereign* in 1852. In contrast to the spare, self-effacing Donald, Lauchlan was tall, stout, bewhiskered, and authoritative. He was also a driver. Despite a gale that tore away the *Sovereign*'s fore and main topmasts, he took her to San Francisco in 103 days. Most of the crew deserted to the gold fields, and McKay had to sign on a gang of untrained Polynesians at his next port of call, Honolulu, where he loaded a cargo of sperm oil from New England whalers using the Hawaiian Islands as their base. McKay then set sail for New York on February 13, 1853. One month later, the *Sovereign* made history.

Her performance was all the more remarkable because she was so dangerously undermanned and had just sprung her fore-topmast in a series of South Pacific rain squalls as she approached Cape Horn on March 18. Groaning and creaking under the mounting westerlies and straining against its iron hoops, the topmast was gaping open in two places. But McKay could tell that the big clipper was nearing record speed, and he gambled by keeping her royals flying until she reached an unprecedented 19 knots. With her lee rigging sagging and her weather shrouds strumming like piano wire, the *Sovereign* maintained this speed for three hours. Then McKay doused her royals; the *Sovereign* still roared along at 18 knots. By noon the next day she had set another record: 411 nautical miles in 24 hours, the first sailing ship to exceed four hundred nautical miles in a day's run.

A clipper captain's wife faced a difficult choice: She could resign herself either to a year or more of loneliness ashore or to the same period of cramped quarters, danger, and, what was even worse, tedium. Cordelia Waterman accompanied her husband on only one voyage aboard the *Sea Witch*. Her reason for deciding to stay ashore after that is not recorded; but it may have been a silent commentary on the difference between her husband's behavior at home and on his quarterdeck. Eleanor Creesy was Captain Josiah Creesy's greatest asset. She not only plotted the course for her husband's ships but also watched over the crew, keeping an eye on the cook and nursing the sick and injured. During one voyage she looked up from her chart table in time to see through the porthole a man who had fallen overboard, unnoticed by those on deck. Running up the companionway, she sounded the alarm; Captain Creesy lowered two boats, which searched until they found the man, on the point of drowning. Eleanor Creesy's reputation along New York's waterfront probably had a lot to do with the fact that her husband managed to round up the last few able seamen when the *Flying Cloud* sailed in June 1851.

When Sarah Tucker of South Danvers, Mass., became Mrs. Charles Low, she decided to join him aboard the new Low clipper named for Nathaniel Palmer on his voyage to China. Charles and Sarah Low made a handsome couple,[7] and the parties they gave aboard the clipper in the Chinese ports became so popular that the *N. B. Palmer* was locally known as "the yacht."

But Sarah Low discovered that life aboard a clipper ship was not all entertainment. She found that her jovial husband could be tough when he had to, quelling a mutiny, disarming the crew, and flogging the ringleaders en route to Cape Horn. The Lows' first son was born in January 1853, a few hours after the *N. B. Palmer* had run at eight knots onto the sharp reefs of Broussa's Shoal in the South China Sea. The ship had been kedged off the reef with a huge hole in her bow, the water in her hold was gaining on the pumps, and she was sinking while Low raced for the harbor at Batavia when Sarah went into labor. Alternately serving as midwife and maneuvering the sluggish, water-laden ship into Batavia Harbor, Low managed to anchor in shallow water just as "my first-born came into the world." Their second son was too impatient to await the clipper's arrival in New York at the end of another voyage a year and a half later, being born off Sandy Hook just after the pilot came aboard.

Captain Nat Palmer's wife and niece accompanied him on one voyage to China. Captain Samuel Very's wife joined him aboard the *Hurricane*. Captain David Babcock's young wife,

Charlotte, made a home in the crowded cabin of the *Sword Fish* for their nine-month-old daughter Nellie and her nurse; Charlotte also accompanied Captain Babcock in the enormously successful *Young America*. Mrs. Charles Brown bore a son aboard her husband's *Black Prince*. Captain Edgar Wakeman's wife, Mary, went around Cape Horn with him three times and had two children at sea (they named the first one Adelaide Seaborn Wakeman). When the *Red Gauntlet* nearly foundered off Cape Horn, her rudder smashed, her sails blown out, her bow leaking, and her hold sloshing with five feet of water, Mrs. Thomas Andrews kept the nearly frozen crewmen working by supplying them with warm food and hot tea while they fought the cape's gales for 29 days. But the all-time heroine of the clipper ship era was Mary Ann Patten.

She was sixteen when she married Captain Joshua Patten in Boston in April 1853, and eighteen when she accompanied him aboard Foster & Nickerson's big clipper *Neptune's Car;* he was twenty-eight. On that voyage, perhaps out of sheer boredom while the *Car* was becalmed in the Pacific, Mary Patten set out to teach herself navigation. Despite eight days of calm, Captain Patten reached San Francisco in just under 101 days. By the time the *Neptune's Car* had crossed the Pacific to Hong Kong and taken a cargo of tea to London en route home to New York, Mary Patten had become a skilled navigator. She also cared for the *Car*'s crew members who were injured when lightning struck the clipper and damaged the foremast in mid-Atlantic. Joshua Patten complacently announced at the end of the voyage, "Mrs. Patten is uncommon handy about the ship, even in weather, and would doubtless be of service if a man." He added that his wife could have passed the examination for a master's certificate if she had wanted to take it. On the *Car*'s next voyage she proved him right.

The *Neptune's Car* set sail for San Francisco on July 1, 1856. Two other clippers, the *Intrepid* and the *Romance of the Seas,* set out at virtually the same time, the *Intrepid* on July 1 and the *Romance* two days later. Both were fast vessels. The *Intrepid* was one of William Webb's clippers, making her maiden voyage. Donald McKay had built the *Romance of the Seas;* she had beaten a rival, the clipper *David Brown,* on a similar race around Cape

Horn the previous year. Many bets were placed at the Astor Bar on which of the three clippers would win the race.

From the outset the *Car's* first mate, a man named Keeler, was a troublemaker. He was abusive to the crew. He napped on watch. Worst of all, he shortened sail against Patten's orders.[8] By the time the *Car* was nearing Cape Horn, Patten had become enraged at Keeler's insubordination and had confined him to his cabin. The second mate, named Hare, was a good seaman but illiterate and incapable of working up the logarithms to plot the ship's position. Mary Ann Patten took over the duties of navigator.

By now she knew that she was pregnant with her first child. And by now the situation aboard the *Car* had gotten much worse. Joshua Patten was suffering from advanced tuberculosis.[9] His condition worsened; he lapsed into delirium, then into a coma. Mary Patten took command of the clipper, and Hare agreed to serve as her first mate. Keeler sent her a message warning her of the difficulties rounding Cape Horn and promising to take the ship to California if freed. She rejected his offer. Keeler threatened to unite the crew against her. Mrs. Patten summoned the men to the break of the quarterdeck. A foremast hand recalled the spectacle of the slight figure of the nineteen-year-old standing at the railing as she told them of her husband's illness and asked them to help her get the *Neptune's Car* around Cape Horn to California. The crewmen answered her with three cheers.

The winter of 1856 was one of the worst in the memory of Cape Horn veterans. Ahead of the *Neptune's Car,* the clipper ship *Rapid* was battling a succession of gales with hurricane-force winds. Captain Phineas Winsor thrashed back and forth against the towering seas, making no headway and nearly destroying his ship. So wild were the storms and punishing the waves that ten of his men were killed or swept overboard; ten more were injured too badly to work the ship. Winsor turned back and limped to Rio for repairs. En route the *Rapid* passed the *Neptune's Car,* about to confront the same storms without her captain or first mate and with a pregnant nineteen-year-old in command.

It took Mary Patten 50 days to round Cape Horn. For a

month and a half she drove the 1,616-ton, 216-foot clipper into the head-on seas, shouting orders through a speaking trumpet as she relentlessly beat southwest, then northwest, making little progress to westward. The skies rarely cleared long enough for her to use her sextant and fix the *Car*'s position; most of the time she navigated by dead reckoning, trying to measure the clipper's speed, guessing at her drift, and plotting her course on the chart. She said later that she never had time to change her clothes during those 50 days and rarely slept for more than a few hours. During one storm she was on deck for 48 hours. What time she could spare was spent nursing her husband, who was alternately comatose and delirious. In the lurching cabin, with the seas thundering against the *Car*'s hull, she studied her husband's copy of Dr. Lowe's *Sailor's Guide to Health* and the few other medical manuals in the cabin's bookrack, trying to find some treatment. There was nothing she could do but bathe his sweating face and tie him to his bunk so he would not be pitched out by the roll of the ship.

Finally the blue-back clouds broke long enough for Mrs. Patten to shoot the sun and confirm her reckoning that she had rounded the bottom of South America. She altered course to north-northwest and ran up the Pacific. And Joshua Patten showed signs of recovery. His temperature dropped and he began to have lucid moments. By the time the *Car* was nearing Valparaiso, he was sitting up in his bunk. Too weak to stand, he could at least help with the navigation while his wife directed the crew from the quarterdeck. Realizing how exhausted she was, he decided to give the first mate another chance.

A couple of days later Mary Patten, checking the compass heading and the charts, found that the mate had them on a course for Valparaiso. She reported to her husband, who ordered Keeler confined again. The *Neptune's Car* was racing up the South American coast when Captain Patten had a relapse, this time losing his sight. For the rest of the voyage, with her husband blind and frequently unconscious, Mrs. Patten commanded and navigated the clipper to San Francisco. The last ten days were the most frustrating, with the *Car* drifting aimlessly in a flat calm almost within sight of her destination. At last she reached the Golden Gate, 134 days out of New York. She had beaten the *Intrepid* by 12 days. But the *Romance of the Seas* had won the race by 22 days. Mary Patten brought her husband back to New York by steamer and across the Isthmus to another steamer. Captain Patten recovered slightly, then sank into a deeper coma and came ashore in New York on a stretcher with his wife walking beside him. She then took him to their home in Boston.

The New York Insurance Company, which had insured the *Neptune's Car,* sent Mrs. Patten a letter of commendation— "We know of no instance where the love and devotion of a wife have been more impressively portrayed . . ."—and a check for $1,000. Since she had saved the company nearly $100,000, it was suggested that she should receive at least $5,000, but the directors pleaded poverty; it had been a bad year for the insurance companies. If any of the directors had a twinge of conscience, it probably was not helped by Mary Patten's reply:

> I am sincerely grateful to you and all of those you represent for the very kind expressions of sympathy, and for the liberal inclosure which you have transmitted to me in their behalf. I feel very sensibly, gentlemen, that kindness which has prompted you to commend the manner in which I have endeavored to perform that which seemed to me, under the circumstances, only the plain duty of a wife towards a good husband, stricken down by what we now fear to be a hopeless disease, and to perform for him, as well as I could, those duties which he could not perform for himself, especially when it was to carry out his own expressed wish. But I am, at the same time, seriously embarrassed by the fear that you may have overestimated the value of those services, because I feel that without the services of Mr. Hare, the second officer, a good seaman, and of the hearty cooperation of the crew to aid our endeavors, the ship would not have arrived safely at her destined port. Be assured, gentlemen, that through all the trials which may be before me, and while I live, your considerate kindness will ever be held in thankful remembrance.
>
> By yours very respectfully,
> Mary A. Patten

On March 10, 1857, two weeks after Mary Patten wrote her letter of thanks, Joshua Adams Patten was born. On July 25, Captain Joshua Patten died without knowing he was a father. A group of well-wishers in Boston collected $1,400 as a testimonial to their local heroine. Another group, the leaders of Boston's new feminist movement, triumphantly proclaimed Mary Patten's example. But when they tried to enlist her in their cause, she rejected their overtures. Meanwhile she found that she had contracted her husband's tuberculosis. On March 17, 1861, four years after his death, she, too, died of "consumption," as the *Boston Daily Courier* called it—a nineteenth-century term for tuberculosis. She was twenty-four.

6

Trouble in the Forecastle

MARY ANN PATTEN HAD the "hearty cooperation" of an able crew. Robert Waterman was not so fortunate. The problem was at the source of supply. Gone were the days when most young Easterners wanted to sign aboard a sailing ship and when many of them were determined to become captains. Now the United States offered many more options for the ambitious as well as those simply looking for a job. The opening West provided the newest challenge, both an opportunity to stake out a more prosperous life and plenty of work for all.

Along the Eastern Seaboard more and more factories and textile mills were competing with ships for American labor. During the decade from the mid-1840s to the mid-1850s, U.S. manufacturing more than doubled. The fast-spreading network of railroads required thousands of laborers to build and operate them. And the shipping industry itself provided thousands more jobs in the shipyards along New York's East River as well as in Boston and other East Coast ports. While wages ashore were low, they generally were better than the $8 to $10 a month earned by an ordinary seaman on a voyage to California.[1] And the mills and factories, the railroads and shipyards offered far better working conditions than did a merchant ship. Even the 10- to 12-hour day of a New England factory was preferable to the round-the-clock drudgery and danger at sea.

The young man who signed a ship's articles subjected himself to a form of voluntary slavery, at the command, even whim, of the ship's master for the duration of the voyage. Discipline was strict and often brutal, and a sailor could not quit his job. His food, such as it was, cost him nothing; but he had to provide his own fork, knife, and tray, as well as his clothing and the straw mattress (which he called a "donkey's breakfast") for his bunk. If he had not had the foresight to bring these essentials aboard in his sea chest, he had to buy them, often at extortionate prices to be deducted from his pay, from the ship's "slop chest."

The seaman lived amid vermin, worked hardest in the worst weather, was wet and half frozen much of the time, had little or no contact with home, and had the shortest life expectancy of any laborer: One study of sixty deaths at sea during a six-month period in 1850 found the average age of the victims to be twenty-eight. And life aboard a clipper ship was the hardest and most perilous of all. Not only did clipper captains reef sail only at the last, most dangerous moment; they also changed sail more frequently in their constant drive to keep the ship moving under every condition of wind and weather. The clippers' extra sails atop taller masts made sail-changing riskier, and the huge press of canvas caused more frequent dismastings. Clipper ships traveled the heavily trafficked trading routes, all of them racing headlong through storm and fog. It was no wonder that veteran seamen preferred the slower, safer merchant trader to the swift, precarious clipper.

When the California Gold Rush drained the Eastern Seaboard of hundreds of thousands of able-bodied young Americans, even fewer hands were available to man U.S. ships—and at the very time when the demand for them was at its height. During the 1840s and 1850s some thirty thousand vessels were flying the American flag and employing a quarter of a million sailors. The clippers were the largest ships, requiring the largest crews. The result was a massive imbalance of supply and demand. The clipper ship era, which had been made possible by the fortuitous timing of ship design and a new breed of captain, came at exactly the wrong time for an expert crew.

Nathaniel and George Griswold, like all the other shipping merchants of New York and Boston, were well aware of the problem. Nor could they have been unaware of a simple solution: the inducement of better pay. But although they were willing to gamble $150,000 on the *Challenge* and a $10,000 bonus on Captain Robert Waterman, they refused to increase the wages of the ordinary or even the much-sought-after Able-Bodied seamen. They were not alone in this parsimonious attitude toward their crews.

A few veteran seamen made up the nucleus of a clipper ship crew. There were rare old-timers who followed a favorite clipper captain from ship to ship. Others maintained a fierce devotion to a particular clipper.[2] Pride in a ship brought some sailors back to sea on voyage after voyage. A natural yen for roving motivated others. Occasionally a young American still shipped out for his health. Such men formed the background of a clipper's crew. Much of the muscle, however, came from the "packet rats" of the transatlantic trade who had been lured into the California run. But for most of them the lure was gold; they made only one voyage, deserting as soon as their ship reached San Francisco. Most came from the Liverpool waterfront, and they prided themselves on their independence as well as their hardiness. Transatlantic packet captain Samuel Samuels accurately described them as "the toughest class of men in all respects. They could stand the worst weather, food, and usage, and put up with less sleep, more rum, and harder knocks than any sailors." However, he added, "They had not the slightest idea of morality or honesty, and gratitude was not in them. The dread of the belaying-pin or heaver [a stout bar twisted to tighten the rigging] kept them in subjection. I tried to humanize these brutal natures as much as possible, but the better they were treated the more trouble my officers had with them."[3] Captain Samuels reported a fellow skipper studying one of the Samuels' crews and commenting, "I never saw such a set of pirates in my life." Samuels handled them with brute force when necessary, assisted by his big dog, named Wallace, who was trained to hold a man down while Samuels or a mate applied the handcuffs.

At least the packet rats were good seamen who worked the ship efficiently if only for their own safety. But there were not enough of them to man the ever-larger new clippers. So the rest of the crew was provided by waterfront kidnappers.[4] A major supplier of manpower was the boardinghouse keeper. He would offer a sailor free board in return for an advance on the wages for his next voyage, so it was in the boardinghouse keeper's interest to find his tenant a berth before the advance was used up. And if the sailor was not ready to sign on, his landlord got him drunk or drugged him. Each port also had its army of crimps who simply knocked out the sailor with liquor, opium, laudanum, or hydrate of chloral before robbing him and selling him like a slave to the shipowners' recruiters. The crimps often worked in league with prostitutes or brothelkeepers who ensnared their victims and delivered them sometimes within hours of debarkation from their last ship.

So scarce had the supply of seamen become by midcentury that even the shipowners who deplored the practice were forced to depend on the crimps. When on one occasion New York's merchant shippers attempted to boycott the crimps, dozens of vessels waited at their piers for two weeks without crews until the shipowners relented. The usual payment was one month's advance of the man's wages; sometimes the crimp could hold out for even more, all of which was deducted from the sailor's pay. The sort of sailors provided by this system was graphically described by the daughter of a clipper captain: "A motley crew they were indeed; most of them were intoxicated. They staggered over the side of the ship, bringing with them their few possessions. . . . Several were 'dead drunk,' as it were, drugged perhaps. These were hoisted on board like bales of merchandise." Many of the crimps stole their victims' belongings and dumped their unconscious bodies aboard ship with nothing but the clothes they wore.[5]

A large proportion of the clipper crews were foreigners who had come ashore from a voyage to New York and had fallen afoul of the boardinghouse, saloon-, and brothelkeepers or the prostitutes and crimps of Water and Cherry streets. The shipmasters' favorites were the sturdy, steady Scandinavians; but most of them had chosen life ashore or had been blown off a yardarm in the North Atlantic. What the recruiters turned up by midcentury were Finns, Italians, Welshmen, a few French, Germans, Dutchmen, Portuguese, Greeks, and some Latin Americans and Chinese, many of whom spoke no English and could not understand a mate's commands. Many had intentionally obscured their origins. In 1817, when there had been many fewer U.S. vessels, Congress had passed a law to give American seamen a priority by stipulating that two thirds of the crew aboard a ship flying the U.S. flag must be U.S. citizens. But with the diminishing supply of American volunteers, the law frequently was circumvented by falsifying the ship's roster. Captain Arthur Clark recalled having a Chinese cook who was signed on as George Harrison of Charlestown, Mass.[6]

There had been a few attempts by concerned shipowners to establish school ships to attract young Americans to merchant shipping. In the 1830s Thomas Goin, a Manhattan ship broker and school ship advocate, polled New York's captains and found that the average number of Americans in their crews was only 20 percent. In 1837, New York's merchants petitioned Congress for a federally funded training ship, without success. By the 1850s, with the problem clearly acute, there were a few more attempts to raise private funds for some sort of training school afloat; but the merchant shippers, perhaps apprehensive about Americans demanding better pay, withheld their support.

The few Americans, as well as the Finns and Greeks, Welshmen and Mexicans who were available for the clippers all called one another "Jack" and referred to themselves as "tars," a name emanating from the tar with which they coated their straw hats to make them water-resistant. In wet weather the clipper sailor who could afford them wore an oil-soaked jacket and pants. Some had oiled boots, but most found that bare feet were safest in the rigging. The true clipper man prided himself on what he called a "sea tan," a sun-browned complexion further darkened by oil and tar. He also, in the custom of the time, regarded naturally black- and yellow-skinned men as inferior. Most clipper cooks were black or Chinese; they were constant targets of racial slurs from the crew and discriminatory discipline from the officers and always were blamed for not making the ship's food more palatable.

Usually the ingredients were more to blame; the most ingenious chef could do little to improve the tainted salt pork, weevily biscuits, and maggot-infested bread found in many clippers' holds. There were some exceptions. Aboard the clipper *Mary Whitridge,* according to one foremast hand, the food "was very good and unlimited in quantity," though "limited in variety." The *Whitridge*'s officers, however, on such special occasions as Thanksgiving, dined on oyster soup, salmon, roast fowl, and huckleberry pie. A clipper ship's provisions frequently were supplemented by fresh fish or birds caught by the crew off watch in calms or light airs. And many clippers left port with a small barnyard, usually consisting of pigs and sheep, chickens and ducks, enclosed in pens forward on deck, to provide fresh food as long as they lasted. China clippers putting into Anjer stocked up with fresh provisions, including local livestock, along with pets and souvenirs purchased by the crew members. One of them wrote, "Our ship looks like a farm yard: Chickens, geese, Ducks, monkeys, Goats, minoes, Paraquetes, Cockatoes, Java Sparrows, Doves. The lower rigging is all full of fruits looking like a forest and the Jib Guys are full of Bananas."

The noisy birds and animals sometimes kept the crew awake, and a favorite diversion of mischievous crew members was to turn the pigs loose. One of the least popular chores was that of the sailor appointed as "Jimmy Ducks," in charge of the menagerie and cleaning the pens. Yet many a Jimmy Ducks admitted that he hated even more the chore of slaughtering one of the animals, despite the prospect of fresh meat, because he had become attached to them. In any case, a clipper ship's barnyard was empty by the time the vessel neared Cape Horn; its pens and cages would not survive the cape's deck-sweeping seas. So for most of the voyage the clipper crew subsisted on the staples in the barrels that had been loaded in her hold.

Hugh Gregory of the *Sea Serpent* complained in his journal, "The way we are fed is truly outrageous," and listed a typical week's "bill of fare," as he sarcastically called it:

Sunday, Scouse—Duff	Bread	& Beef
Monday, Mush—Spuds	"	"
Tuesday, Scouse—Beans	"	"
Wednesday, Scouse—Rice	"	"
Thursday, Mush—Duff	"	"
Friday, Scouse—Beans	"	"
Saturday, Scouse—Cape Cod Turkey	"	"

A good scouse (or lobscouse, as it was better known) was a stew usually consisting of salt meat, potatoes, onions, bread, and spices. But Gregory described the *Sea Serpent*'s version as "a miserable compound of crackers and salt beef made like hash . . . a libel on pig fodder." The crackers, of course, were the infamous ship's biscuit called "hardtack," which over the weeks and months in their barrel attained the consistency of oak. Mush was a porridgelike mess of bread and water, sometimes flavored with molasses. As Gregory characterized the *Sea Serpent*'s food, "the mush is never cooked, the beans are awful and Cape Cod turkey, or in plain English, codfish, is the meanest mess of all. The coffee and tea, which we have morning and night, is a muddy compound not fit for any civilized man to drink." The only palatable dishes were sea pie and duff,[7] which usually were served as a treat on Sundays and Thursdays. Gregory noted that on these days "always 5 minutes before 8 bells, a numerous array of tin pans can be seen hovering around the galley door." And even the rest of the food seemed more palatable as the sailors got accustomed to it, especially after a hard day on deck or in the rigging. For all his complaining, Gregory admitted, "I am always so hungry I can eat what is set before me without a second bidding." Second only to the complaints about the quality of most clippers' food were the complaints over not getting enough or a fair share of it.

A major deprivation was fresh water. In many clipper ships the water supply was carried in a tall cylindrical tank reaching from the keelson, just above the keel, to the deck and containing as many as four thousand gallons; some of the later, larger ships carried two such tanks. Normally enough water to provide a gallon per man was pumped into the scuttlebutt[8] on deck, where it was issued as needed, usually under the supervision of the ship's carpenter. But not all the clippers provided such an abundance. Some carried their water in casks, and what had been fresh water at sailing time became stagnant and took on the taste of the cask, which had not always been purified before refilling. A clipper could not load enough fresh water for the entire voyage and depended on rain as a supplement en route; many an off watch was summoned on deck during a storm to trap rainwater in an extra sail while the crewmen on watch worked the ship.[9]

If there was anything the clipper sailor complained about more than the food, it was the condition of his living quarters. Life aboard ship in the nineteenth century was ruled by rigid unwritten laws of class. The officers lived aft, the men forward, and no common seaman went aft unless ordered to. The sailor's home was the forecastle (called the foc's'l), so named from the fore castle at the bow of the early, high-riding galleons. In most of the clippers the forecastle had been moved from the bow of the ship to a house forward on deck. Some were divided by a bulkhead so each watch had its own quarters, and a well-ventilated deckhouse was a big improvement over the damp dungeon at the bows of the earlier vessels. But even the best-designed forecastles usually were infested with a vast variety of cockroaches, bedbugs, fleas, lice, ants, rats, and tarantulas. Mosquitoes and biting flies swarmed through the vessel. One seaman complained that the rats aboard his ship

> seemed to increase in numbers and boldness every day. They ate holes over-night through the hardwood cabin partitions, stole socks out of our shoes while we slept, also balls of twine and beeswax used in sail-making, and dragged them into their nests between the partitions where they seemed to produce a fresh family over-night. It was no trick at all when you turned out in the morning to find one or two drowned in your water pitcher, and to be awakened in the night by their running over your face.

On arrival in port, an exterminator was hired to clean out the ship; he caught 624 of them. The roaches aboard another vessel, a seaman complained, were "actually as large as mice."[10]

The sailors themselves added to the malaise of the forecastle. Landlubbers who had been kidnapped and delivered aboard a clipper awoke to a deadly combination of hangover and seasickness, and their illness became infectious. "Oh dear, I'm so sick," scrawled one unhappy neophyte in his journal. "Will somebody throw me overboard?" The forecastle's atmosphere became progressively worse in the first heavy weather, with the men staggering back to their bunks and turning in without changing their wet jackets and pants. The ship's chores contributed to the man-made odors. The clipper's standing rigging was tarred frequently as a preservative; men who had been working on the shrouds came back to the forecastle with tar-covered clothes. "Jimmy Ducks" returned from his duties with the effluvium of the pigpen.

But the dirtiest job was slushing the masts and spars: With a bucket of grease from the galley, a sailor rode a bosun's chair and slopped the grease over the mast or spar so the parrels holding the yards could move with less friction, or climbed the rigging to grease it and keep it pliant. The *Sea Serpent's* Hugh Gregory never did master the slushing job without spilling this "truly vile compound" all over his clothes, and the rancid stink of grease permeated the forecastle when he changed. When in good weather the sailors washed their filthy, lice-infested clothes, they were not permitted to use fresh water. Salt water did a poor cleansing job, and some men tried the scouring effect of ashes or urine, adding to the forecastle's funk when the clothes became wet again. In bad weather, with everything battened down, the smog grew so dense that one could scarcely see the length of the room. The men could not eat on deck, and the forecastle became littered with bits of food. Water from boarding seas sloshed back and forth, sending sea chests, sodden clothing, and garbage washing from bunk to bunk.

In bad weather, however, even the forecastle was preferable to the deck. The flaring clipper bow shouldered aside the sea in moderate weather. But because the clipper sliced through the waves instead of pounding over them, as its predecessors did, a great deal of water washed aboard when strong winds stirred up high seas. At its worst in a Cape Horn gale a clipper's deck was swept by chest-high icy waves that sent the men gasping and tumbling against the deckhouses or the rail. The work on deck was difficult as well as dangerous. Staggering about in water-filled boots, the men were washed away from the halyards and braces as they tried to trim the yards. Netting along the bulwark openings saved most of the men from being washed overboard. But many a clipper sailor broke an arm or leg, and there was no anesthetic for the crude surgery performed by the captain with his splints, knives, lancets, and saws.

The most perilous work, of course, was aloft. Even on a moderately smooth sea the gentle roll of the ship was magnified the higher the sailor climbed. The worst peril occurred in the Cape Horn gales, with the winds whipping the footropes beneath him, yanking the heavy, wet—sometimes frozen—canvas from his bleeding fingers and slamming it against him on his plunging perch. A fall almost always meant death on the deck nearly a hundred feet below or in the freezing sea. Hugh Gregory, again, described a typical episode when a "heavy sea and drizzling sleet made it extremely dangerous aloft." Two seamen named Tilly and George climbed the *Sea Serpent*'s rigging to furl the mizzen royal. Then . . .

> just as Tilly got onto the yard he slipped and fell, going overboard. . . . George said the first he heard was a shriek and, looking, saw to his horror Tilly falling; he struck the spanker gaff [the mizzenmast's fore-and-aft top] and then, falling inboard, went like a shot thro' the foot of the spanker, falling overboard. Charley Koerner, who was at the wheel, says he saw him for a second ere he passed out of sight, and that he cried "Help! Help!" or something to that effect. Everything was done that man could do to save him; the Captain, at the first alarm throwing a life buoy over, but going as we were at 12 knots an hour, long before it touched the water he was out of sight. There were many different opinions about his fate, but by far the most merciful one is that he died before he struck the water. . . .

Fair weather offered little leisure to the clipper sailor. When not changing sail he was expected to perform the many other chores of shipkeeping. Besides slushing the masts and tarring the rigging, he was put to work holystoning the decks. Working on his knees with a piece of sandstone the size of a Bible (thus "holystone"), he laboriously scraped the deck clean for hour after hour; and anyone who paused at the job was put back to work by a clout from a heaver or the sting of a rope's end. A favorite seaman's saying was:

TROUBLE IN THE FORECASTLE

* * *

Six days thou shalt labor and do all thou art able,
And on the seventh—holystone the decks and scrape the cable.

Holystoning dislodged some of the oakum in the decks'
seams, which had to be replaced. Even a new clipper leaked;
being driven at full speed opened seams in her hull, and at least
a few hours were required at the pumps. After a bad pounding
off Cape Horn, the pumps often had to be manned almost constantly. Near the end of the voyage the deck work increased.
Because most captains wanted their vessels to appear shipshape
on arrival, the last few days were devoted to scraping, painting,
and varnishing the ship as well as her masts and spars. The
rigging was tarred anew and the decks scraped until they gleamed.
The exhausted clipper sailor who flopped into his bunk at the
end of his watch and fell asleep immediately was still tired when
only four hours later a banging on the forecastle entrance announced the time for his next watch.

Nor was deck work completely safe in good weather. Frequently someone in the rigging dropped a tool or paint pot,
which from such a height could knock a man out. A seaman
who was too careless at the braces could become entangled in a
line and be whisked aloft or over the side. In an age when the
best shoreside doctors resorted to bleeding, poulticing, and
purging, a seaman could hardly expect very effective medical
treatment from an untrained captain. Broken bones were set
with crude splints, and amputations were performed with the
carpenter's saw. And always there was the contagion of the many
illnesses—malaria, dysentery, venereal disease—brought aboard
and spread by the forecastle's unsanitary conditions. Frequently
the captain's medical prescriptions only made it worse. Either
because of his own lack of knowledge or his suspicion of malingering, many a captain prescribed medicines such as castor oil
or mustard plasters that made a sick seaman even sicker. Well
aware of the officers' suspicions of ailing crewmen, many sailors worked on despite an injury or illness until they dropped.

In fair weather or foul, aboard a well-ordered clipper ship
the work went to the tune of a chantey. The chantey was comparatively new, evidently originating in the 1840s and derived

from the work songs chanted by black stevedores loading cotton aboard packets in the southern American ports.[11] Aboard the clippers there were chanteys for nearly every job, from hoisting the anchor to furling the last sail. The first chantey of a voyage was sung at the anchor capstan, with a chanteyman leading a grunting chorus as the seamen—those who could stand—leaned into the wooden bars of the capstan and stumbled about it in a circle to winch up the anchor cable. The chanteyman, usually chosen for his strong, clear voice (and his knowledge of chanteys), would start the work song with the verses; everyone in the work detail joined in the chorus. Clipper captains agreed that a good chanteyman was worth half a dozen men.

As soon as a vessel was under way and it was time to raise her topgallant or royal yards, the chanteyman sang out a long-haul work song. The mate had loosed the proper halyard from its belaying pin,[12] and the foredeck men in his watch formed a line as in a tug-of-war. Facing them, the chanteyman provided the rhythm leading up to the synchronized pull on the halyard—a sophisticated version of the simple "Yo, heave ho!" In the chantey called "So Handy," the pull came with each shout of *handy* (as shown in italics) in the chorus:

> Handy high and handy low,

Then the chorus, and the pull with each *handy:*

> *Handy,* me boys, so *handy.*

The chanteyman picked up with another verse:

> Growl you may, but go you must.

And the men chorused and pulled:

> *Handy,* me boys, so *handy.*

The chanteyman:

> Just growl too much and your head they'll bust.

The men:

> *Handy,* me boys, so *handy.*

The chanteyman:

> Now, up aloft from down below,

Chorus:

> *Handy,* me boys, so *handy.*

The chanteyman:

> Up aloft that yard must go.

Chorus:
Handy, me boys, so *handy.*

And on the chantey went until the yard was in place.

There were chanteys for nearly every chore aboard ship. There also was plenty of singing by the crewmen off watch, but to the sailors these were songs for leisure, not chanteys. Because the ship's work hours were divided into four-hour shifts called watches and the seamen into two watches, half of the crew worked while the other half rested. During daylight hours most of the crew was awake anyway, and those not on watch entertained themselves with song and story. Nearly every ship had at least one storyteller who could spin yarns for hours, especially for the benefit of the landlubbers. Even more popular was the seaman who had brought along his fiddle, flute, or accordion. The younger sailors favored sentimental songs about home and mother and girls left behind; the veterans liked to sing about famous prostitutes. The convivial songfests in the forecastle or on deck around the foremast in warm latitudes were limited to fair weather in which the clipper was steadily moving along; whenever the wind changed, all hands were summoned to the sheets and halyards and into the yards.

Few holidays were observed aboard a clipper ship, which had to be worked every day. Some of the more religious clipper captains observed Christian holidays and tried to slack off such unpopular work as mast-slushing and deck-holystoning on Sundays, giving the sailors a bit of free time to wash and mend their clothes and try to delouse their bedding. These captains also usually forbade such popular activities as card games, dice, or other gambling; a few even outlawed the sailor's hornpipe. An important occasion for many foremast hands, however, was "Dead Horse Day": The sailor who had been dumped aboard by a crimp usually spent his first month or two paying off the advance; the popular phrase was that he spent that time working to pay for a "dead horse." So the end of the term was understandably celebrated with song and, if the captain could be persuaded, a tot of rum.

Boredom in the forecastle sometimes reached the point where some of the sailors put on performances of dancing and singing or even plays and revues, with the less burly men playing women's parts.[13] But the most popular shipboard event was the ceremonial crossing of the equator, during which veteran sailors initiated first-timers into the rites of King Neptune. The usual procedure consisted of blindfolding the neophyte and announcing the arrival of Neptune as the vessel reached the equator. Neptune, played by one of the old hands and assisted by other shipmates who had crossed the line before, dunked the initiates in a tub of water, shaved them, and pronounced them Sons of Neptune. Even a driving clipper captain usually permitted this harmless diversion, if only because in the calms and doldrums near the equator there was little need for sail-changing. Some skippers also permitted another ration of grog at the end of the ceremony. For most young hands it amounted to a rite of passage into the fraternity of around-the-world sailors. Usually at the end of the ceremony the new Son of Neptune was given a certificate attesting to his initiation; he carried it with him thereafter to prove his new standing—and to avoid a repetition of the initiation. After his baptism, Hugh Gregory of the *Sea Serpent* declared, "I may now say that I am a son of Neptune with truth, and privileged to play pranks off on the uninitiated."

But few clipper captains relaxed the ship's work long enough for King Neptune if a fresh breeze arrived and there were sails to be changed. No means were spared to get the most out of the clipper's crew. Historian-Captain Arthur Clark, perhaps more candidly than he intended, described the typical clipper master's attitude:

> Sad enough, no doubt to the captain of a clipper ship bound round Cape Horn, compelled to stand by and see his canvas slatting to pieces in the first bit of a blow outside Sandy Hook, because he was cursed with a crew unable or unwilling to handle it. But this seldom happened more than once aboard of an American clipper in the fifties, for such a crew was taken in hand and soon knocked into shape by the mates, carpenter, sailmaker, cook, steward and boatswain. Belaying pins, capstan bars, and heavers began to fly about the deck, and when the next gale came along the crew found that they would get aloft and

make some kind of show at stowing sails, and by the time the ship got down to the line, they were usually pretty smart at handling canvas. As the clipper winged her way southward, and the days grew shorter, and the nights colder, belaying pins, capstan bars, and heavers were all back in their places, for system, order and discipline had been established.

Clark's analysis was oversimplified. Frequently the mates' weapons of persuasion continued to be used. "Belaying-pin soup and handspike hash" was the sardonic term the clipper sailors used to describe their lot. A seaman could get a belaying pin across his back even for neglecting to call a mate "mister" or for answering him without a "sir." Any sign of disobedience or delay was dealt with brutally. Clipper captains and mates were convinced that instant obedience was necessary for the safety of the ship as well as for the primary objective of reaching port in record time. And the more determined the captain, the harsher the punishment for such offenses as foot-dragging or shirking duty. Josiah Creesy was a stern taskmaster, and Robert Waterman was even tougher, especially with malingerers who hid out or pretended illness; idlers aboard a Creesy or Waterman ship were "started" by a rope's end or beaten with a heaver. Anyone who was so unwise as to strike back in defense could spend the rest of the voyage "in irons," shackled hand and foot to a bulkhead in the hold.

A law passed by Congress in 1853 provided legal penalties for a ship's officer who out of spite should "beat, wound, or imprison a member of his crew or inflict any cruel or unusual punishment." And a small legion of waterfront lawyers made a career out of meeting homecoming sailors and using their testimony to sue ships' mates and captains. One of their most successful tactics was to wait until a captain was about to sail, in hopes of a quick out-of-court settlement. New York's Marine Court was often clogged with cases of sailors versus their captains. Understandably, Captain Clark scornfully complained that these lawyers "degrade an honorable profession," claiming that the sailor rarely saw any of the money that his lawyer collected; Clark maintained that the sailors themselves regarded these lawyers with contempt. "One of the most insulting epithets which a sailor could apply to another was to call him a 'sea lawyer,' " Clark wrote, "and there was a particularly ravenous species of shark which used also to be known as the 'sea lawyer.' "

There was one "sea lawyer" who won the respect of the sailors if only because he had been a sailor himself. Richard Henry Dana, Jr., had been one of those young New England aristocrats who had gone to sea earlier in the century. He had been about to start his junior year at Harvard in 1833 when an attack of measles left him weak and impaired his eyesight so that it was painful to read. The family doctor, in the custom of the times, suggested a sea voyage to help the young man recover his health. So Dana signed on as an ordinary seaman aboard the 86-foot *Pilgrim,* bound around Cape Horn to California to collect hides for Bryant & Sturgis, one of Boston's major leather dealers. Within a week at sea his eyesight was improving and he was gaining weight. And in his leisure hours he started keeping notes for a journal of his experiences.

The *Pilgrim* was not a happy ship; her captain, Francis A. Thompson, was a tyrant of the quarterdeck. Dana soon realized that the New Englanders who campaigned against slaveholding in the South condoned a similar form of bondage aboard their own ships. After a few months of cruising the California coast loading "California bank notes," as the *Pilgrim*'s sailors called the hides, Dana managed to get himself transferred to another Bryant & Sturgis hide drogher, the *Alert,* which was on her way home. Debarking in Boston on September 22, 1836, his health restored, he resumed his studies at Harvard, graduated at the top of his class, and entered law school. Meanwhile, in hopes of making enough money to get married, he wrote his journal and found a publisher.[14]

Two Years Before the Mast became an immediate best seller, was also published in England, and was translated into a dozen languages. Dana's straightforward, lucid, and simple description of life aboard a nineteenth-century sailing ship—especially his descriptions of fighting winter storms at sea (which "must have been written," said Herman Melville, "with an icicle"),[15] caught the attention of sailors and landlubbers alike; the British

edition, for example, sold out in Liverpool in one day to seamen who lined up to buy a copy. One of the book's most chill-
ing scenes occurred while the *Pilgrim* was anchored in San Pedro
Harbor taking on hides from the nearby ranchers:

> For several days the captain seemed very much out
> of humor. Nothing went right, or fast enough for him.
> He quarrelled with the cook, and threatened to flog him
> for throwing wood on deck; and had a dispute with the
> mate. . . . But his displeasure was chiefly turned against
> a large, heavily-moulded fellow from the Middle States,
> who was called Sam. This man hesitated in his speech,
> and was rather slow in his motions, but was a pretty good
> sailor, and always seemed to do his best; but the captain
> took a dislike to him. . . . The captain found fault with
> everything the man did.

When Sam refused to admit that he had been insubordi-
nate, the captain ordered him tied to the rigging and flogged:

> Swinging the rope over his head, and bending his
> body so as to give it full force, the captain brought it
> down upon the poor fellow's back. Once, twice—six times.
> "Will you ever give me any more of your jaw?" The man
> writhed with pain, but said not a word. Three times more.
> This was too much, and he muttered something which I
> could not hear; this brought as many more as the man
> could stand; when the captain ordered him to be cut down,
> and to go forward.

Captain Thompson, "his eyes flashing with rage, and his
face as red as blood," turned his attention to a sailor called John
the Swede, who had asked why his shipmate was being flogged,
and ordered him triced to the rigging as well. John complained:

> "Have I ever refused my duty, sir? Have you ever
> known me to hang back, or to be insolent, or not know
> my work?"
> "No," said the captain, "and it is not that that I flog

you for; I flog you for your interference—for asking questions."

"Can't a man ask a question here without being flogged?"

"No," shouted the captain; "nobody shall open his mouth aboard this vessel, but myself;" and began laying blows upon his back, swinging half round between each blow, to give it full effect. As he went on, his passion increased, and he danced about the deck, calling out as he swung the rope,—"If you want to know what I flog you for, I'll tell you. It's because I like to do it!—It suits me! That's what I do it for!"

That evening, Dana recalled, lying in his bunk and listening to his two groaning shipmates, "I thought of our situation, living under a tyranny . . . and then, if we should return, of the prospect of obtaining justice and satisfaction for these poor men; and vowed that if God should ever give me the means, I would do something to redress the grievances and relieve the sufferings of that poor class of beings, of whom I then was one."

The proof of *Two Years'* popularity with the common sailor soon became apparent in the waiting room of Dana's law office, which, some fastidious Bostonians complained, resembled a forecastle and frequently smelled like one. Dana quickly established a reputation as the sailor's advocate.[16] Preparing his cases with thoroughness and bringing his seafaring experience to bear, he won all of his cases in the first eighteen months of his law practice; in his first four years he won forty-five of the forty-eight cases in which he represented the plaintiff. His name rapidly became a malediction among Boston's captains and shipowners, who lumped him with the "sea lawyers" preying on affronted sailors. Whenever a seaman threatened to sue his skipper, the sneering response was that it "was a case for Dana to pick up."[17]

Some of the shrewder shipowners, however, recognizing Dana's undoubted ability in court, overlooked their distaste for the sailors' advocate and enlisted his aid in their salvage and insurance suits. These cases were much more remunerative than the small settlements Dana was winning for his forecastle clients, and gradually he concentrated his practice on admiralty law. Dana had married Sarah Watson of Hartford, Conn., who was turning out to be a social climber and something of a spendthrift. Dana himself felt that his profession required a prosperous appearance, staffing his home with a butler, a cook, and a governess for their four daughters. He also made some real-estate speculations that lost money. Despite a healthy income from his law practice, he was nearly always in debt.

But another reason for neglecting his sailor clients was Dana's own personality as an aristocratic snob. He had overcome his inborn inclinations aboard the *Pilgrim* and the *Alert;* but once he was back in Boston he reverted to character. Even while suing Boston's shipowners, he remarked, "I never had trouble with the upper class of merchants." Indeed, as a successful lawyer he courted the company of the bankers and Brahmins. He publicly voiced his distaste for the Irish immigrants pouring into New England and New York, and he remonstrated with his wife for her donation to famine aid in Ireland. When some friends urged Dana to enter politics, he demurred, explaining that it was beneath the dignity of a gentleman to seek votes from the common people. He continued to write articles on seamen's rights; but he also defended flogging when a sailor was guilty. He advocated temperance aboard ship and a plentiful supply of Bibles. Many sailors, he maintained, were "abandoned men. . . . A bad crew," he argued, "will make a bad captain."

As his case load increased, he referred more and more indigent sailors to other lawyers. By 1846 he boasted to his father than he had handled only a couple of sailors' cases in the past year; such suits, he wrote, "must fall mainly into the hands of persons who do little else. I am hoping to be clear of that predicament. . . . There is no progress in it," he explained, "it stands in the way of rise in the profession." Soon he was defending shipowners and captains against suits by their crew members. One of the cases he took in 1854 was reminiscent of the scene he had described aboard the *Pilgrim:* This time he defended a captain accused of beating a sailor to death. And this time he lost.

But others were taking up the seamen's cause. One was a friend of Dana's. The Reverend Edward Thompson Taylor's preaching at Boston's Seamen's Bethel drew landsmen and sailors alike for forty years, starting in 1833. Father Taylor attracted seamen because he spoke their language: He had been a foremast hand for a decade as a young man and had been captured by the British during the War of 1812 and sent to England's notorious Dartmoor Prison. Some of Dana's earliest sailor clients were referred to him by Father Taylor. San Francisco's counterpart to Father Taylor was Father Fell, who tried to find safe lodgings with honest boardinghouse keepers for arriving seamen and who advocated monthly pay for merchant sailors with no advances for San Francisco's crimps. In New York as early as 1843 the Reverend Benjamin Parker of the Young Men's Church Missionary Society was attempting to attract seamen to his chapel, strategically situated over a saloon.

Not many sailors took to the Christian missions at first. Few were interested in—indeed, many were put off by—the ministers' recruiting and the tracts, hymnals, Bibles, and prayer books they handed out. The shipowners continued to deal with the crimps to such an extent that a sailor who chose a church boardinghouse found it difficult to get a berth aboard a ship. Father Parker in New York at least managed to catch the sailors' attention with the YMCMS's Floating Church of Our Savior, a small gothic-style church complete with steeple, mounted on two pontoons, which tied up on the East River at the foot of Pike Street in February 1844. The floating bethel had pews for five hundred, a pipe organ, and a marble baptismal font in the shape of a capstan with a scallop shell for holy water. Hundreds of sailors went aboard the Floating Church of Our Savior, more out of curiosity than religious zeal, giving Father Parker an opportunity to persuade some of them at least to stay sober during most of their time ashore.[18]

Another New York missionary group, the American Seamen's Friends Society, provided bed and board for five hundred in their Sailors' Home on Cherry Street in the heart of the city's sailortown.[19] There also was a haven for seamen who were ill. Largely through the efforts of a former captain elected to the New York State legislature, a Marine Hospital opened on Staten Island in October 1831; within six months it had admitted three hundred patients. Their range of illnesses revealed the occupational hazards of the nineteenth-century sailor: Syphilis was the most common, followed by rheumatism, various fevers, and frostbite. In that period only twelve died in the Marine Hospital; the deadlier diseases such as smallpox, typhus, and yellow fever were treated at the nearby quarantine hospital.

But for every sailor who went to a bethel, a hundred preferred the brothel and the saloon. The homecoming sailor shaved his beard with his knife, donned his cleanest white ducks and checked shirt, tied a black silk ribbon to his tarred hat, and strutted ashore. The sailor on liberty, particularly the hardworked clipper sailor, was chiefly interested in three amenities he had been denied at sea: fresh food, alcohol, and sex, not necessarily in that order. In San Francisco, where the wharves were so crowded that the clippers had to anchor to wait for space, most of the crew went over the side into boats provided by the crimps attempting to lure them to their saloons and bordellos and pick their pockets before they headed for the gold mines. For those who tarried in San Francisco on the way to the mines, there were such havens of refreshment as the Noggin of Ale, the Bird in Hand, the Magpie, the Jolly Waterman, Faust's Cellar, and the famous Bella Union; the latter's level of entertainment was indicated by an actor named Oofty Goofty, whose performance consisted of smearing himself with tar and prancing around the stage shouting "Oofty goofty!"—usually to a small audience, since most of the sailors were fondling the Bella Union's waitresses (for a price) in the saloon's curtained booths. But the unwary sailor who visited these establishments often did not make it to the mines, instead awaking stupefied aboard another clipper. The most notorious crimps' bar was run by a Miss Piggott, whose "Piggott's Special," laced with laudanum, could drop a sailor in his tracks right at the bar. A convenient trapdoor delivered him to the runner in the cellar, who rushed him to the next departing ship before he came to.

New York Harbor had its Whitehall boats full of runners vying for the returning sailors' seabags and whatever wages they had earned. But most of the clippers tied up at their wharves, and the clipper sailors could fan out through the saloons, dance halls, and brothels of lower Manhattan. Those who set out to get drunk first had the widest choice. Water and Cherry streets had hundreds of dives, each usually consisting of a rough wooden bar presided over by the owner, who doubled as bouncer when his customers became unruly. Whiskey was dispensed from a barrel, rum from a jug, and a bucket on the bar contained the cheapest drink (2 cents a shot): whiskey diluted with Cayenne pepper, kerosene, or creosote. One of the most notorious saloons was The Hole in the Wall, managed by "One-Arm Charley" Monell and featuring as bouncer a rugged Englishwoman named "Gallus Meg," who subdued recalcitrant clients by biting off their earlobes. (She kept a jar of trophies behind the bar as a warning.) The Hole in the Wall was closed by the police after seven men had been murdered there in the same number of weeks.

Most of the saloons swarmed with prostitutes. Some were a bit formal about it, offering a dance hall in the back room. The music usually consisted of a fiddler, though John Allen's Dance House featured a string orchestra. Among the more picturesque saloon dance halls were Liverpool Mag's and Kit Burns's Rat Pit and Dance Hall. In most of the establishments the entertainment was deceptively free: There was no charge for a sailor to select a dancing partner; but he soon found that he was expected to buy a drink for her after each dance. Those who tried to skip a round were promptly ushered from the premises by the bouncer. The dancing sessions grew shorter and the drinks more frequent as the evening wore on. As the saloon owners had learned, it did not take many drinks to affect a sailor who had abstained, however involuntarily, for half a year or more. And for those with a good capacity the bartender had laudanum or opium to spice the rum or whiskey. Soon the girls were leading their partners upstairs, where the victims usually awoke to find they had been robbed. An entire voyage's wages could disappear in the first night.

If he managed to avoid being robbed in a brothel or doped in a bar, the sailor encountered dozens of other waterfront thieves and crooks on the lookout for seamen on leave or between vessels. A favorite fraud practiced on a prospective seaman was to sell him a flashy outfit of sailor's blouse, pants, and hat plus shiny, pointed shoes, all useless at sea. Another scam was the sea chest switch, in which the chandler sold the sailor a chest with a complete seagoing outfit at an exorbitant price, offered to deliver it to the ship and, as soon as the customer had left the shop, took out all but a top layer of clothing, filling the rest of the chest with rocks or sand. What with the crimps, the girls, and the crooked chandlers, the sailor usually found himself in a strange forecastle, suffering the acute hangover of drug as well as drink, a dose of "ladies' fever," as the sailors called venereal disease, and a switched sea chest. In the eloquent words of one chantey,

> The next I remembers I woke in the morn,
> On a three skys'l yarder bound south round Cape Horn;
> Wid an ol' suit of oilskins, an' two pair of sox,
> An' a bloomin' big 'ead, an' a sea-chest of rocks.

"As a matter of fact," Captain Arthur Clark maintained, "the lives, limbs, and morals of sailors at that period were very much safer at sea than they were on land." But most clipper sailors did not see it that way; certainly the forecastle conversation did not compare life aboard favorably with liberty ashore. Captain Clark spoke for many of the clipper masters when he called the new class of sailors from Europe and South America "outcasts." The clipper captains, he argued, were forced to sign on these derelicts from other ports

> because they could get no other men. They provided them with better food than they had ever seen or heard of on board vessels of their own countries, supplied them with clothes, sea boots, sou'westers, oilskins, and tobacco, restored them to health, paid them money which many of them never earned, and for the time being, at least, did their utmost to make men out of them. If anyone imagines that this class of sailors ever felt or expressed the least gratitude toward their benefactors, he is much mistaken.

Clark did admit that "there were many American clipper ships with crews that were for the most part decent, self-respecting men." But most clipper crews, he maintained, "were amenable to discipline only in the form of force in heavy and frequent doses, the theories of those who have never commanded ships or had experience in handling degenerates to the contrary notwithstanding. To talk about the exercise of kindness or moral suasion with such men," he argued, "would be the limit of foolishness; one might as well propose a kindergarten for baby coyotes or young rattlesnakes."

Captain Josiah Perkins Creesy, for one, would not have regarded himself as his crew's "benefactor." Neither would he have compared his sailors to coyotes or rattlesnakes. Although the roster of the *Flying Cloud* has been lost, no doubt her owners were forced to ship a number of foreigners to make up her complement. But the difference between Captains Creesy and Waterman was that Creesy carefully supervised the selection of his crew, while Waterman depended on N. L. & G. Griswold and the first mate to recruit the men for the *Challenge*. It was to become a crucial difference when the *Challenge* and the *Flying Cloud* set out on their competing voyages around Cape Horn.

7

Challenge vs. Flying Cloud I

ON WARM JUNE AFTERNOONS in 1851, one of the most popular spots in New York City was Battery Park. The railed promenade along the shore at the southern tip of Manhattan usually bustled with people watching the harbor spectacle. Ladies with parasols and gentlemen in top hats strolled along the promenade. More common folk wandered about the lawn or leaned on the promenade railing, alternately admiring the fashion parade and the view of the harbor. Young boys in tattered undershorts dived from the seawall for pennies. An occasional beggar or prostitute worked the crowd. The harbor was full of ships moving in every direction at once. Steamers puffed to and from their North River piers; pilot boats skimmed out toward the Narrows; schooners, brigs, and sloops of every size slanted across the harbor; a ferry thunked toward Staten Island; and ponderous merchantmen, most of them under tow by little steam tugs, proceeded upharbor toward the East River. Dominating all of these smaller craft was the occasional stately clipper ship.

June 2 was a blustery day with a brisk northwesterly ruffling the harbor and kicking up whitecaps. A particularly large crowd had gathered to watch the magnificent new clipper *Flying Cloud* set sail on her much-heralded maiden voyage to San Francisco. Clipper-watching had become a popular sport; one of them took its majestic departure every few days. And everyone knew of the mounting rivalry between the *Flying Cloud* and the *Challenge,* which still was loading but would soon set sail in hopes of catching the *Flying Cloud.* All morning there was no sign of the *Flying Cloud* off the Battery, and the number of watchers grew as the air of expectancy increased.

The *Cloud* still lay gently rolling and creaking at Pier 20 in the East River at the foot of Maiden Lane. In the captain's cabin, Eleanor Creesy was arranging her chart table and unpacking her aids to navigation: the Dent sextant, the chronometers, the five-place logarithm tables by Bowditch, Matthew Maury's *Wind and Current Charts* and *Sailing Directions,* and the pads of foolscap for her calculations. Her husband meanwhile studied the ship from his quarterdeck to make sure she was sea-ready. A harbor pilot came aboard and joined Creesy, the helmsman, and the first mate on the quarterdeck. Finally, at 2 P.M., Creesy turned to the mate and gave the order. The lines were cast off. A tug took the clipper's bow hawser and puffed out into the swirling East River.

Riding the outgoing tide, the *Flying Cloud* shortly came into view off the Battery. Along the promenade hats waved, handkerchiefs fluttered, and hundreds cheered. Her topsails loosed to the gusty breeze, the clipper grandly followed her tug down the harbor and through the Narrows. At 7 P.M. the pilot scrambled down the ship's ladder to his pitching pilot boat. Creesy kept the clipper at anchor overnight, and at dawn called for full sail and anchor aweigh. The *Flying Cloud* rapidly gathered speed before a moderate southwesterly and ran out into the North Atlantic on her maiden voyage around the Horn.

In the *Cloud*'s log Creesy contentedly recorded for the first three days "Moderate breezes fine weather," perfect conditions for training his crew. Most of them needed training. Grinnell, Minturn's recruiters, under Creesy's careful supervision, had been able to scrape up a few "A.B.'s" (veteran Able-Bodied seamen) despite the scarcity of experienced sailors along the New York waterfront. But most of the rest must have been landlubbers shipping out as an inexpensive way to get to the gold fields; and the *Cloud* probably had her share of derelicts kidnapped by the crimps. From the start, Creesy had trouble with his first mate, whom he accused of malingering. Creesy was not an easy master to work for. But he knew how to train a crew with or without help from his officers, and he put the first three days of fair weather to good use.

The first lesson a sailing ship crewman had to learn was the names and uses of some 130 lines forming webs above the deck[1] and converging along the pinrails. He had to know the correct belaying pin holding each of these lines and to be able to find it in the dark on a pitching deck; to cast loose the wrong one could mean disaster. Even more daunting was the work high in the yards.

Setting a clipper's sails required an intricate orchestration of teamwork by the men on the yardarms and others manning the braces on deck. By custom the few experienced men went aloft first and were assigned to the outer ends of the yards for the perilous task of securing the earrings at the corners of the sails. The landlubbers gingerly followed them, climbing the easier windward side of the rigging and trying to remember what the mates had told them: Don't look down. But as each man edged along the footropes swinging under his feet, he could not resist a glance to make sure of his foothold, whereupon he usually froze in terror. Far beneath him the *Cloud*'s hull looked slimmer than ever, and each roll of the ship, carrying him out over the ocean, seemed to last forever. Urged on by a mate, the neophyte edged along the yardarm to his position where he found his gasket, one of the lines that tied the furled sail in place.

At a command from below the men on the yards untied the gaskets and the heavy cotton duck fell free. More orders echoed up from the deck. The braces creaked in their blocks, and the bottom ends of each sail, the cringles, were hauled in. Bellying in the breeze, the sails filled and the big clipper increased her speed. Slowly each man shuffled back along the footrope, holding his breath as he grabbed for the sturdy, laddered rigging, and climbed downward, finally jumping onto the deck, legs shaking and heart pounding from his brush with death. No one who made that first climb aloft ever believed he could do it again, much less with the agility of the few veterans who seemed to run along the swinging footropes.

The next lesson for all landlubbers was the complicated procedure for tacking a square-rigged ship. Unlike a sloop or schooner with triangular fore-and-aft sails, the square-rigged *Flying Cloud* could not whip about through the eye of the wind and quickly fall off on the other tack. Bringing a square-rigger about was a ponderous yet delicate maneuver usually requiring most of the crew. The first step was to get up as much speed as possible so as to give the ship the momentum to carry her through the arc of the head wind. So the helmsman let the ship fall off onto a more favorable slant with the wind nearly at 90 degrees to the vessel. The next command was, "Hard a-lee!" at which the helmsman spun the wheel to leeward (away from the wind), thus making the rudder move to windward.[2] The *Flying Cloud* started to swing into the wind. At that point the lines to her jibs and staysails—the fore-and-aft sails that caught the wind more quickly on the other side—were cast loose. Her foretopsail—the square sail first to catch the head-on wind—also was loosed to be ready for trimming to the wind on the other side.

This was the critical moment, with the wind blowing straight at the clipper's bow and all her loose sails and lines flying and flogging. If she had enough momentum, she continued her swing past the direction of the wind and began to take it on her other side. At that point the *Cloud*'s fore-and-aft jibs and staysails were sheeted in, helping to move her about on her new tack. Meanwhile, the square sails on her foremast were backwinded; but slowly they moved with the ship through the eye of the wind and also began to catch it from the other side. That was the moment for the command "Mainsail haul!" Everyone hauled on the lee braces of the *Cloud*'s big mainsail, yanking it around to catch the wind from the new direction.

Everything depended on the split-second timing of the command and the swift response of those hauling the mainsail about. If the maneuver were delayed too long, the ship would be driven backward and her swing through the head wind would halt. Gradually she would fall back on her previous tack and the entire procedure would have to be repeated. In a heavy sea she would meanwhile be unmaneuverable and at the mercy of the waves. But if the timing were right and the men at the braces responded promptly and with enough strength—it took a great effort to haul the big mainsail against the wind—the *Flying Cloud* would fall off on her new tack. The braces were then trimmed in and she began to pick up speed on her altered course. During the first days of the voyage she probably missed a good many tacks and had to repeat them. But at least the moderate winds helped by making the maneuver less dangerous during the learning process. Evidently the *Cloud*'s men learned fast during the first three days under the careful tutelage of Creesy—as they proved in the near-disaster that occurred on the fourth day.

It had happened to Donald McKay's fine-tuned vessels before and it would happen again. As the northwesterly winds piped up to a full gale and the big clipper labored in the heavy seas, there was an ominous crackle aloft and most of the *Flying Cloud*'s top-hamper wrenched free of its stays. Her main topgallant and topsail, about half the upper length of her mainmast, toppled to one side and crashed onto the deck and into the sea, dragging her mizzen topgallant with them. In one minute of flying spars and thundering canvas the big clipper lost a third of her sail area and everyone was enveloped in a tangle of canvas, hemp, and splintered wood.

Creesy had dealt with partial dismastings before. In a salvage operation on the run, he first had the fallen spars fished aboard so they would not hole the hull. Through the days and nights of June 6 and 7, all hands cleared the giant spider's web of fallen shrouds and rerigged the *Cloud*'s main and mizzen masts. In his laconic style, Creesy merely noted in the log for June 6: "Lost Main & Mizen Topgallant mast & Main Topsail yard." Only 24 hours later he tersely added, "Sent up Main Topsail Yard. Set all possible sail." In 48 hours without pausing, Creesy had kept his clipper on course while restoring all her sails. The *Cloud* picked up speed again and raced on down the Atlantic.

The clipper now began to run out of the North Atlantic's trade winds and into the horse latitudes.[3] Fitful breezes came and went, and during one of the breezier periods Creesy wrote in the log: "Discovered Main Mast badly sprung below the hounds." The toppling main topgallant mast had split the lower mast where they were joined (the "hounds"), weakening the mainmast's entire structure. Creesy strapped the splintered section of the mast and kept the *Cloud* on the run. By June 21 the clipper had passed through a buffeting series of squalls and into the doldrums. Next day she was adrift on a flat sea, her yards banging and her empty sails flogging as she rolled in the ocean's oily swells. Creesy for once lost his imperturbability long enough to complain in the log: "Calm. Calm. Calm."

But Eleanor Creesy had noted Matthew Maury's admonition to drive directly south; and following the shortest route indicated in Maury's *Wind and Current Charts,* she eased the *Flying Cloud* through the doldrums in under four days. Most sailing ships floundered in this area for a week or more. By June 24 the clipper had picked up the South Atlantic's southeast trade winds, and Creesy was recording "Gentle breezes. Fine weather." Two days later he was tacking off to the northeast on a temporary slant to round Cape de São Roque, the great bulge in the Brazilian coast, and the shoals that fan out from the cape.

Eleanor Creesy was following Matthew Maury's advice again. His *Wind and Current Charts* and *Sailing Directions* warned navigators running down their southing, as they called it, not to take a long slant of easting to round the formidable obstacle of the cape and its shoals. Instead, he advised, they could stay close to the coast and pick up favorable offshore winds and currents to round the cape. That was exactly what Eleanor Creesy did, plotting a course out and around the big promontory. So close did his wife navigate the *Cloud* to the cape that Creesy noted in the log on July 3: "Land in sight all day." Next day, on the lookout for the cape's shoals, he ordered a mate forward with a sounding line, which was dropped over the side throughout the day and into the night. At 2 P.M., the water had shoaled to 20 fathoms. Four hours later it was only 17 fathoms, and no doubt Creesy made ready to tack again toward deeper water; he prided himself on not being a slavish follower of Maury's recommendations and sometimes disregarded them despite his wife's advice. But Eleanor Creesy's calculations were exactly on the mark. The water deepened to 20 fathoms. By 1 A.M., the line read 30 fathoms. Free of the cape's deadly sandbanks, Creesy took the *Flying Cloud* south again, running down the coast of Brazil under a gentle easterly.

He began to suspect that they were in for some heavy weather when the wind hauled into the northeast. During the four days from July 8 to July 11, the wind went around the compass, to north, then northwest, then west, then southwest, bringing with it a succession of thunderstorms, squalls, and finally a howling gale. The latter probably was a *pampero,* the infamous storm that frequently sweeps down from the Andes and blasts seaward off the South American coast. Because he was on the lookout for it, Creesy had shortened sail, and by the time the gale winds struck, the *Flying Cloud* was carrying nothing but reefed topsails and staysails. But the gusting winds were too much even for them, and just after noon on July 11, all of the staysails were ripped to ribbons. The *Flying Cloud* heeled over until, as Creesy recorded, she was "shipping large quantities of Water over lee Rail." Under the intense pressure, her weakened mainmast began to shake in its base. Slashing rain obscured the horizon; but between downpours Creesy noticed a brig not far off to the east. As he watched, her top-hamper gave way and crashed into the sea; Creesy was too busy saving his own ship to offer her any assistance. Sending his few experienced men into the tossing rigging, he brought down the main royal and topgallant spars. Relieved of their weight, the *Cloud*'s mainmast seemed more secure. By that time the brig had disappeared over the horizon.

Sporadic gales continued out of the southwest through the night of the eleventh and the morning of the twelfth. The *Flying Cloud* was plunging through mountainous sea, slicing into them and sending sheets of water across the deck. Her lee rail was still nearly under even though she carried only a couple of reefed topsails; without them she would have been wholly at the mercy of the wind and water. At midafternoon, with the gale still blowing, the ship's carpenter reported that the forecastle was flooding.

The *Cloud* had taken a great deal of water over her bow and rail, but nearly all of it had drained off through the scupper holes and the openings in the bulwarks designed for the purpose. The water level in the forecastle was gaining on the pumps and had risen enough to suggest a serious leak. The carpenter suspected the port hawsehole; this entry for the anchor cable had a stopper to prevent leakage, but it had been taking a heavy beating for two days and perhaps had been knocked loose. Since it was on the leeward side, it was beneath the surface most of the time because of the clipper's angle of heel. Despite the strength of the storm, Creesy had kept the *Flying Cloud* beating as close to due south as possible. But now he reluctantly fell off to eastward, running before the wind at a more even keel so the hawsehole would be above the surface and could be restoppered.

The carpenter had guessed correctly. Standing belowdecks in water nearly to his waist, he replaced the stopper. Yet still the water gained on the pumps. At that point one of the sailors, perhaps unnerved at the sight of all the water below, gave away a shipmate whom he suspected of drilling a hole in the hull. Sloshing through the floating debris in the flooded forecastle, the carpenter found the leak. It was under a bunk on the leeward side: Two neatly bored holes had been joined to make a rectangular opening nearly four inches across and all the way through the *Flying Cloud*'s thick planking. This part of the ship's hull had been some three feet below the waterline when she heeled under the force of the wind, and the sea had poured in. The carpenter patched the hole, reported to the quarterdeck, and Creesy immediately ordered the *Cloud* back on course. She had been on her eastward tack for only one hour. And the wheel had scarcely stopped spinning before an investigation was under way to find out who had tried to sink the ship.

It had been not one man but two, and they were quickly apprehended because they had been so clumsy. The first man had bored two holes under his own berth; he was in the larboard (port) watch, so his bunk was on that side, to leeward when the wind came from the west. The shipmate who turned him in had seen him leaving the forecastle with an augur in his hand. His accomplice had used a marlinspike to join the two holes; and unbeknownst to him he had been seen in the act. Obviously the two men had agonized over the *Flying Cloud*'s sprung mast and had hoped that the captain would put into Rio to replace it. When it became evident that Captain Creesy had no intention of wasting that much time, the men decided to add to the ship's damage by holing her hull, trusting that Creesy would then have no choice but to put into Rio, where they would have a chance to desert ship. Instead they were put in irons. Creesy released them the following day only long enough to help clean up the wreckage from the storm.

By July 14 the *Flying Cloud* was below Rio and running for Cape Horn. Through mast-breaking gales Creesy had kept her on course for all but a few hours, and she had gained a long lead over her rival the *Challenge,* which was only now setting sail from Sandy Hook.

Robert Waterman gave the Battery Park onlookers a better show than Josiah Creesy had. Instead of boarding the *Challenge* at her South Street pier, he sent her downriver to await him off the tip of Manhattan. There on the morning of July 13, 1851, she rode at anchor, a swan among the geese, the largest clipper ship afloat. Her bowsprit pointed into the east wind and her rippling pennant seemed to repeat her name and her purpose: CHALLENGE. Dozens of small craft danced attention around her long black hull while Whitehall boats, the harbor's taxis, rowed out from the Battery with last-minute provisions, her officers, and her four passengers. But the man everyone at the Battery was waiting for was her captain.

Waterman knew how to make a dramatic departure. He had just completed his customary call at the Griswold counting-house at 71–72 South Street to pick up the *Challenge*'s manifest and his two mahogany-encased chronometers.[4] His carriage now came whisking along the Battery promenade, escorted by boys waving their caps as they ran alongside. It halted at the steps leading down to the landing stage, and while the horses stamped and snorted, the crowd surged forward. His chronometers under his arm, Waterman nodded to his audience. His beaver hat caught the summer sun; his frock coat was molded to his broad shoulders; and his narrow trousers were impeccably creased. Striding down the steps, he hopped into the waiting Whitehall boat and stood in the stern as it moved away. The people jamming the promenade railing broke into cheers and applause. Turning back to face them, Waterman lifted his top hat in acknowledgment.

Soon he was a tiny figure climbing the rope ladder and vaulting over the rail onto the *Challenge*'s quarterdeck. Within minutes the crowd at the Battery could hear the distant screech of the capstan and the clank of chain as the clipper's anchor rose from the harbor bottom. A waiting tug surged forward; the towline rose dripping from the water, and the big ship began to move down the harbor. As she did, the watchers on the shore could see a few tiny figures scampering up the rigging and out along the yardarms. Shortly, in a burst of white, the *Challenge*'s new topsails were loosed and canted to the easterly to steady her on her way. With a few more cheers and yells, most of the clipper fans dispersed. But some remained, watching at the Battery's railing until the big black hull was below the horizon and nothing but her white topsails could be seen against the southern sky.

It was a different Robert Waterman who stood on his quarterdeck beside the pilot and helmsman as the *Challenge* rode her towline through the Narrows and out into the Lower Bay. The beaver hat, the morning coat, and the silk cravat had been discarded in his cabin. And the genial arrogance with which he had accepted the cheers of his shoreside well-wishers had given way to simmering anger. One glance along the deck of the *Challenge* had confirmed his fears. Few of the men nimbly climbing the rigging were members of his crew. He recognized nearly all of them as longshoremen on special duty to help get the ship out of the harbor. Most of the *Challenge*'s men were still below in their bunks, some sleeping off their last binge, others drugged into insensibility. When the pilot went ashore, the longshoremen would depart with him, leaving the ship's work to the handful of stumbling creatures on deck and their comatose shipmates below.

But it was worse than that, as Waterman realized when he studied the ship's roster. He had resigned himself to a barely competent crew. He was well aware of the shortage of experienced seamen in New York; it was one of the reasons he had decided to retire. He knew that the dozens of ships that had sailed that summer had swept the waterfront of virtually every competent sailor. The *Flying Cloud* had taken the pick of those who remained, and the *Telegraph,* which had sailed earlier that day, had scooped up the rest.[5] Nonetheless, he had assumed that with about a dozen Able-Bodied seamen he would be able to make serviceable sailors out of the rest of them. But the situation he now faced was appalling.

The crew complement for such a large, heavily sparred vessel was about sixty men. The *Challenge* had fifty-six. Instead of a dozen "AB's," he had three. Out of the entire crew, only six men had ever had a hand on a ship's wheel. Half of the crew had never been to sea. Some of the landlubbers had signed on for a free ride to the gold fields. Others were released jailbirds. Most of them had been delivered, drunk and drugged, by New York crimps. Half a dozen of the crewmen were derelicts from European ports, immigrants still unable to understand commands in English.

The more Waterman studied the *Challenge*'s roster the angrier he became. And by the time the ship was anchored in the Lower Bay, he was taking out his anger on the first mate, whose responsibility it was to accept the crew. The first mate made the mistake of talking back. Waterman fired him and ordered him to leave the ship with the pilot. Shortly the mate, pilot, and longshoremen had climbed down into the bobbing pilot boat; and Waterman was left to consider his predicament.

He was in command of the largest merchantman in the world, with loftier sails than had ever been handled before. The *Challenge* carried a cargo worth $60,000 in New York and at least three times that amount in San Francisco, a cargo so diversified that her manifest was 28 feet long. He was expected to take this enormous ship and her precious cargo down the Atlantic and through the gales off Cape Horn at the worst time of the year—and in record time—with a gang of landlubbers and derelicts who had never climbed the rigging in their lives.

As he later confessed to friends, Waterman all but decided to return to the *Challenge*'s East River pier; better to try for at least a nucleus of experienced seamen than to court disaster. But when he considered the money that the Griswolds had paid out for the cargo and advance wages and, most important, the urgency of reaching San Francisco while demand was still high, he could not bring himself to return. Waterman's friends, however, must have recognized another factor in the equation, and that was Robert Waterman himself. To him, returning would be slinking home. He had never let his shipowners down. He had not even lost a spar. No insurance company had been called on with a claim from a ship commanded by Robert Waterman. He must have realized by now that he should have taken a part in recruiting the *Challenge*'s crew. But he had whipped landlubbers into shape before and had made record voyages with them. Most of all, there was the *Challenge*'s challenge. The *Flying Cloud* was well out ahead of him, and there was little chance of catching her; but the important point was to better her time to San Francisco. Waterman was well aware that a lot of money had been invested in getting the *Challenge* there faster. He also was convinced that the only ship that should be able to outsail the *Flying Cloud* was the *Challenge;* and the only captain who could make her do it was Waterman. Supreme confidence was as much a part of his makeup as his aquiline nose and jutting jaw. It was this confidence, perhaps hubris, that made it impossible for him to turn back.

The wind continued to come from the east. It would be difficult to tack out into the Atlantic from the Lower Bay, and in any case, most of the *Challenge*'s men still were barely able to stagger on deck, much less climb out onto the yardarms. Chafing at the delay, Waterman watched the coastwise schooners beating out past Sandy Hook. Not far from the *Challenge,* a transatlantic packet lay at anchor; she was the *Guy Mannering,* just arrived from Liverpool and awaiting a flood tide to help take her up harbor to her berth. Waterman was considering whether or not to promote his second mate, Alexander Coghill, to first when he noticed a ship's boat putting out from the *Guy Mannering.* Rolling in the easterly swells, the boat approached the *Challenge,* and the man sitting in the stern hailed the quarterdeck.

Waterman recognized him as soon as he climbed over the rail. James Douglass was known on the transatlantic run and in every bar in New York and Liverpool as one of the toughest first mates in the packet trade. He greeted Waterman and came right to the point. The *Mannering* had had a difficult crossing, he explained, and he had been forced to knock his crew about a bit. They were a rough bunch even for packet rats, and some of them had made it clear that they were planning their revenge as soon as they got ashore. Douglass had decided that he would be safer at sea. Could Waterman use a first mate? Waterman replied that he certainly could.

He must have known what he was letting himself in for. A hard-fisted driver who had earned the nickname "Black Douglass," the burly, two-hundred-pound mate had been heard to boast that he "would rather have a knock-down fight with a lot of sailors than eat a good dinner." But Douglass was an experienced ship's officer, and experience was what the *Challenge* needed, experience and a willingness to beat an incompetent crew into shape and get the most out of it. Waterman may not have known that Douglass often made no distinction between harsh discipline and brutality. What Waterman did know was that he needed a firm hand on this voyage and that Douglass was the man to supply it. So with no way of foretelling what calamity it would bring to the decks of the *Challenge,* he signed on James Douglass as first mate.

It was near dusk by now, and the lamp could be seen flickering on Sandy Hook's low lighthouse. The easterly wind had moderated. Waterman called for a foretopsail and ordered the anchor raised. The half-dozen men who were able to climb the rigging loosed the *Challenge*'s sails. Others staggered around the capstan, leaning into the wooden bars as the revolving drum drew up the anchor line. A few men, aided by the second and third mates, hauled on the braces. With her anchor dripping at its cathead, the *Challenge* slowly edged past Sandy Hook into the open Atlantic. Waterman set her course as close-hauled to the easterly as she could point, bound down the Atlantic and around Cape Horn on her historic, ill-starred voyage.

Sunset was still reddening the horizon and the *Challenge*'s sails when Waterman summoned the crew aft. Not all of them could get out of their bunks, and those who could presented a sorry sight. Many were only now realizing that they were at sea and not in the saloon or boardinghouse where they had been drugged. Those who had signed on to get to the gold fields were wary and sullen. Some were barely able to stand and supported themselves by clinging to the rail or to a shipmate. Some still wore flimsy shore clothes; many were barefoot. Only a few were properly outfitted in duck jackets, sturdy pants, and boots for work on deck and the narrow, swaying footropes of the rigging. Among them were half a dozen eager young ship's boys, inexperienced but attentive as Waterman addressed them.

It would be interesting to know the exact wording of the speech that Waterman traditionally gave at the beginning of a voyage, but he never wrote it down. The gist of the message, he claimed, was that everyone would be treated fairly and fed well as long as he did his work promptly and exactly as ordered—the safety of the vessel and all hands depended on immediate obedience. But anyone who shirked would regret it. No doubt Waterman, being Waterman, emphasized the last point, especially to this crew. And he took his time, because while he had the men's attention, Douglass and Coghill were, at his orders, inspecting the chests and seabags in the forecastle. As Waterman expected, they found hidden stores of rum, a dozen daggers, slingshots, bowie knives, and knuckle-dusters, and a few pistols, which they tossed over the side. And when Waterman finished, the mates herded the men into a line filing past the main hatch. There Michael Gallagher, the ship's carpenter, nicked the tip off every man's sheath or pocket knife. A sailor needed his knife for a dozen different chores aboard ship; but a blunt-ended knife was a less lethal weapon.

Next came the division of the crews into watches. By custom the first and second mates "chose up sides" as in a modern sandlot ball game: First choice went to Douglass; then Second Mate Coghill chose a man, then Douglass until each mate had his watch detail. The first mate's was known as the larboard (port) watch, the second mate's as the starboard.[6] It was while supervising this procedure that Waterman fully realized what an incompetent crew he had. Of the 56 men aboard the *Challenge,* three were Americans. The rest included only a few Britons and Frenchmen and one Swede who had had sea duty. Among the others were half a dozen who scarcely spoke English. Waterman decided that the six men who had some experience at the helm should be reserved for that duty; he promoted them to quartermaster, which meant that they would not stand watch. Besides the three U.S. seamen, the only Americans were the ship's boys, signed on as servants and errand-runners; they were not expected to serve watches. Nor were Hugh Patterson, the third mate, and the half-dozen crewmen with specific jobs, including Carpenter Gallagher, the cook, and the sailmaker, who would have a full-time task mending the *Challenge*'s torn and blown-out canvas.

That left few experienced men for Douglass and Coghill to select: John Leggett, already a veteran at nineteen; Fred Birkenshaw, a former Royal Navy sailor; and Charles Pearson, who had been to sea for forty years and who later confirmed Waterman's analysis of the crew: "We had not more than eight or ten good men," Pearson claimed. "Most were miserable trash." Among the near-useless men who made up the rest of the two watches were George Lessing, a practiced malingerer who soon earned the nickname "The Dancing Master" for his nimbleness in avoiding a rope's end; John Nisrop, a Frenchman who knew no English; an Italian whose illiterate signature on the roster was "Pawpaw" and who had come aboard with no shoes or socks; and an illiterate Finn with no English variously known as Smith and Smiti, whose shirking soon antagonized even his shipmates. These were the men who managed to make it to the deck. Half a dozen others, in advanced stages of dysentery, tuberculosis, or venereal disease, rarely left their bunks. In fact, so many of the *Challenge*'s crew were ill that Waterman converted the ship's sail room into a sick bay, partly in hopes of preventing the spread of infection.

Bad as the situation was, a tradition of the sea made it worse. By long-established custom a seaman stood his watch for four hours, then was off for four hours, then on again for another four and so on through a 24-hour period.[7] But by the midnineteenth century most captains had adopted the "dog watch," which was designed to change the schedule daily. Some four-hour periods were less popular than others, and the dog watch relieved a man from standing watch during these periods day after day. It accomplished this by dividing the 4 P.M. to 8 P.M. period into two-hour dog watches, resulting in a schedule that looked like this:

8 P.M. to midnight	First watch
Midnight to 4 A.M.	Middle watch
4 A.M. to 8 A.M.	Morning watch
8 A.M. to noon	Forenoon watch
Noon to 4 P.M.	Afternoon watch
4 P.M. to 6 P.M.	First dog watch
6 P.M. to 8 P.M.	Second dog watch

Thus James Douglass' crew took the first watch, from 8 P.M. to midnight, then was off watch until 4 A.M., then went back on duty from 4 A.M. to 8 A.M. Without a dog watch,

Douglass and his men would have repeated this schedule every day, and meanwhile Coghill and his crew would have been standing the other watches, including the most unpopular one, from midnight to 4 A.M. By "dogging the watches" the schedule changed every day: Douglass' crew, having stood the noon to 4 P.M. watch, was relieved not for the next four hours but only for two hours, coming back on deck at 6 P.M. and retiring again at 8 P.M. Now, instead of taking the 8 P.M. to midnight slot, they came on duty for the midnight to 4 A.M. period, which had been Coghill's watch the night before.

So the two watches shared such unpopular periods as midnight to 4 A.M. (Some sailors considered the next one, 4 A.M. to 8 A.M., as worse; sometimes it was called "the death watch" because most accidents occurred during these early-morning hours.) But while the practice of dogging the watches had been instituted for humane purposes, it actually had the opposite effect, for a reason no one realized in the nineteenth century: the circadian rhythms of all animals, including man (who later called it "jet lag"). Our built-in time clock, by which we become accustomed to regular hours of sleep and wakefulness, is thrown off when we change these hours by night shifts or travel to different time zones. And the human system reacts by making us wakeful at bedtime and sleepy while trying to work. It adjusts to the new hours after a while. But by changing the watches every day, Robert Waterman inadvertently made sure that his incompetent crew would be more incompetent still.

One of the ship's boys, E. A. Wheeler, wrote a long letter to his parents[8] after his arrival in California. From him we know that on the first leg of the voyage, from New York to the equator, "the weather was very fine and light winds." Very fine perhaps for Wheeler but maddening for Waterman because the *Challenge* had been built for strong, not light winds. Day after day the big clipper ship sailed grandly—and slowly—down the North Atlantic while her captain tried in vain to get more speed out of her. Day after day Douglass and two of the experienced seamen went to the weather rail to "cast the log" and measure the *Challenge*'s speed, knowing ahead of time the disappointing reading they would get.

The "log," the nineteenth-century device used for a ship's speedometer, was an ingenious contrivance consisting of a wood chip, a long line wound onto a reel, and an hourglass. The wood chip was shaped like a generous slice from a small pie; its round edge was weighted so its tip would stay upright in the water. The long line was attached to the tip of the wood chip; and two short lines ran from the ends of the curved bottom to a plug attached to the long line. The other end of the long line was rolled onto the reel, which one of the sailors held shoulder-high at the quarterdeck rail. The second sailor stood ready with the hourglass, a small version holding 28 seconds' worth of sand.

Douglass tossed the wood chip overboard. The line whirred off the reel and through his hand. Shortly a knotted bit of cloth whipped past, indicating that the wood chip was far enough astern to be out of the *Challenge*'s wake. He called out, "Turn!" and the man with the hourglass flipped it over. The sand flowed through the glass's neck as the wood chip rushed astern and the line reeled out. The moment the top of the glass was empty, its holder shouted, "Stop!" Douglass snubbed the line; the resistance of the wood chip broke the plug that had been holding it vertical in the water; the two short lines fell free and the long line pulled the chip to the surface, where it danced on the wavetops as Douglass hauled it in.

The point where he had snubbed the line marked how much of it had been drawn off the reel by the wood chip during the 28 seconds. And since the line was calibrated for the 28-second hourglass and marked for each half knot, the one nearest Douglass' hand indicated the *Challenge*'s speed. Rarely during those first weeks did the ship move fast enough to draw out more than half a dozen knots.

Robert Waterman was the skipper who was always able to find enough wind to send a clipper along at 12 knots of more. Now he could find nothing but fickle breezes. With each day the record that he and his shipowners hoped for—not to mention the $10,000 bonus—was already beginning to evaporate. Lack of wind, the curse of the clipper ship captain, must have exacerbated Waterman's annoyance; he was a man with a short-fused temper. And his frustration certainly would have been infectious as he and Douglass kept trying to catch every breath of breeze with inexperienced sailors who took so long to change sail that often the breezes were lost.

Like the *Flying Cloud,* the *Challenge* provided better crew

quarters than most nineteenth-century sailing vessels. Instead of
the customary damp dungeon in the bow of the ship, the *Challenge*'s forecastle was a forward deck cabin illuminated by four
portholes during the day and an oil lamp at night. Each man
had his own bunk; and so many of the crew were in sick bay
that the forecastle was less crowded than usual. But even the
gentle roll of the ship made most of the landlubbers seasick, and
their retching soon turned the forecastle into a noisome hold.

Seasickness was one malady that nearly everyone recovered
from in a few days, and soon there were more men on deck.
Those who knew anything about ships found the *Challenge* a
marvel of efficiency, her rigging designed by Waterman for ease
of sail handling in the heaviest weather. Because nearly all lines
led to the main deck, few had to climb onto the wave-washed
foredeck during a storm to handle the sails. Shrouds and stays,
bitts and belaying pins were all of the latest design and sturdiest
construction. William Webb had been told by the Griswolds to
spare no expense, and the result was the most efficient clipper
ship afloat.

But the *Challenge*'s amenities were lost on those who had
never been to sea before and had nothing to compare with this
new clipper; they knew only how daunting it was. They were
appalled by the bewildering complexity of the miles of running
rigging and the hundreds of belaying pins, each for a different
purpose and all looking alike. Confronted with the dismaying
task of learning to distinguish among all these lines, the kidnapped landlubbers tried to avoid duty entirely—all the more
so when they were forced up into the rigging.

During the first weeks the *Challenge* was spared the sudden
squalls that dismasted the *Flying Cloud*. But like every tall-masted
clipper, she required frequent fine-tuning of her delicately bal-
anced shrouds. Her rigging, made of four-strand Russian hemp,
had extra strength but stretched under the strain and had to be
tightened through dozens of wooden deadeyes. Waterman reported later that the entire rigging had to be seized up at least
three times during the first leg to Cape Horn. Her stiff new sails
had to be set. And her masts had to be slushed regularly with
grease. They were the world's tallest. A man on her skysail
yard was more than 230 feet above the water, as if perched on

the windowsill of a 23-story building during an earthquake. In the light winds of the first weeks the *Challenge* rolled with the long ocean swells, her masttops drawing circles against the blue sky and her spars creaking as they dipped from side to side. Not surprisingly, most of the *Challenge*'s neophytes quailed at the prospect of climbing out along those dipping spars. But Douglass changed their minds with a flick of a rope's end; the only escape was aloft.

Furling and loosing the *Challenge*'s sails were frightening enough, but Waterman added a task that was more hazardous even in fair weather. Because of the light winds, he called for the clipper's studdingsails. These extra stretches of canvas extended out over the sea from the tips of the yards. The sails were brailed to their own yards, which were hauled aloft to be fitted into hoops at the end of each yardarm. It was dangerous work, hanging over the water and pushing the studdingsail yard out to its end while the ship's roll threatened to dip it into the heaving sea. The studdingsail's far tip was supported by a line running upward and through blocks back downward to the men on deck who hauled it into place. With her studdingsails set, the *Challenge*'s 90-foot main yardarm was nearly twice as long, stretching 160 feet from port to starboard leach.

Only one maneuver was more dangerous than setting the studdingsails, and that was bringing them back in. The reason was that no self-respecting clipper ship captain doused these extra sails until heavy weather made it absolutely necessary. And Waterman kept his studdingsails flying longer than anyone else. By that time the ship was rolling heavily and the waves were reaching up to pluck the men from their footropes. Work on the yards taking in sail was terrifying, and the teamwork of men aloft and on deck was essential. The braces could be loosed only in stages, so there was just enough slack as the men swinging on the footropes grabbed the heavy canvas and tucked it against the yardarm; if there were too much slack, the swirling, slatting sail could sweep a man from his perch. And the procedure had to go quickly, the men on deck easing the braces while the men aloft fisted in the loose canvas, bunched it along the yard, and finally tied the gaskets to hold it in place.

But handling these sails in a gale of wind was a test still to come; the *Challenge*'s mild weather continued. July and August are hurricane months in the North Atlantic. But if there were any hurricanes, they stayed away as the big clipper sailed south. A white bow wave creamed away from the yellow copper sheathing protecting her hull. An orange-hot sun rose from the east every morning and sparkled on the blue sea at midday. By evening, near the end of the second dog watch, the ocean to starboard shimmered wine-red in the sunset. Below Bermuda flying fish darted under the *Challenge*'s bowsprit, and floating pastures of planktonic weed marked the western edge of the Sargasso Sea. The clipper's new masts creaked and groaned with the weight of the sails pulling her southward. To those who saw her, aboard packets crossing her path and steamers chugging to and from the Isthmus, the *Challenge* was like a towering ghost ship, her clouds of white sail overbalancing her slim, glistening hull.

But the *Challenge* was better seen from a distance. On her quarterdeck Captain Waterman fretted and cursed at the fickle breezes. On her main deck Douglass vented his displeasure with the recalcitrant crew. Only a few were showing any inclination to learn the intricate business of the ship—the proper hauling of lines and the technique of working on the footropes. Nearly a dozen men were still in the sail room sick bay; some were too feeble to stand, but most of them, Waterman and Douglass were convinced, were feigning illness. Those who appeared on deck were learning ways to avoid work more readily than the ways of ship-handling. And already it was apparent that nothing aroused Douglass' ire more quickly than a malingerer. Partly to set an example for the others but mostly because of his violent temper, Douglass used a rope's end, a belaying pin, a heaver, or his huge fists to beat anyone who tried to dodge work or responded to an order less than instantly.

Whether or not Waterman began to worry about his first mate's brutality is not known. But Waterman had always believed in strong—harsh, if necessary—discipline for the safety of the ship and the lives of the crew. Nowhere could disaster strike more quickly than aboard a high-sparred, slim-hulled clipper ship when a squall struck and the crew did not respond in time. Most of this crew, however, not only avoided duty but

also spent the time squabbling and skirmishing. Waterman recalled later, "I think it was the worst crew I've ever seen. . . .
They would fight among themselves, cut, gouge, bite and they
kept in a continual row." Now, to make matters worse, the
Challenge entered the horse latitudes and the even calmer waters
of the doldrums.

No doubt Waterman, like Eleanor Creesy, followed Matthew Maury's advice; he also used Maury's *Wind and Current
Charts* and the *Sailing Directions* in plotting his course. Still, there
was no avoiding the deadly, frustrating calms completely. The
Challenge slowed to a crawl and sometimes sat still in the water,
her sails slatting as she rolled with the ocean's swells. The deck
turned hot enough to blister bare feet and the air belowdecks
was stifling. The men dipped buckets into the glassy sea and
poured water over their heads, with little relief. Tropical downpours drenched the ship, and the few men who had oilskins
found them coated with mildew. The steaming heat brought
out boils that chafed under the men's clothes and smarted when
they poured water over themselves. Tempers flared; crewmen
shirked duty even more; and Douglass beat them more frequently. Even Charles Pearson, the forty-year veteran who
complained about the rest of the crew, later claimed that he had
been "frequently struck myself." Then the first man died; Richard Cleaver had never recovered from whatever disease he had
had when brought aboard. By the time the *Challenge* finally
drifted out of the doldrums below the equator, she was a hotbed
of rebellious men, with open mutiny awaiting only a spark to
touch it off.

On August 17 she was running down the coast of Brazil,
near the area where the *Flying Cloud* had been sabotaged. It was
a deceptively pleasant, sunny Sunday with a soft, steady trade
wind filling the *Challenge*'s sails. The quartermaster known to
everyone as "Big Jerry" was at the wheel alternately watching
the compass binnacle and the set of the sails to keep her steady
as she went. Douglass had the forenoon watch, but there was
not much work to do. The white sails pulled gently at their
yards; all canvas was set and drawing, and there was no need
to change the trim. Passengers William Masten and Cornelius
Sterling, along with two of the ship's boys, were lounging in

the longboat atop the main cabin, mesmerized by the swish of the sea alongside and the parabola of the *Challenge*'s white masts that seemed almost to touch the fat clouds above them. From their vantage point they could see Waterman and Douglass conversing aft on the quarterdeck. Douglass descended to the main deck, walked to the forecastle companionway, and bellowed for all hands to bring their seabags and chests on deck.

Douglass later explained that a seaman had complained that some of his gear had been stolen. This sort of pilfering had been going on throughout the voyage. The *Challenge,* like all ships of the time, had a slop chest, but most of the *Challenge*'s men preferred to steal from one another. When Douglass reported the newest complaint, Waterman angrily ordered him to search the men's belongings and make an example of the culprit.

Everyone in the forecastle and all those who could stagger from sick bay were hounded on deck. The men were sullen and slow, and Douglass laid into them with his heaver. As seaman Birkenshaw reluctantly shoved his sea chest across the deck, Douglass swung his club at him, knocking him down. A few others were similarly hurried along until all the bags and chests were set out in the waist of the ship. At Douglass' command they were opened and their contents dumped out. Douglass, by his account, was about to ask if anyone could identify his own gear in anyone else's sea chest. But he made the mistake of not lining up the men where he could watch all of them.

He was bending over to inspect one man's belongings when he was grabbed from behind. Fred Birkenshaw pinioned Douglass' arms and, as if at a signal, most of the others rushed him. George Smith grabbed Douglass by the throat and half a dozen men tackled him. Douglass' heaver clattered to the deck, and the writhing mass of men fell across an overturned ship's boat. As Douglass toppled under the weight of his attackers, he felt a knife slash at his thigh.

Transfixed by the spectacle, the two passengers and ship's boys looked aft and saw Captain Waterman at the *Challenge*'s weather rail. It was nearly noon and he was raising his sextant to take the ship's position when he—and everyone else aboard the *Challenge*—heard Douglass bellow "MURDER!"

Masten jumped down from the longboat to alert Waterman; but the captain had already reacted. It took him only a few seconds to run down the steps to the main deck and plunge into the melee. Douglass had already struggled to his feet and had almost shaken himself free. Blood stained his pant leg, and his two-hundred-pound frame swayed in the grasp of half a dozen men. George Smith still had a death grip on his throat. Snorting and roaring, Douglass kicked and lashed out at them as Waterman arrived and smashed his sextant over Smith's head. Smith let go and turned on the captain, who grabbed him, dragged him to the rail, and secured him with a couple of turns of rope.

Some of the men scattered, and Douglass managed to wrench himself free. Ripping off his jacket, he handed it to Masten, grabbed up his heaver, and waded into the rest of his attackers, cutting them down like hay. Most of them scrambled up and ran for their lives. Together Waterman and Douglass rounded up half a dozen who had not escaped and tied them to the rail.

Waterman was examining Douglass' wound when the second mate appeared. Coghill had been off watch in his bunk when he heard the scuffling on deck. He was still trying to take it all in when Douglass shouted, "Mr. Coghill, I want you to look for that man and be damned quick about it!"

"What man?" Coghill asked.

"That Fred in your watch," Douglass answered. Fred Birkenshaw, after igniting the attack, had slipped away. Coghill went looking for him, and Waterman helped Douglass limp down the companionway to the cabin, where he dressed the mate's wound. It was a long, deep triangular gash in the thigh; probably it would have been much deeper if the point had not been knocked off the knife.

Waterman and Douglass were back on deck by the time Coghill returned to report that he could not find Birkenshaw. One man claimed to have seen him jump over the side, apparently preferring drowning to Douglass' rage. It seemed unlikely to Douglass, so he made a search himself; but he could not find Birkenshaw either. Hobbling back on deck, his bandaged thigh oozing blood, he growled to Coghill, "God damn their souls, I'm damned glad the row has occurred. I can lick them as much as I like and they can't do anything with me when I get to

California." Clearly Douglass was thinking of the lawyers who made a career of hauling captains and mates into court for mistreating their crews. Now that the *Challenge*'s crew had attempted mutiny, Douglass felt he had an unassailable defense.

Waterman ordered George Smith put in irons. The other men at the rail were untied and taken to the forecastle to await their punishment. Coghill's men took the afternoon watch, and Douglass limped to his bunk. Waterman and his four passengers sat down to dinner—and to a discussion of the morning's event. The *Challenge*'s main cabin was one of the most luxurious afloat, paneled in rosewood with upholstered sofas, large windows, and a wall-size mirror reflecting the enameled cornices and gilt-carved moldings. Seated around the large table with the sunlight off the sea dancing on the ceiling and the cabin stewards bustling about serving the meal, the passengers must have found it difficult to believe the seething resentment on deck that had so recently reached the flash point. Waterman himself, Masten recalled, seemed to be in a reflective mood, wondering aloud whether it had been an isolated flare-up or a planned mutiny. He tended toward the latter explanation.

Masten went to his stateroom after dinner; but shortly a steward knocked on his door and asked if he would come to the captain's cabin. Two other passengers, Sterling and Richard Morse, were also there; evidently Waterman wanted them as witnesses while he interrogated Douglass' attackers. The first man brought before the captain was George Smith. He was manacled; his guard had shaved the back of his head and put a plaster on the wound inflicted by Waterman's sextant.

Waterman started the interrogation calmly, according to Masten, reminding Smith that his offense deserved the most severe punishment; however, if Smith would confess and name his accomplices, his sentence might be lessened. Had the attack been planned?

Smith denied any conspiracy, claiming that it had been a spur-of-the-moment reaction to Douglass' beatings. Further questions brought the same sort of answers. Waterman's voice became threatening. Smith's punishment would be even worse, the captain promised, if he continued to lie. Smith's resistance collapsed and he admitted that some of the men had indeed planned a mutiny. The plotting had started only a few days after leaving Sandy Hook. The plan was to kill both Waterman and Douglass and take the *Challenge* into Rio. The timing originally had been set for the previous night, but the scheme had failed because the captain and first mate had not been on deck at the same time during the night watches. Smith hastily added that he had not been a member of the group planning the mutiny; he had only heard about it.

He was marched to the brig. Nine more men were brought before the captain. Confronted with Smith's confession, all admitted that a mutiny had been planned; and all but one, a defiant seaman named Ralph Smith, claimed that they, too, had heard of the mutiny but had not been among the conspirators. On the basis of the interrogations Waterman decided that George Smith and eight others were guilty. One of the nine was Birkenshaw, who would be dealt with when he was found, if he were still aboard. Waterman ordered that Smith and the seven others be flogged.

Congress had outlawed flogging aboard merchant ships the previous year; but Waterman was not the only captain to ignore the new law. The eight men were marched to the waist of the ship, their shirts were stripped off, and their wrists were tied to the rigging. The rest of the crew was summoned on deck to watch. Swinging a heavy whip made of knotted ropes, Douglass went to work with sadistic pleasure. He later claimed that he could not recall whether he administered a dozen or two dozen lashes per man; one dozen would have been more than enough. The knotted ropes quickly reduced each man's back to a pulpy mass. Blood spattered the deck and Douglass' arm as he grunted with each lash. Most of the victims screamed at first, then subsided into semiconscious groans, crying out for the last time when the traditional bucket of cleansing salt water was splashed over their lacerated backs. Some were able to stagger to their bunks when cut down from the rigging; others had to be carried.

Douglass later claimed that the rest of the crew watched in silence. But he had no illusions that the example had subdued the mutinous resentment of the *Challenge*'s sailors. He decided never to go on deck without a sheath knife, this one with its point intact, and he advised Coghill to do the same. "I considered myself liable to be seized by them at any moment," Douglass later explained. Waterman disdained such protection on his quarterdeck, but from this time on he kept a gun by his bunk when he slept.

They were approaching Cape Horn now; and they still were far behind the *Flying Cloud*.

Courtesy of the Peabody Museum of Salem

The *Challenge* was the world's largest, and presumably fastest, clipper ship; Robert Waterman (*left*) was the most successful clipper captain. It should have been a perfect combination. The *Challenge* was painted (*above*) in Hong Kong after Waterman had left her in San Francisco at the end of a disastrous voyage.

Photograph by Charles E. Steinheimer, courtesy of the Haley Family

Courtesy of the Smithsonian Institution, photo #32596

John Willis Griffiths, designer of the first clipper ships.

Courtesy of the Peabody Museum of Salem

While the *Flying Cloud* was loading in New York (*above*) for her maiden voyage to San Francisco, Josiah Perkins Creesy prepared to take command. Creesy is shown (*right*) during the Civil War, but was already a grizzled thirty-seven-year-old when he took over the *Cloud* in 1851.

Courtesy of the Peabody Museum of Salem

Donald McKay, builder of the *Flying Cloud*.

All rights reserved. The Metropolitan Museum of Art. Gift of I. N. Phelps Stokes, Edward S. Hawes, Alice Mary Hawes, Marion Augusta Hawes, 1937.

William Webb (*right*) designed the *Challenge* with towering masts which were made even taller by Captain Waterman. In the sail plan (*below*) Webb's proposed rigging is indicated in black lines, with Waterman's additions in dotted lines.

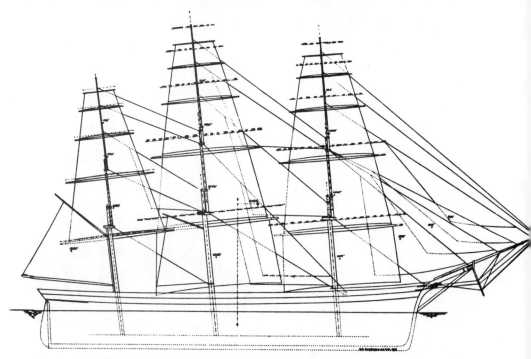

Courtesy of W. W. Norton & Co., Inc., and the Smithsonian Institution

Courtesy of the Webb Institute of Naval Architecture

*From an 1853 daguerreotype, courtesy of the Smithsonian
Institution, photos #38416-C and #38416-D*

By midnineteenth century San Francisco's harbor had a ghost fleet of hundreds of ships abandoned by sailors who had rushed off to the gold fields.

Left, Captain Robert Waterman, retired and a ranch owner, at sixty-seven. *Top right,* Cordelia Waterman at about the time of her marriage. *Bottom,* as a housewife in California.

Courtesy of Gary Odaffer

Captain Robert Waterman's ranch house today.

8

Challenge vs. *Flying Cloud* II

FORTUNE HAD FAVORED the *Flying Cloud* off Cape Horn. It had not seemed so at first, though. As he approached the Strait of Le Maire on July 22, Creesy reported a "Hard Gale with Rain & sleet" that threatened to drive the ship toward the South American coast. He was forced to bear off and wait for clearer weather. The Strait of Le Maire provides a shortcut to the waters off Cape Horn between the mainland, where Cape San Diego juts out into the Atlantic, and Staten Island off the coast. But it is a treacherous passage of swirling currents and countercurrents, boiling with riptides and buffeted by contrary winds. Slipping through the strait in a sailing ship required good weather as well as excellent navigation. Just before the storm took away all visibility, Creesy spotted Cape San Diego only 15 miles off his starboard bow, whereupon, he "wore ship at 5 P.M. to NE." Through the night, with the storm driving out of the southeast, he tacked back and forth from east to west while his wife checked her charts against Maury's *Sailing Directions,* plotted the clipper's position, and navigated a course to bring them back to the strait by daybreak.

At 6 A.M. the storm was nearly spent. The visibility improved. And there, dead ahead as Eleanor Creesy had calculated, lay the entrance to the strait, with Cape San Diego 10 miles to starboard. Creesy set more sail. But he kept the mainmast's upper spars on deck; he would have to take her around the Horn without those sails because of the weakened mast. The crosscurrents of the strait helped instead of hindered the

Flying Cloud—and no doubt Maury's *Charts* helped Mrs. Creesy plot a favorable tide. The *Cloud* ran through in just 12 hours, encountering a strong head tide only after she emerged into the open water south of the Horn.

Experienced skippers dreaded the Cape Horn passage more than any other stretch of ocean. Sailors called the area "Cape Stiff" and "The Widow-Maker." For a sailing ship the east-to-west passage was the deadliest: The prevailing winds are head-on from the west. Unimpeded by any landmass, they gather massive momentum as they cross the Indian and Pacific oceans, and they funnel between South America and Antarctica at speeds of up to a hundred miles per hour. With the winds come towering waves, mast-high mountains of white-capped green water that block the way for any sailing ship whose crew cannot make the most of every changing slant of wind. In the nineteenth century that meant following Matthew Maury's advice and sailing south toward the dangerous ice fields off Antarctica, where the bergs can be fifty miles long and nearly as wide. Constantly on the lookout for these floating islands, the nineteenth-century skipper usually tried to set a course a little west of south. Then he tacked onto a northwest leg back toward Cape Horn, the rocky island off the tip of the South American continent.

At 55° 59' south latitude, 67° 16' west longitude, Cape Horn is one of the island outcroppings that were formed when the last of the Andes gave way to the relentless attack of wind-driven sea. Its latitude is thirteen hundred miles south of the Cape of Good Hope and six hundred miles below the bottom of New Zealand. Warm air moving down from Chile meets the frigid air from Antarctica and produces squalls, blizzards, hail-storms, or ice storms almost daily, and the circulating winds send them spinning eastward, forcing every westbound ship to change sail constantly to take advantage of each wind shift and to reef down for each squall.

Once clear of the Strait of Le Maire, Creesy tacked for a short run northwestward instead of going farther south. It was a dangerous maneuver that close to land, but the skies had cleared, and Eleanor Creesy was sure of their position. At 8 A.M. on July 23, a rocky, ice-sheathed beach and a snow-covered cliff rose from the mists of the sea only five miles ahead. It was

Cape Horn. Heavy rollers smashed against the glistening rocks, and clouds of ducks flashed along the coast. Glaciers loomed behind the shore and, behind them, beech trees rimmed the snow line of the mountains. As the *Flying Cloud* came about onto the starboard tack and headed back out to sea, a fast-moving snow squall blotted out the land.

More snowstorms pelted the clipper and her crew. But the winds unaccountably turned favorable. Instead of the howling westerlies usually encountered off Cape Horn, Creesy found moderate northeasterlies and even easterlies. With "all sail set," the *Flying Cloud* raced across the bottom of the world. Creesy had no need for long tacks to the south; the *Cloud* never went below 56° 04' south latitude; and she faced little threat of icebergs in these waters. Not until July 26 did the wind haul into the west, and by that time Creesy had turned the corner. The *Flying Cloud* made it from "Fifty to Fifty"—50° south latitude in the Atlantic to the same latitude in the Pacific—in a record seven days.[1] By July 27, Creesy had "Sent up Main topgallant & Royal Yards" again and "set all possible sail." Under a light southwesterly the *Cloud* set out northward on her last leg for California.

Two days later Creesy was fretting: "Calm. Calm." But not for long; a brisk breeze soon filled in from the northeast and the *Flying Cloud* went thundering up the western coast of South America. By July 31 the northeasterly had swung southeasterly and freshened. "High sea running, ship very wet," Creesy noted; he brought in his studdingsails, then had to furl his royals. With slightly reduced sail the *Cloud* still was slicing along so fast that when the mate cast the log, 18 knots of line rushed out before the glass emptied. That night when Eleanor Creesy completed her computations for the day, her husband jubilantly recorded: "Distance Run this Day by observation 374 miles, an average of 15 7/12 knots"—faster than any ship up to that time. The wind increased to a gale, forcing Creesy to reef down his foretopsails and mizzentopsails. But the minute the wind showed signs of moderating, he piled on sail again and kept her speeding northward.

There was little to do at this stage but let her run. The wind held strong and steady from the east-southeast and the

Flying Cloud was on a long reach, a fast and efficient point of sail for a clipper ship. Crewmen off watch spread out on the deck soaking up the welcome sun. The helmsman merely kept her steady on her heading, his eye on the mizzen royal: If it was full, the others would be, too. Creesy's only problem at this point was an old one, and he finally did something about it. He and his first mate were still at odds, Creesy accusing him of shirking his duty. Now that the *Flying Cloud* was safely around the Horn and running up the Pacific, Creesy suspended the mate from duty. With his wife as navigator, he was quite capable of taking the ship on to her destination without the services of a first mate.

For twelve glorious days Creesy repeated "fine weather." On the thirteenth day he downgraded it only to "fine at intervals"; but the "Light Squalls of Rain" that also came out of the southeast pushed the clipper ahead even faster. On August 12 she crossed the equator. The wind swung into the north-northeast and increased in velocity. The *Flying Cloud* went roaring north for two more weeks before she was temporarily deserted by her winds. But the "Light and unsteady breezes" that Creesy complained about in his log were enough to provide a spectacle for the passengers aboard a vessel that the *Cloud* overtook on August 25.

The British bark *Amelia Paquet,* also bound for San Francisco, was lumbering north along the California coast when the people on deck saw a clipper ship coming up on them at great speed. They lined the rail to marvel at the long, narrow hull and the huge clouds of white canvas; she was carrying twice as many sails as their bark. She seemed almost motionless despite her speed, with her sharp bow knifing through the waves as she overhauled them. So fast did she slip past them that there was barely time for the two captains to exchange hails through their speaking trumpets: the *Amelia Paquet,* 180 days out of London, and the *Flying Cloud,* only 83 days out of New York. For a few minutes the British passengers had time to admire the *Cloud*'s figurehead, an angel holding a trumpet, the lofty whiplike masts groaning under the pull of her huge sails and the blue, red, and white swallowtail house flag rippling and popping at her main-truck. Then she was gone; within an hour the *Flying Cloud* was hull down on the northern horizon. And nobody aboard the *Amelia Paqeut* ever forgot the sight.

By the 27th Creesy was reporting "fresh breezes" again. They were followed by intermittent squalls that added to the *Cloud*'s speed. Creesy was tasting a new record, and he kept nearly everything aloft despite the squalls. As a result, on August 29 the strongest gust toppled his foretopgallant mast. But Creesy was not to be denied his victory. Despite "heavy squalls with high sea," he got the wreckage cut away and the fore-topgallant mast reset in 24 hours.

His luck held; the frequent calms and fogs around San Francisco gave way to more squalls that sent the *Flying Cloud* romping north so fast that in the predawn darkness of August 31, Creesy "hove ship too for Daylight." By Eleanor Creesy's calculations, they were in danger of running right past the Golden Gate. At 6 A.M., in the early light, there was South Farallon, one of the islands marking the entrance to San Francisco Harbor. One hour later a pilot boat was alongside. And at 11 A.M. Creesy made his final entry in the *Flying Cloud*'s log for the San Francisco leg of the voyage: "Came to anchor in five fathoms water off North Beach San Francisco Harbor."

Oddly for such a record-seeker, Creesy said nothing in the log of the *Flying Cloud*'s historic accomplishment: She had raced from New York to San Francisco in 89 days, 21 hours.[2] Not only had she bettered the previous record, set by the *Surprise,* by seven days, but also her record time would never be beaten by a sailing ship—except by the *Cloud* herself four years later, when she shaved it by 13 hours.

Her achievement electrified San Francisco. And when the news reached New York more than a month later, the *Herald* proudly announced the "EXTRAORDINARY PASSAGE OF THE 'FLYING CLOUD.' " New Yorkers, it happened, were still exulting over another sailing triumph, one that had occurred across the Atlantic. While the *Flying Cloud* was running down her last leg to San Francisco, the New York-built schooner *America* outsailed fourteen British yachts off Cowes, England, astonishing the complacent European yachting community and winning what became known as the America's Cup. With patriotic hyperbole the *Herald*'s headline proclaimed:

THE SMARTEST NATION IN ALL CREATION

Aboard the *Challenge,* which had never closed the gap, there was no such mood of exultation. The crew had reacted to the floggings with a sullen, silent rebellion. Nearly everyone found ways to avoid duty or hide out. Many more feigned illness, and the sick bay became even more crowded. Fewer hands came on deck each day. During one night watch so few men reported that Douglass went into the forecastle looking for malingerers. He had hardly entered the room when someone blew out the lamp. In the darkness Douglass stopped and listened. The only sounds were the muffled boom of the storm outside and the groan of the *Challenge*'s timbers as she fought the storm. The threat in the dark forecastle was palpable. Douglass did not have to be reminded of the day off Rio. He retreated to the deck.

Waterman also was increasingly outraged at the obvious shirking, and he, too, was resorting to the heaver and the belaying pin. Some of the crew members were indeed weakened by dysentery or crippled by swollen arms and legs. But the *Challenge* required a large crew to man her yards and braces, and Waterman felt he had no choice. Moreover, he knew that the worst was still to come when they reached Cape Horn. He had rounded the Horn before in the *Natchez* and the *Sea Witch,* and no doubt his memory of the winds and seas off the cape had contributed to his decision to retire instead of entering the San Francisco run. Now he faced this stormy passage in the world's largest sailing vessel with less than half of his crew capable of handling a ship in a crisis, with more than a dozen men in sick bay, and with most of the rest ducking duty.

At first the *Challenge* was favored with an easy approach to the cape, including some fair, strong winds. Along the coasts of Brazil and Argentina the southeast trades move into the southwest and gather speed. The *Challenge* was in what sailors call the "Roaring Forties"—40° south latitude—and here at last she showed the speed she had been built for, thundering down the last leg of the South Atlantic under a deep blue sky. During the night watches the Southern Cross hung low overhead. On a broad reach with a strong, steady wind, there was little need for shifting sail. Instead, this was the time to prepare for the cape. The clipper's sails had to be replaced with storm canvas. Chafing gear had to be wrapped around the rigging wherever one line could rub against another. The new rigging needed more tightening for the increased stresses it would undergo. Everything movable had to be battened down. The ship's boats were brought in from their davits and lashed firmly to the cabintops. Netting was strung across the bulwark openings to keep the boarding seas from sweeping the deckhands overboard.

Now the *Challenge* was greeted by the first messengers from Cape Horn: swift little storm petrels rocketing past the masts, cape pigeons bobbing alongside the ship, and ungainly albatrosses wheeling over the stern. The cook knew that the albatross was too tough and gamy to eat, but he strung baited hooks astern to catch a few plump cape pigeons, the main ingredient of pigeon pie, which some sailors considered to be better than chicken stew.

A blustery indication of the weather the *Challenge* would encounter was the *pampero,* the sudden, hurricane-force squall that had given Creesy and the *Flying Cloud* so much trouble. The *pampero* often could be seen approaching in the form of a large, fast-moving black cloud. At night its signal was lightning; the first flash was the warning to shorten sail. Usually there would be a breathless pause, an ominous calm during which the grateful men in the tops furled the canvas and knotted the gaskets. But anyone who had not scrambled back on deck before the first blast could be swept overboard, because the storm arrived in smashing gusts bringing rain and sometimes hailstones. The winds were strong enough to knock a man down; those holding fast to a stanchion or the rail had to turn their backs, and even then they found it difficult to breathe.

Almost certainly the *Challenge* encountered one of these gales. If, as is likely, Waterman was flying his lighter sails until the last possible day to keep the *Challenge* running at full speed, the sudden winds probably reduced some of them to tatters. If he had already shifted to his storm canvas, the *pampero* gave it a good test.

Gradually the steady southwest trades became fitful, swinging about the compass and rapidly changing velocity. The

Challenge was leaving the Roaring Forties for the lower, even windier latitudes that the sailors called the "Fearful Fifties." The blue sky turned leaden and the water became gray-green. But the fair winds took the *Challenge* through the Strait of Le Maire. To port was the rocky promontory of Staten Island, close enough to hear its thousands of screaming seabirds; and to starboard was the near-tundra of the bottom of South America, lit at night by the bonfires of the Stone Age inhabitants who gave the desolate place the name Tierra del Fuego (Land of Fire).

At first it looked as if the *Challenge,* too, would have a fast passage around the Horn. Waterman took her on a favorable slant to the southwest, came about, and worked his way northwest on another leg, gradually gaining some westing until he calculated his position as already past the cape itself. But the island is only a quarter of the way across the bottom of the South American continent, and the *Challenge* still had a lot of westing to make before she could turn northward into the Pacific. She was on another southwest leg, approaching Diego Ramirez Island, when the first gale struck. Its sudden severity, with a horizontal onslaught of snow, had the earmarks of a quick, slashing squall that would rush on past. But August is midwinter in the Southern Hemisphere; the *Challenge's* (and the *Flying Cloud's*) owners had been too anxious to get their goods to San Francisco to wait six months. With little moderation the squall settled into a full-fledged winter storm that showed no sign of letting up.

The moment the wind increased, Waterman ordered the *Challenge's* topsails furled. Douglass hobbled about the deck bellowing for all hands, and Coghill led half a dozen men up the slippery rigging of the mizzenmast. Pushing and kicking those who froze in terror at the sight of the wild ocean below, he drove them out along the pitching footropes. The *Challenge* was taking the seas nearly head-on, slicing beneath each one and shouldering it aside in two hissing clouds of white spray that swept as high as her lower yards. Under the force of the wind she heeled until her yardarm tips brushed the waves rolling past her. The sea had become a menacing bilious green marbled with white spume. As each wave, towering as much as sixty feet high, bore down on the clipper, its crest crackled and broke into a white mane which the wind batted off to eastward. "Cape Horn snorters," the sailors called these rollers. The long-familiar creak and moan in the *Challenge*'s rigging had changed to a high-pitched scream, so loud that Coghill and his men on the mizzentopsail yard could scarcely hear Douglass below them. He was yelling that if Coghill and his "sons-of-bitches" couldn't move faster he would come up there himself.

Lined up on deck and trying to keep their balance as the clipper rolled, Douglass' watch started to loose the mizzentopsail braces so the sail could be furled. They released too much of it. Whipped by a powerful gust, the loose canvas filled with a boom like a cannon shot and recoiled against the yardarm, smacking one of Coghill's men off his perch. Head over foot, screaming all the way down, he plummeted into the ocean. There could be no attempt to rescue him in such a sea; in any case, the ice water would kill him almost instantly.

Coghill shouted at Douglass to cant the yardarm and spill the wind from the sail. It was out of control and flogging wildly. Snatching at whatever they could catch, his men folded some of the canvas against the yard and held it with one arm while trying to grab for more. The rogue sail filled again in a thunderclap and whipped back against the yard. Two more men toppled downward, one dropping overboard and one onto the deck.

The *Challenge* was shipping huge seas; with each roll her rails went under and more water cascaded on deck. Waist-high waves of frothing white water caught Douglass and his men, sweeping most of them across the deck and sending them thudding against the bulwarks. Under the first mate's lash they staggered back to the pinrail and tried to get the topsail brace under control. Shouting, swearing, bleeding, the two teams finally managed to furl the mizzen-, main-, and foretopsails. The *Challenge* eased to a less perilous heel. Coghill's beaten, exhausted survivors inched down the ratlines and stumbled to their bunks while Douglass checked the braces to make sure they were secure. Meanwhile the seaman who had fallen to his death on deck was bundled below. The next day, as soon as the storm moderated slightly, he was wrapped in a tarpaulin with a weight at his feet and toppled over the side to join his two shipmates.

The names of all three have gone unrecorded except for seaman E. A. Wheeler's later reference to one of them as "Stevens," who also was mentioned during the trials at the voyage's end.

The storm increased again, with a blue-black mass of rolling clouds and stinging sheets of sleet. The winds exceeded hurricane force—up to 80 and 90 knots in gusts. Pushed by such power, the sea rose like a moving mountain range; and large as she was, the *Challenge* fought a losing battle. Even her sharp bow could not cut through such towering waves. As each one came rumbling down on her, she rose slowly and climbed its slope. At the top, with the wind at full blast, each wave broke into a giant white comber that crashed over her bow, sending more tons of water flooding the length of her decks. Everyone grabbed hold, but the overwhelming impact of the rushing water swept most of them off their feet.

The *Challenge* seemed to pause at each summit. Then everyone aboard, above and below, shuddered with her as she pitched forward and rode the roller coaster down the back side, diving in a sickening plunge toward the deep trough between waves as if she were headed for the bottom of the sea. In the trough she fetched up as if she had hit a wall. Even a veteran held his breath as the big ship wallowed in the deep seaway, her timbers groaning as the next wave, high as her masts, bore down on her. Slowly, like a stunned animal, the clipper shook herself, raised her bowsprit, and started her next climb.

At her helm two men fought the big spoked wheel to keep her head into the wave. Occasionally, despite their full weight on the wheel spokes, the *Challenge* would start to sideslip. This usually happened as she topped the crest of a wave, pitching forward and momentarily lifting her long rudder out of the water. As she started her descent, she would roll off to leeward, her lee rail under and her lower yardarms dipping into the sea. Sliding sideways down the wave, she would nearly broach to (capsize). But in this ultimate test the new clipper proved William Webb's sure design. Always her keel and rudder took hold in time; always, with agonizing slowness, she moved back to meet head-on the toppling crest of the next wave.

In such weather even a driver like Waterman had to shorten down to one or two small storm jibs at her bow, perhaps a fore-and-aft staysail between the masts to help keep her on course and reefed topsails—partly because they were smaller than the lower sails but mostly to catch what wind there was in the deep valleys between the waves. Without this minimum sail area the ship would have been completely out of control. Even with these few sails on her, the *Challenge*'s leeward shrouds sagged and her windward shrouds were taut and whining. And at the height of the storm, gusts approaching a hundred knots blew out even this heavy storm canvas. With a sharp slatting noise the sail would rip along a seam, and within seconds there was nothing left but ribbons streaming in the gale. Or with a crackling report like gunfire the boltropes would yank loose from the clew of a sail. Then the men had to scramble into the rigging again to reef or replace the flogging canvas before the wind whipped it to shreds. The shrouds and footropes were sheathed in ice. The *Challenge*'s new canvas, stiff, unwieldy, and frozen, cut the men's chilblained hands and the blood crusted on their blue fingers, while surging gusts alternately pinned them to the yardarm or threatened to blow them off. Below them, rolling in wide circles over the heaving sea, the *Challenge* seemed more under water than on it, her decks constantly awash in foaming waves.

But the one thing no Cape Horn sailor ever forgot was the sound of the wind, a never-ending, keening wail so loud that it hurt. At its height no one could make himself heard unless he bellowed into the other man's ear. The wind knocked men down, made them turn their backs, took their breath away. But it was its incessant scream, night and day, that got to everyone's nerves even more than the threatening sea, the paralyzing cold, the clattering hail, and the sickening plunge of the ship.

The Cape Horn weather swelled the numbers in the *Challenge*'s sick bay. Men who had been brought aboard in New York with no warm clothes were unprepared for the freezing temperatures of the Fifties. Even the few old salts who had their own foul-weather gear found it nearly worthless in the cape's storms. After being washed the length of the deck, they were soaked through. Their jackets froze on their backs. Whenever they had a few hours off watch, they tumbled into their wet bunks in their icy clothes, paralyzed with exhaustion, and tried to jam themselves into a corner to keep from being pitched out by the roll of the ship.[3] Some came down with pneumonia. Nearly everyone was frostbitten. Many who had been smashed against bulkheads or bulwarks by boarding seas had broken arms or legs. At one point the *Challenge*'s sick bay was crammed with 17 sick and wounded seamen. And many more feigned illness or pretended that their disabilities were greater than they actually were.

The unrelenting assault of wind, ice, snow, and pounding seas was utterly demoralizing to those who had never seen Cape Horn before. And when three men were killed while they looked on, they were terror-stricken. Some crept on deck, stared at the overwhelming seas, listened to the shrieking wind and thundering sails, and retreated to the forecastle. Water sloshed around the bunks and the forecastle's air was a nauseating mixture of sweat, urine, and vomit. But it was better than the violent world on deck and far preferable to what seemed like certain death in the rigging. James Douglass, still limping from his leg wound, came on deck in the midst of one storm and, he later claimed, "found it nearly deserted."

For almost three weeks the *Challenge* was battered by a series of storms. Waterman testified that he did not go below to his cabin for 18 days and nights, never changing his frozen clothes and catching what naps he could on a bench in the chart house near the companionway. Meanwhile he kept fighting for a bit of westing against the head-on gales and seas, occasionally making a few miles, only to be driven back in the next heavy blow. Searching for the favorable winds that Matthew Maury had found farther south, Waterman took the *Challenge* all the way down to 60° S, only a few miles north of Antarctica. But still he could not find an easterly.

Frustrated, exhausted, outraged at the shirking crew, Waterman and Douglass resorted to a reign of terror. The first to feel the lash of their anger was twenty-year-old George Lessing—"The Dancing Master" who was so adept at avoiding punishment. During one of the storms off Cape Horn Douglass ordered Lessing into the rigging and Lessing refused, pleading dysentery. In a flash of rage Douglass shouted, "Go aft! The captain will cure you!" Waterman was on the main deck at the time, just leeward of the mainmast. Shoving Lessing before him, Douglass reported that he had refused an order. Waterman growled, "I think we'll baptize him," grabbed Lessing, and threw him into the lee scuppers.

The *Challenge*'s decks were awash and her scuppers were filled with frigid water. Lessing surfaced, gasping; Douglass jumped onto him and tried to hold his head under. The two men thrashed in the gurgling scuppers until Douglass finally yanked Lessing to his feet, marched him to the weather rail, and tied him there. Lessing was wearing a flannel shirt, a thin jacket, and trousers. He was barefoot, and the deck ran with slush. For nearly an hour he shook in the freezing wind until Douglass cut him free and let him go below. Whether or not he had dysentery then, he did have it a few days later, and it was not helped when passenger William Masten visited him and mistakenly gave him a dose of castor oil. Thin and emaciated from the time he had come aboard, Lessing weakened and died in sick bay twelve days after his brutal baptism.

Waterman certainly realized by now that James Douglass had an uncontrollable streak of sadism; when he was disciplining someone he often went berserk. And nothing got his blood up more than a skulker or even one he suspected of avoiding duty. Another crewman, complaining that he could not work because of swollen, chilblained legs, was given a similar baptism in the slush that had collected on deck. Second Mate Coghill, evidently taking the cue from Douglass, caught seaman John Brown trying to escape from his watch and gave him such a kick in the groin that Brown had to be carried to his bunk. But Waterman apparently did nothing to curb his mates' cruelty; evidently he was convinced that desperate measures were necessary to get the *Challenge* through the cape's storms. He could not punish the reluctant crew members by putting them in the brig; he needed the manpower and had to force them to work the ship. If cruelty was the only way, Waterman was in no mood for leniency.

Douglass' rage reached its limit during one of the storms off the cape. A particularly inept member of the crew was the illiterate Italian listed on the ship's roster as "Pawpaw." Evidently swept up in a South Street crimp's dragnet, Pawpaw had come aboard with no shoes; he still was barefoot despite the snow and ice on the *Challenge*'s deck. Unable to understand orders, Pawpaw had a maddening response, which was to stand still and shake his head. At the braces during a change of tack, Pawpaw heaved with the rest but dumbly continued to heave after everyone else had obeyed the command to let go, nearly fouling the split-second timing necessary for bringing the ship through the eye of the wind. Enraged, Waterman beat Pawpaw on the back with a belaying pin until he let go of the line. Next day, when all hands were called out during a squall, Pawpaw refused to leave his bunk.

Douglass went into the forecastle, pulled Pawpaw from his bunk, dragged him on deck, and ordered him aloft. Pawpaw did not budge, muttering in Italian and pointing to his bare feet. They were swollen, perhaps from frostbite, and he evidently was protesting that he could not walk. Douglass' temper flared again and he drove a fist into the Italian's ribs. Pawpaw doubled over, then demonstrated that his feet were well enough for him to scamper back into the forecastle. Douglass exploded into an insane fury. Following Pawpaw into the forecastle, he stood him up and pummeled him in the head and chest. Finally, panting and cursing, he dumped the groaning man in a heap.

A witness in the forecastle was Charles Weldon, one of the ship's boys, who later testified that Pawpaw's eyes were swollen shut and that he was barely conscious when Weldon lifted him into his bunk. Weldon went on deck, and within an hour a shipmate sidled up to him to whisper that Pawpaw was dead. Another *Challenge* sailor, George Hill, later added a poignant postscript. Waterman himself, Hill claimed, came to the forecastle with a glass of water and a glass of wine for Pawpaw just before he died.

This brutal incident must finally have convinced Waterman that his first mate was out of control. But if he did anything about it, there is no record. So the hellish voyage continued, with the *Challenge* fighting one storm after another and the captain and mate beating and terrorizing a surly, furtive crew. For eighteen days, with never enough men to handle the rigging, Waterman stubbornly kept tacking the huge clipper north and south. There was no sign of the sun in the leaden sky, so he could not fix his position; he could only guess whether the *Challenge* had made any progress or had been driven back, perhaps even eastward of the Horn. At last, suddenly and with no warning, the wind veered around into the east and the big clipper roared for the Pacific with the rolling hills of water now pursuing her and threatening to poop her from astern.

As each sea approached, the *Challenge*'s counter rose under it. The wheel was nearly torn from the helmsmen's hands as the wave passed under her, its crackling white crest breaking over both rails. But this was a blessed relief after nearly three weeks of pounding into such seas. Shortly the sun appeared, and Waterman's first sight indicated that the *Challenge* was nearly around the corner. By the time the clipper had reached 75° south longitude and could begin her turn to the northwest, the forecastle was pumped out and the forward deck was strung with drying gear. Now there were white, fleecy clouds instead of lowering skies and sleet. At night the stars sparkled again. And the still sea left a soft wake astern. But the ceaseless battering of the cape's storms had taken the heart out of nearly everyone aboard. There was a deckful of storm wreckage to clear away, and the men turned to only when forced. Douglass' leg evidently still pained him. And Waterman was in a foul mood. He realized by now that only a miracle could save his $10,000 bonus.

Again he took out his frustration on the crew. Ever since leaving New York he had been forced by the shortage of manpower to postpone one of the normal ship's routines: holystoning the decks. With the *Challenge* around the Horn, Waterman took advantage of the fair weather by ordering the watch to clean and polish the storm-roughened decks. The Finnish crewman known as Smiti joined his shipmates on their knees but spent most of his time watching them work. Enraged, Waterman beat Smiti on the head. Smiti muttered in Finnish and gestured to his scurvy-swollen legs, evidently complaining that he could not move about. Waterman later testified that Smiti was "always skulking." He gave him a few more whacks, and Smiti got to work.

Almost by habit Waterman kept the *Challenge* driving. He realized that he had little chance of making it to San Francisco in 90 days; she was 66 days out and still below the equator. But he was determined to avoid an ignominious passage. The lethargy of his dispirited crew made him all the more frustrated and angry. And by now two more men in sick bay had died of dysentery. So Waterman was in no mood for leniency when suddenly Fred Birkenshaw, the leader of the mutiny, was found.

James Douglass had never believed that Birkenshaw had deliberately jumped overboard, and was convinced that the man was hiding somewhere in the ship. But not until a month after Birkenshaw's disappearance did someone betray him by telling Douglass where he was. Douglass waited until the next time all available hands were on deck and in the yards reefing for a threatening squall. Summoning Charles Weldon, he told the ship's boy to inspect the lower forecastle, a dark cave in the ship's bow that was used to store spare cordage. Weldon squirmed into the cramped space, touched something alive, yelped, and ran on deck. Only because he feared Douglass' wrath more did he obey the first mate's order to go below again. Birkenshaw was crawling out of the hiding place where he had survived for a month while his friends had brought him food and water.

Emerging on deck, blinking in the sunlight, Birkenshaw mumbled to Douglass, "I will make a full confession. Don't hurt me." Douglass grabbed him and shoved him aft. Waterman was on the quarterdeck, and Douglass triumphantly announced, "I've got the son-of-a-bitch!" Waterman replied, "Put him in irons."

"Captain, he has some confession to make," Douglass answered. "You had better hear it first." Waterman picked up a heaver, came down to the main deck, and faced the culprit.

Fred Birkenshaw was one of the few veteran seamen aboard the *Challenge;* he had been at sea for sixteen years, twelve of them in the Royal Navy. Waterman felt that he had made a point of sparing such experienced seamen; that one would repay him by leading a mutiny was particularly galling. And instead of taking his punishment, Birkenshaw had hidden out during the passage off Cape Horn, when his skill had been needed most. So Waterman's temper was at the flash point when Birkenshaw was brought before him.

"Have I ever ill-used you in any way?" Waterman asked. Birkenshaw murmured no.

Waterman asked him about the mutiny. Birkenshaw, apparently losing his nerve, denied any part in it.

Everyone Waterman had questioned on the day of the mutiny had implicated Birkenshaw; many had claimed that he was the ringleader. At his denial of any complicity, Waterman exploded.

"Down on your knees, you son-of-a-bitch!" he shouted. Birkenshaw knelt. Waterman swung his heaver. Birkenshaw raised an arm to ward off the blow and, he said later, "I felt the bones of my arm crack when he hit me."

Still Birkenshaw maintained his innocence. Waterman ordered one of the ship's boys to set up a block and tackle in the rigging. Taking one end of the line, he whipped it into a hangman's noose, which he slipped over Birkenshaw's head. He then pulled on the other end of the line until Birkenshaw was on tiptoes. Birkenshaw decided to confess.

At Waterman's request, passenger Sterling took down Birkenshaw's account of the conspiracy, which included most of the crew. He also claimed that Second Mate Coghill had been involved and had promised to provide handcuffs to use on Douglass and Waterman. Now Birkenshaw received the handcuffs; Douglass snapped a pair on him and led him below to sick bay where, Birkenshaw later claimed, his injured arm was left untreated.

Waterman meanwhile confronted Coghill, who indignantly denied any part in the uprising, arguing that he had been asleep in his berth at the time of the attack on Douglass. Waterman decided to give Coghill the benefit of the doubt, but he kept a wary eye on him for the rest of the voyage.

Like the *Flying Cloud*, the *Challenge* picked up the Pacific's southeast trades and bowled along toward the equator. Unlike the *Flying Cloud*, the *Challenge* ran into a belt of calms as soon as she had crossed the line. Again, as in the doldrums of the Atlantic, the *Challenge* wallowed in the long, glassy swells while her sails slatted and the pitch oozed from the seams in her deck. At last the North Pacific's northeast trades set in, and the *Challenge* showed more of the speed she was capable of. In only two weeks she was off the coast of California. And then, in a final stroke of misfortune, she ran into another airless patch. For four days she drifted aimlessly in the Pacific while Robert Waterman nearly went mad. Her last day's run was a humiliating 35 miles.

Not until October 29, 1851, did the *Challenge* ghost past the foggy Farallons into San Francisco Harbor. Instead of 90 days, she had taken 108. Indeed, if the *Challenge* had reached San Francisco only nine days earlier, Waterman could have watched the *Flying Cloud* drop down harbor and go out through the Golden Gate, already unloaded and bound out to Hong Kong for a cargo of tea on her way home.

9

⤜∞⤏

Chase, Riot, and
a "Waterfront Jury"

THE *Challenge* CAME IN through the Golden Gate flying her distress flag. And the bubbles were still rising from her anchor when the U.S. revenue cutter *Lawrence* warped alongside. First Mate Douglass already had eight handcuffed men lined up on deck, and they were herded aboard the cutter to be held and tried for mutiny. One of them was Fred Birkenshaw; at the moment no one, including Birkenshaw, mentioned his injured arm. Next day the *Lawrence*'s Captain Ottinger was told that one of the prisoners had a fracture. He inspected them all, including Birkenshaw, and found no broken bones.

Captain Waterman had not been surprised when the harbor pilot had told him he would have to wait two days for wharf space. So the *Challenge* rode to her anchor off Bird Island and was promptly surrounded by the skiffs, wherries, and Whitehall boats of the crimps, so many of them that within hours every sailor who could walk had tumbled over the side into a crimp's boat and was on his way to the saloons, gambling halls, and bordellos of San Francisco's waterfront. Only Waterman, his mates, and the men still too ill to leave the *Challenge*'s sick bay remained aboard—plus one sailor who died just after the *Challenge* had anchored. Seaman E. A. Wheeler reported in his letter home that the ship's carpenter made a coffin for the man, identified by Wheeler only as "J.W."; Waterman gave Wheeler the keys to J.W.'s seachest "and told me to take care of it till we get home." Next day the coffin was rowed ashore for burial in one of San Francisco's rapidly expanding cemeteries. And it was another day before the *Challenge* could be towed to a berth alongside Pacific Street Wharf. Her stevedores were waiting for her, and so was a milling, threatening mob.

The *Challenge*'s arrival was not only late but ill-timed as well. San Francisco's newcomers had included an abnormally high proportion of thugs, thieves, and chronic troublemakers, the most notorious of whom were known as the Hounds and the Ducks. Many of the Hounds had come from New York, sent off as soldiers in the 1st New York Volunteers to secure California during the Mexican War. By the time they had arrived, the war was over; and instead of being brought home, they had been mustered out of service. Few wanted to go home, anyway. They were former Plug Uglies and Dead Rabbits from New York's Five Points and the Bowery, and they knew an easy mark when they saw one. The few who tried the gold fields quickly found digging too much work, and they were such troublemakers that the other miners ran them out of the camps. They straggled back to San Francisco and set up a paramilitary gang headquartered at the corner of Kearny and Commercial streets in a big tent they called Tammany Hall. They lived by thievery and extortion and earned their nickname, the Hounds, by hounding the city's South Americans and Chinese. The Hounds always were ready to join a riot or foment one.

The only gang worse than the Hounds was the one whose members called themselves the Ducks; most of them were ex-convicts from Australia who had settled in an area along the waterfront between Broadway and Pacific streets that they called Sydney Town. The Ducks managed to outdo even the Hounds in depravity and rabble-rousing. Many of San Francisco's frequent fires were blamed on the Ducks; the conflagrations mysteriously broke out when the wind was blowing away from Sydney Town, and one Duck was caught in the act of setting a fire. The Ducks were prominent among the looters of the rubble, and were even more riot-prone than the Hounds. It became a San Francisco phrase to explain nearly any noisy commotion by saying, "The Sydney Ducks are cackling again."

To make matters worse, San Francisco in 1851 had a largely ineffective police force. The city was managed by a First Alcalde, or mayor, and a board of selectmen, most of whom regularly looted the treasury and lived in fear of the Hounds and the Ducks. A new mayor made the gesture of converting one of the harbor's abandoned vessels into a floating jail. But the few criminals who were arrested and imprisoned easily slipped over the side and swam ashore. By the spring of 1851, when the *Challenge* was launched in New York, San Francisco was on the verge of anarchy. In only a few recent months more than a hundred murders had been committed without one conviction. This was the tinderbox that awaited the spark of the *Challenge*'s angry sailors who swarmed through the waterfront saloons telling their stories and improving on them with every drink.

It happened, though, that a large group of San Francisco's merchants and miners had only a few months earlier banded together to combat the city's growing lawlessness with an assumption of authority on their own. On the night of June 10, 1851, just before the *Flying Cloud* sailed from New York and while the *Challenge* was loading for her voyage, two hundred San Franciscans met secretly in a warehouse to sign the constitution for what they called a Committee of Vigilance. The preamble provided a clear description of the situation:

> Where it has been apparent to the citizens of San Francisco that there is no security for life and property, either under the regulations of society as it at present exists, or under the laws as now administered, therefore the citizens whose names are hereunto attached do unite themselves into an association for the maintenance of peace and good order of society and the preservation of the lives and property of the citizens of San Francisco.

The committee members (who, despite legend, did not call themselves "vigilantes") pledged to administer their own *ad hoc* brand of justice to murderers, robbers, and rioters who were currently escaping punishment "either by quibbles of the law, the insecurity of prisons, the carelessness or corruption of the police or a laxity of those who pretend to administer justice." The Committee of Vigilance established its own headquarters in a building on Battery Street with its own blue-and-white flag, a large holding cell, and two stout beams under the roof to support hangman's ropes. The members also agreed on a signal to call them into action: two strokes of a bell "repeated with a pause of one minute between each alarm," at either of two centrally located firehouses half a mile away from each other, the California Engine Company and the Monumental Fire Company.

The committee lost no time in suiting its constitution to action. On the same night as its founding, committee members apprehended a Sydney Town Duck who had stolen a safe, tried him, convicted him, and hanged him within a few hours. In succeeding weeks other Ducks and Hounds were given such summary treatment, and as early as autumn the committee, criticized by frustrated public officials[1] but praised by many otherwise law-abiding San Franciscans, seemed to have most of the Hounds and Ducks at bay. And in the meantime San Francisco had a tough new mayor, the city's fourth. Charles Brenham was a grizzled ex-ship captain with no patience for unruly hoodlums. As it happened, the San Francisco *Daily Evening Picayune* ironically chose the day of the *Challenge*'s arrival at Pacific Street Wharf to publish a complacent if slightly incoherent editorial claiming that "the city has remained quiet to a most gratifying degree. The nervousness of the people which has been so remarkable among our people and which is exemplified in the facility with which a crowd can at any time be collected in our streets, is evidently giving place to a better feeling and a confidence is being engendered that our darkest days have passed and that hereafter order and quiet will prevail." The *Picayune*'s editorial turned out to be premature.

As the *Challenge*'s lines were made fast to the wharf, the jostling crowd converged on the clipper's gangway. Other men in boats rowed alongside her, obviously less interested in the largest clipper to visit San Francisco than in her captain. At the sight of him a few threatening shouts were heard. Waterman strode down the gangway into their midst. The mob parted as he walked through them. There were taunts from the fringe of the crowd, and a muttering chorus as he walked up the pier. But no one made a move for him, and he continued up Pacific and California streets to the squat building housing the offices of Alsop & Company, the San Francisco agents for N. L. & G. Griswold.

Inside the Alsop offices he was greeted by Charles Griswold, the firm's representative in San Francisco. Waterman had lost out on his bonus by taking more than 90 days, but congratulations were in order nonetheless. A 108-day passage was excellent for the winter season off Cape Horn, and while the *Challenge* had not caught up with the *Flying Cloud,* she had beaten the *Telegraph,* which had left the same day as she (and would not arrive for another two weeks). Waterman delivered the *Challenge*'s long manifest. Evidently he also met with a few reporters, because the local newspapers briefly quoted him on the voyage. The *Daily Alta California,* for example, reported in a masterly understatement, "Captain Waterman is not satisfied with the ship's record on this maiden voyage. Her largest run in 24 hours was 300 miles; the most she made in one hour was 14 knots, with sky sail set and wind abaft the beam. . . . Captain Waterman said he had no chance during the entire voyage to try her speed." But he also praised the *Challenge* saying that she "is a noble sea boat and behaved well off Cape Horn during the heavy blows."

By the time James Douglass was ready to go ashore, the mob on the wharf had grown and become more menacing. The first mate had had enough experience with vengeful crewmen ashore; it was why he had left the *Guy Mannering* and joined the *Challenge.* Whether or not he recognized any *Challenge* sailors among the men milling about Pacific Street Wharf, Douglass obviously decided that it would be dangerous to walk into their midst. And presumably he feared that they might come aboard after him, because he decided to slip away if he could.

The stevedores were hard at work unloading the *Challenge,* hoisting crates and barrels over the side on slings and carting them down the wharf through the jostling mob. Some of the clipper's cargo was being lowered into barges on her water side. The dock workers were employed by Commodore T. H. Allen, who specialized an off-loading New York clipper ships. The *Challenge*'s cargo was larger than any that had been brought to the city. It included flour and coffee; molasses and butter;

stationery and wallpaper, a vast variety of glassware ranging from water tumblers, goblets, and lemonade, wine, and champagne glasses to decanters, lamps and 150 boxes of window glass, plus a hundred dozen lamb's-wool undershirts and ten dozen silk hats. Amid the confusion of the unloading, Douglass watched and waited until he noticed that the only boats alongside the *Challenge* were Allen's; for the moment the angry men in their skiffs and Whitehalls had converged farther up the wharf. And among the boats at the *Challenge*'s side was that of Allen himself, supervising the procedure. Douglass seized the moment and signaled to Allen. Shouldering his seabag, Douglass climbed down the rope ladder and dropped into Allen's boat. Allen bent to the oars and set out for nearby Commercial Wharf. But he had no sooner pulled away from the *Challenge* than a cry went up. Someone had spotted Douglass in Allen's boat, and half a dozen more boats went after them. Allen was quickly cut off from Commercial Wharf. He set out across the bay toward the only promising refuge, the fleet of abandoned ships off Rincon Point about a mile away, with a growing posse of skiffs and rowboats in hot pursuit.

By the autumn of 1851, the ghost fleet of deserted vessels in San Francisco Bay had increased to nearly five hundred. They presented a petrified forest of masts clustered offshore. A skilled oarsman who knew the bay well, Allen made it to the fleet a couple of hundred yards ahead of the yelling pursuers and went skimming into the shelter of the abandoned ships.

They were in a dripping, echoing maze of rust-streaked hulls. Above them rose a canopy of masts, their spars canted randomly and their rigging forming tangled webs against the sky. Tattered canvas hung from the spars like Spanish moss. Sheets and halyards had rotted, parted, and now swung from their masts to the roll of the ships. Shrouds and stays sagged and unraveled into loose rope ends. The forlorn hulls, their paint peeling, creaked as they swung to their anchor lines. Green-stained copper plates formed jagged patterns at the waterline where they had ripped away from the hull, and the unprotected wood sprouted long beards of weed that waved in the water. The smell of tar, grease, and decay pervaded the shifting avenues and alleys formed by the swaying ships. The tall hulls blocked the sunlight, and the chasms between them were shadowed and labyrinthine. In the silent canyons the drip of Allen's oars and the thump of the oarlocks seemed magnified as the boat went whisking through the maze. Shortly there was the louder sound of pursuit as the other boats came racing into the floating jungle in a shouting chase.

Allen took a zigzag course, attempting to disorient the pack on their heels. At times Douglass must have worried that they had lost their way and might blunder into the midst of their pursuers. But Allen obviously had been here before. Sometimes the bellowing of the men after them sounded closer, echoing and reechoing down the avenues of the ghostly hulls. But Allen left them floundering about in the corridors of the fleet and soon shot free of the maze. He had calculated perfectly; they were headed straight for Rincon Point. A few of their pursuers emerged in disarray but dangerously close. Allen put his last strength into the remaining few hundred yards. Douglass clambered over him into the bow, and the moment the boat crunched onto the sand he was off and running through the scrub, disappearing before the other boats reached the shore. Baying like foxhounds, some of the men raced off into the brush. By the time they had returned empty-handed, Allen had wisely rowed away.

The disappointed posse returned to Pacific Street Wharf, where most of the mob had melted away. But the *Challenge*'s voyage remained the topic of the hour in most of the saloons. The newspapers had also begun to take notice. The *San Francisco Daily Herald* reported rumors of mistreatment of the *Challenge*'s sailors, claiming that some of them had hired lawyers to press charges against Waterman and Douglass. A few had come to the *Herald*'s office to give their accounts of the affair; others had denied the charges, maintaining that only the necessary discipline had been used to control a mutinous crew. "We are not prepared to express an opinion as to which of these counterstatements is correct," the *Herald*'s editor piously announced. But by November 1, the *Herald* reported that placards had appeared in the city proclaiming that the U.S. marshal had issued warrants for the arrest of Waterman and Douglass, offering a $500 reward for each.

Meanwhile, the other newspapers were regaling their readers with the sailors' stories, which became more exaggerated as they were retold: that second mate Coghill had knocked a man out of the rigging and first mate Douglass had sewed him up in a sail and tossed him, still groaning, over the side; that Waterman had knocked a helmsman down for letting the *Challenge* slip off course; that he had beaten sailors for having dirty hands; that he had shaken four men out of the rigging; that he had shot a man from a yardarm; that he had cleared the deck by training a swivel gun on the crew; even that he had killed his own son (Waterman had no children). But the most inflammatory outcry appeared in the *California Courier* on the day the *Challenge* reached her wharf. James M. Crane, publisher of the *Courier,* was already known for his intemperate journalism. But the November 1, 1851, issue outdid most of his previous efforts:

> The ship *Challenge* has arrived, and Capt. Waterman, her commander, has also—but where are nine of his crew? And where is he and his guilty mate? The accounts given of Captain Waterman towards his men, if true, make him one of the most inhuman monsters of this age.
>
> If they are true, he should be burned alive—he should never leave this city a live man.
>
> The scene at this time on board of the ship beggars all description. Five of them are mangled and bruised in the most shocking manner. One poor fellow died today, and five others, it is expected, will soon be in the embrace of death. One of the men now lying on his deathbed has been severely injured in his genitals, by a kick from this brute in human form. Had these poor men been put in a den with bears and panthers, they could not have been much more inhumanly and shockingly maimed. They are all now lying in the forecastle of the ship. The captain, the vile monster, has made his escape, and so has his brutal mate.
>
> It is an infamous outrage to have such a bloody murderer to command a ship. He is noted for his cruelty everywhere, and in the streets of New York he does not dare show himself, nor dare he hereafter show himself in this city.

The *Courier*'s editorial finally set the spark to the tinder. A surly group of men converged on Pacific Street Wharf, just in time, it turned out, to watch the rest of the *Challenge*'s men being taken from her sick bay to San Francisco's Marine Hospital. Most were on stretchers; they were victims of dysentery, scurvy, and venereal disease rather than "shockingly maimed" by Waterman and Douglass. But the sight of the long line of stretchers was all the mob needed.[2] A cry went up to get Waterman, and the crowd set off up California Street for the Alsop Building.

Waterman was still in the Alsop offices conferring with Charles Griswold and Captain John Land, the *Challenge*'s next commander, when the mob arrived. While Griswold went to the door, Waterman slipped up the stairs toward the roof. At the sight of Griswold, the shouting men started to rush the entrance. Griswold stood his ground. Someone called out for him to produce Captain Waterman. Griswold replied that Waterman was not there. There was a chorus of booing and cursing and another rush for the door. Playing for time, Griswold announced that if the men would select a group of six, he would let them search the offices. The ploy worked. It took some minutes for the arguing men to select their delegation, and by the time Griswold let them into the building, Waterman had reached the top floor of the Alsop Building, climbed a ladder through the scuttle onto the roof, and pulled the ladder up after him. Leaping to the roof of the building next door, he ducked out of sight into the top floor, where he waited in hiding for the crowd to disperse.

The six men pounding through the Alsop Building found no Waterman. They responded by grabbing Captain Land and dragging him out into the street. Someone shouted to Griswold that if he did not produce Waterman, they would hang Land from the nearest lamppost.

The riot had meanwhile brought San Francisco's mayor, Charles Brenham, to the scene. Just before leaving his office he had been visited by a leader of the Committee of Vigilance with an offer of aid: The committee stood ready to disperse this rabble if the mayor called for them. Brenham mounted the steps of the Alsop Building and called for order. The mob paid no attention to him. Captain Land's captors produced a rope and began to fashion a noose. The noisy confusion was suddenly brought up short by a familiar sound: two loud clangs of the nearby Montgomery Street Engine Company's fire bell.

In the comparative silence that ensued, members of the Committee of Vigilance arrived on the run. Fingering their guns, they formed a ring around the mob. Mayor Brenham called for the crowd to leave. The men still shuffled about; no one left. Brenham took out his gold watch and said, "I shall now give you just ten minutes to disperse, and if you fail to comply, I shall order every last one of you to be incarcerated in the city bastille." He paused. "In other words, I will put every damned one of you in jail."

As the first couple of minutes passed, more vigilantes joined their committee members, until there were some six hundred circling the crowd. A few of the more sober men in the mob began to walk away. More followed. Before Mayor Brenham's watch indicated ten minutes, Pacific Street held only members of the Committee of Vigilance; and a shaken Captain Land hurried back into the offices of Alsop & Co.

Remnants of the mob drifted back to Pacific Street Wharf. There was some drunken oratory, including a proposal that they storm the *Challenge* and burn or scuttle her. But the heart had gone out of the riot, and gradually everyone wandered back to the saloons. With darkness that night, Captain Waterman slipped out of the city and went to his ranch.

James Douglass was not so fortunate. Evidently he over-celebrated his escape from his waterborne posse, because next morning he was found, drunk and asleep, in a cart ten miles south of San Francisco on the road to Monterey, where he apparently intended to catch the next steamer to Panama City. Sheriff Jack Hayes and a couple of aides bound Douglass' hands behind his back, slipped a lariat round his shoulders, and led him back to the city. Still unrepentant, Douglass muttered, "I whipped 'em and I'll whip 'em again." Staggering behind Hayes's horse, Douglass maintained an air of sullen bravado, at one point offering, "Well, gentleman, if you want to hang me, here's a pretty tree. Do it like men." Sheriff Hayes and his deputies formed an armed guard around Douglass as a small crowd gathered and followed them. In San Francisco Douglass was quickly locked up in a temporary jail, mainly to protect him from the mob that was rapidly forming as word of his capture spread along the the waterfront. But he also was being held for trial. By now so many accusations were flying back and forth that the U.S. marshal had decided to charge both Waterman and Douglass with assault and murder.

Robert Waterman later maintained that he had personally insisted on a trial to clear his and Douglass' name. He had also charged the eight ringleaders with mutiny and demanded that they be tried and convicted. For four months, from November 1851 through February 1852, San Francisco was treated to a sensational round of trials.[3] It seemed as if everyone who had been aboard the *Challenge* was suing everyone else. California's first grand jury indicted Waterman and Douglass for murdering George Lessing, Waterman for assaulting Fred Birkenshaw, and Douglass for murdering Pawpaw. The grand jury handed down nearly a dozen more indictments. Second Mate Coghill was charged with kicking two of the *Challenge*'s seamen: one, identified as Stevens, off a yardarm, and the other, John Brown, on deck. A litany of charges came from aggrieved *Challenge* sailors. Besides Birkenshaw, Waterman was accused of beating Alex Nicoll, Jon Smiti, and James McCartney. Douglass was also accused of "malicious cruelty" against Alex Nicoll, Charles Pearson, and Michael Gallagher as well as Smiti, McCartney, and Lessing. The roundup of charges even included one against both Waterman and Douglass for beating Thomas Cleaver; it was quickly dismissed when someone pointed out that Cleaver had died of illness only three weeks out. As for the ringleaders of the mutiny, six of the eight Waterman had had arrested were arraigned: Birkenshaw, Ralph Smith, and seamen named on the indictment as Downey, Johnson, Nick, and Ralph. The prosecutor later added Second Mate Coghill; despite his protestations of innocence, some of the mutineers still claimed that Coghill had been in on the plot.

The scene of the bewildering series of trials, charges, and countercharges was the U.S. District Court in its new courthouse on Merchant Street. The judge, Ogden Hoffman, was a

Harvard Law School graduate who had practiced law in New York before coming out to San Francisco in 1850. After a brief period as a lawyer in the city, he had been named to the bench by President Millard Fillmore. Judge Hoffman was only twenty-nine, but he managed the seemingly impossible task of maintaining some dignity and order in the court despite a raffish spectators' section. There evidently were no major disruptions, though on one occasion, at the request of a witness, a "sneering man in a red shirt and straw hat" was evicted from the courtroom. Judge Hoffman's major problem was jury selection. In the city's poisoned atmosphere most of those called to serve were found to be prejudiced against Waterman and Douglass. It took weeks to impanel a jury. And it was another sign of the times that court had to be adjourned on the day after Christmas because two of the jurors had not sobered up from the holiday's celebrations. But considering the rough-and-ready vigilante mood of San Francisco, the juries were for the most part remarkably thoughtful and careful, especially since they evidently were not forbidden access to the rabble-rousing newspaper reports and editorials that continued to flood the city.

Judge Hoffman and the juries were breaking new ground. There had been many trials in New York and Boston of a captain or mate for cruelty or of a sailor or two for leading a mutiny. As a young law student, Hoffman had known about Richard Henry Dana, Jr.'s, cases and may have attended some of the trials; one of his professors had been the same Judge Story whom Dana had accused of being too lenient toward ships' officers. But rarely had there been a series of such complicated, confusing, and interlocking trials, certainly not in California. Some of the principals were defendants as well as accusers; men charged with mutiny by the captain were in turn charging the captain with assault. The *Challenge* trials also provided a vivid example of faulty memory. Different witnesses swore on oath to exactly opposite versions of what happened aboard the *Challenge*. Discrepancies flew like buckshot. By one witness's account George Lessing had been ducked in the scuppers by Douglass; another witness was sure it had been Waterman who had held Lessing underwater. Birkenshaw, when hauled out of hiding, had confessed his part in the mutiny as soon as he had come on deck, according to one witness's recollection; most remembered that Birkenshaw pretended innocence until nearly strung up by the neck. Pawpaw, the old Italian, was barefoot according to most witnesses, and wore one shoe according to another. The mutineers, by various accounts, received a dozen, two dozen, or three dozen lashes; one sailor claimed that thirty-six men—an impossible number—had been flogged for mutiny. Any conscientious juror must have found it nearly impossible to separate fact from fantasy.

A typical case of baffling testimony came in the first trial, in which Second Mate Coghill was accused of kicking seaman Stevens off the mizzentopsail yard during the gale in which three men were lost. Sailor George Hill testified that when Douglass had shouted from the deck to get "those sons-of-bitches" out on the yard, Coghill had kicked Stevens, who fell into the sea. On closer questioning Hill remembered that he had been on the footropes between the two men and that therefore Coghill could hardly have administered much of a kick to Stevens. Hill finally agreed that the leech of the flapping sail, not Coghill, had sent Stevens to his death. The jury found Coghill innocent of this charge. But he still faced two more: for assaulting seaman John Brown and for conspiring in the mutiny.

At the outset the trial of the mutineers seemed almost hopelessly complicated. As in the other trials, potential jurors, one after another, were excused for bias. Once a jury finally was impaneled, U.S. Prosecutor Calhoun Benham, in an attempt to simplify the procedure, concentrated the charges on the two most obvious men: Birkenshaw, whom many of the *Challenge*'s sailors accused of being the ringleader; and Coghill, who, according to Birkenshaw and others, had promised to provide "irons" (handcuffs) for Waterman and Douglass if the revolt succeeded. The prosecution's charge was that Birkenshaw and Coghill had conspired to "subvert the authority of the master and chief mate and take control of the ship from the officers." The case against them seemed airtight. Waterman's statement to the court put it succinctly: "The truth is that, when my ship *Challenge* was in the neighborhood of Rio de Janeiro about 30 of the crew fell on the first mate, Jim Douglass, with the declared intention of killing him, and, afterward, me. This act they later confessed to, which signed confessions I have in my possession at this time."

James Douglass made a dramatic appearance in a packed courtroom. His name had become a waterfront legend, and he had been seen in public only since his capture, when he had been brought to the U.S. District Court for pretrial examination; a crowd had immediately surrounded the courthouse, and Douglass had been rushed back to the security of the county jail. Now, sober and straightforward, he testified, "I was ordered to make a search of the trunks in consequence of reports that property had been stolen from some of the crew. I was standing on deck seeing the chests overhauled when I was seized from behind and thrown down. About all of the crew were present. While I was falling, I received a wound. I felt the knife as I fell, but did not see who struck me with it. There were several men kicking me."

The most lucid testimony came from William Masten, the passenger who had been lounging in the longboat nearby and had had a ringside seat at the time of the attack on Douglass. Masten swore that he had seen Birkenshaw seize Douglass from behind and hold him while George Smith attacked him. It was a matter of seconds, Masten said, before Waterman waded into the fray, hitting Smith on the head, grabbing him, and trussing him up. Birkenshaw, Masten recalled, slipped away. Masten described how Douglass, his thigh bleeding, ripped off his coat and handed it to him, picked up his fallen heaver, and attacked his attackers. Masten also recalled the scene he had witnessed in the captain's cabin later that day when Waterman questioned and got confessions from the leaders of the mutiny.

But three lawyers named Irving, Randolph, and Ely put on a masterful defense of the mutineers. The jury probably did not give much credence to such testimony as Birkenshaw's claim that all he did was push Douglass away and that Douglass fell against seaman Smith, who happened to have a marlinspike concealed in his shirt which "fell out and struck the mate in the fleshy part of the thigh." The defense lawyers, however, chose not to argue the details of the mutiny itself, instead attempting to shift the blame onto Waterman and Douglass. The attack on the first mate, they argued, had not been premeditated; the crewmen were simply reacting to a constant reign of terror. One after another, *Challenge* sailors took the stand to testify to abuse by Douglass. George Smith, whom Waterman had pulled off Douglass during the attack, complained that nearly everyone was beaten at one time or another. John Leggett claimed that Birkenshaw had not initiated the attack but had been reacting when Douglass had hit him with a heaver while the sea chests were being inspected. Charles Flanders testified, "I was beat with a club myself. I did not disobey orders. The first intimation I had was a crack on the head." Charles Pearson, the Navy veteran, maintained, "I knew of no attempt to revolt or create a mutiny. Yes, I have been frequently struck myself." When Coghill came to the stand, he was even more vehement: "I know nothing of any revolt, mutiny, disobedience of orders, or attempt to do so." And in a curious move, perhaps engineered by the defense lawyers, he praised his fellow defendant who had been his chief accuser. Birkenshaw, he testified, was an excellent seaman who always obeyed orders. On and on, the defense lawyers summoned up a litany of accusations against Douglass and Waterman, clearly on the principle that the best defense was a strong offense. And it worked.

The jury found Birkenshaw not guilty. As a result, Coghill escaped on a legal technicality: Since Birkenshaw was innocent, Judge Hoffman ruled that his confession, which implicated Coghill, was inadmissible. So Coghill, too, went free.

Attorney Benham clearly was taken aback. By gambling on charges against only Birkenshaw and Coghill, he had lost the case against the other alleged mutineers as well. Since Waterman had their confessions, the attorney asked him if they should move for a retrial. But Waterman was convinced that the jury had been prejudiced from the start by the waterfront rumors and the inflammatory newspaper stories. "No," he replied. "With the type of jurors available, it seems utterly useless to continue the matter."

Waterman obviously felt he had a good reason to fear for his fate at the hands of a similar "waterfront jury" in his and Douglass' trial for cruelty to the crew. Again it proved difficult to select a jury because so many who were called admitted animus against the captain and mate. Finally a dozen men were seated in the jury box. The chief accuser was Birkenshaw, who testified colorfully to the beating administered by Waterman after he had been routed from his hideout. He was struck even before being asked about his part in the mutiny, he claimed. Ordered to kneel on deck, he recalled, "I got down on my knees and, as I did so, I saw a stick in the captain's hand coming down on my 'ead. I raised my arm to save my 'ead and the weight of the stick fell on my arm. He struck me several times on my body and on my eye. I felt the bones of my arm crack when he hit me." Evidently somewhat carried away by his account, Birkenshaw testified that he had been kept kneeling for six hours. Under cross-examination by the defense he changed this to twenty minutes and, on repeat questioning, to ten minutes. At another point Birkenshaw claimed that he was already handcuffed when Waterman struck him, evidently forgetting that he had claimed to raise one arm in defense. Another seaman, John Leggett, describing the scene for the prosecution, claimed that Birkenshaw "raised his hands to protect his head—they were free at the time."

The defense produced a damaging witness: Captain Ottinger of the cutter *Lawrence,* who described his inspection of Birkenshaw's arm and his diagnosis that it had not been broken. More important, Ottinger testified that Birkenshaw had blamed his injury not on Waterman but on Douglass who, he said, had beaten him after he had been handcuffed. "I am clear that he stated it was the mate who struck him," Ottinger swore. He was certain on this point, he added, because he was impressed "with the circumstances of Birkenshaw's having been struck when in irons. It seemed so extraordinary." Birkenshaw was brought back to the stand, where he insisted, "I never told 'im that the mate broke it." But Ottinger stuck by his testimony. And the defense lawyers, reminding the jury of Birkenshaw's shifting testimony, made a point of questioning his reliability as a witness.

Waterman's and Douglass' lawyers, named Hamilton, McLane, and Austin, built their defense around the "continuous mutinous intention" of most of the crew, pointing out that more than normal discipline was necessary to keep the ship moving—indeed, to save it from foundering. Waterman took the stand to argue that "the toughs of the crew of the *Challenge* received only such treatment—severe as it seemed to be—as was necessary for the operation of the ship." Douglass followed him to the stand to testify that the crewmen "were in an almost continuous state of disobedience and mutiny."

The trial went on for weeks, with the city's newspapers avidly reporting the details. But by now there was a swing of public opinion in favor of Waterman, if not of Douglass. An anonymous friend[4] of Waterman wrote to the *Herald* an indignant complaint about the inflammatory treatment of the *Challenge* case in the press. Waterman, his friend claimed, had not hidden out to escape justice; he had "concealed himself from a mob, and not from the officers of the law, being most anxious for a legal investigation; but became alarmed at the outburst of public opinion, as indicated by the press, and fled for refuge into the mountains." Making a pitiable case for the captain, his friend even claimed that Waterman "has been reduced to such extremity by famine as to have been compelled to kill his horse for food." The *Herald* huffily defended its coverage of the *Challenge* affair, but the *Alta California,* sensing the changing mood, took the occasion to criticize the demagoguery of its rival newspaper, the *Courier,* which had called for Waterman to be "burned alive." The *Alta California* editorialized:

It should be the duty of all order-loving citizens but particularly of the press, to put down this attempt to forestall judgment in this case, and we cannot but deprecate the course pursued by one of the city papers in the matter. The veriest crime-hardened transgressor is entitled to a suspension of public opinion on his acts when the law has taken cognizance of his offenses, and it is asking no more than justice, that Captain Waterman should receive the full benefit of unprejudiced and impartial public opinion in his case.

The *Alta California*'s editor, however, hedged his bet by adding, "There appears to us no disposition to question the general statement, that Captain Waterman and his mate, Mr. Douglass, treated some of the crew with most shameful and unjustifiable brutality, and it is necessary for the protection of our seamen that this matter should be thoroughly sifted, and dealt with to the utmost rigor of the law." Nonetheless, "we well know that many of the stories that are put in circulation are utterly false, while others are so greatly exaggerated as to scarcely bear resemblance of truth." And the editor added a revealing observation: "Let us not permit so dangerous an example of the insecurity of person and character to be told against us, for if it be said in foreign ports that a vessel arriving here is pounced upon by a furious mob, thirsting for vengeance on its officers because of cruelty during the trip," the shipping merchants of other cities might reconsider sending their vessels to San Francisco. "Our port will be regarded as an unfavorable one to the enterprise and ambition of Yankee shipmasters, and the days of the clipper ships and surprising voyages hither will be over." It was a somewhat naïve conclusion: Yankee shipmasters would not be put off by San Francisco's mobs so long as there was a good profit to be made.

News of the *Challenge*'s voyage had in fact reached the eastern ports. The *New York Herald*'s headline for November 30 trumpeted:

ARRIVAL OF THE CLIPPER CHALLENGE, IN ONE
HUNDRED AND NINE [sic] DAYS—DEATHS AMONG
THE CREW—GREAT EXCITEMENT—CAPT.
WATERMAN AND FIRST MATE
OBLIGED TO FLY FOR THEIR LIVES!

Three days later the *Herald* published a more accurate account. Seaman Wheeler's letter had by now reached his mother in Connecticut, and she had sent it to the *Herald*. Wheeler reported simply, "On Sunday, there was a mutiny aboard." He was unsparing in his description of the conditions off Cape Horn: "Oh, such cold weather I never saw in my life. The ship was rolling her rail under both sides, the sea ran mountains high. . . . We have had the worst passage we could have." And he had nothing but scorn for the *Challenge*'s crew: "Such a set of sailors there never was before in any other ship in this wide world." But Wheeler had not a word of complaint against Waterman or Douglass; in fact, he wrote, "I get along very well with the captain and mate."

Copies of that issue of the *New York Herald* reached San Francisco, by way of steamers and the Isthmus, in mid-January. The *Alta California* reprinted Wheeler's letter, as did the *San Francisco Herald,* which added a letter from another of its readers. "Now, can any responsible person for a moment believe," the *Herald* reader asked, that if the charges against Waterman and Douglass were true, "this young American in writing a private letter to his parent would not have alluded to them?" The letter added a new piece of information: "It can be proved that soon after the *Challenge* arrived here, nine good fellows of the crew, of whom five were Americans, waited on the consignees and expressed their entire satisfaction with the captain on the voyage and their willingness to continue on with him to China."

If the *Herald* reader's claim was true, it is difficult to understand why Waterman's defense counsel did not produce these nine loyal crew members as witnesses. The letter writer was incorrect—and innocently revealed his prejudice—in claiming that "from over fifty men who composed the crew of the *Challenge,* some four or five have been retained as witnesses for the prosecution. It is believed that they are all foreigners, some of them having never sailed in an American ship before." Waterman's accusers numbered more than four or five, and many of them were Americans. But the letter to the *Herald* made no claim to objectivity. Captain Waterman, it concluded, "is a ruined man, ruined for exercising what he considered was his duty to the owners of his ship, to the owners or assurers of the valuable cargo, and for protecting the lives of the passengers and other innocent persons on board by forcing a set of mutineers to bring his vessel safely to the end of her voyage. The loss of employment by having given up command of his ship and the immense expense connected with the protracted law proceedings in this country will leave him without an available free dollar. It's a hard case, ain't it?"

The writer signed himself only with the initial "R." But most friends of Waterman recognized the hand of his partner, Captain Archibald Ritchie, who certainly knew that Waterman was unemployed by his own choice. Presumably the jurors were reading most of this special pleading, if they could wade through it; there is no indication that Judge Hoffman sequestered them from exposure to the press. Meanwhile, Waterman himself was putting up a strong defense, claiming that in thirty years of experience at sea the *Challenge*'s was "the worst crew I've ever seen." As for Smiti, the Finn he was accused of beating, Waterman countered, "He was lazy, dirty, indolent, and always skulking. . . . Yes, I ordered the mate to give him a rope's end and I think he deserved it." When reminded of testimony that Smiti's feet were so frostbitten that he was crawling about the deck, Waterman replied, "He appeared to walk well enough when going to the galley for his tea." The captain and mate were on trial, Waterman maintained, because when the *Challenge* reached San Francisco, "some of the blacklegs or mutineers in the crew, the better to conceal their own guilt, spread slanderous falsehoods and outlandish stories to the newspapers."

When it finally came time to charge the jury, Judge Hoffman chose his words meticulously: "Weigh carefully the portion of the testimony touching the state of discipline and behavior of the crew at the time the offense is alleged to have been committed and whether under a consideration of all circumstances, as detailed by witnesses, a reasonable man would have had cause to fear personal danger or be deprived of the command of the ship and whether this state of affairs warranted the committal of an assault like the one charged in the indictment." On December 22, the jury retired, returning three hours later to announce that the members could not reach a verdict. Judge Hoffman sent them back. By 6 P.M. the jury was in the courtroom again, its foreman repeating the members' inability to agree and asking to be discharged. The judge handed the jury over to the custody of the U.S. marshal for the night. By next morning at 10 A.M. the foreman announced that "it is utterly impossible for us to agree." With the Christmas holiday approaching, Judge Hoffman reluctantly discharged them.

Instead of being retried on the same charge, Waterman and Douglass were tried on the remaining accusations by other crewmen and their lawyers. On the charge that they had murdered George Lessing, "The Dancing Master" who had been dunked in the scuppers, another hung jury (two for conviction, nine for acquittal, one undecided) spared them. The case against them for cruelty to Alex Nicoll came to a ludicrous dismissal when Nicoll and Birkenshaw, attempting to testify for the prosecution, engaged in a slurred shouting match over who was the drunker of the two. Finally tiring of the whole procedure, the district attorney *"nolle prossed"* (withdrew) the remaining cases except for four that looked certain.

The case against Waterman and Douglass for mistreating Smiti got off to a poor start when no interpreter of Finnish could be found so Smiti could testify. But the prosecutor made an appealing case out of the crippled illiterate beaten by the mate and captain. The jury took four hours to bring back a verdict of guilty.

The *Challenge*'s carpenter, Michael Gallagher, helped convict Douglass of assault by a convincing argument that the mate beat him frequently and for no apparent reason.

The evidence was so strong in the case of Douglass' beating of the Italian seaman Pawpaw that the first mate was found guilty of his murder.

And when the assistant surgeon of San Francisco's Marine Hospital testified that seaman John Brown had been effectively emasculated by a kick from Alex Coghill, the second mate was found guilty in less than an hour.

The sentences dealt out by Judge Hoffman were lenient even by San Francisco standards. For kicking John Brown, Coghill was given thirty days, fourteen of which he had already served. Waterman was fined $400 for cruel treatment of Smiti. And Douglass got off the most easily, perhaps partly because Waterman argued that his first mate was merely following orders. Douglass received no sentence for mistreatment of Smiti. For assaulting carpenter Gallagher he was fined $50. And for the murder of Pawpaw he was fined only $200.

There remained the question of establishing the *Challenge*'s exact death toll. It had been variously estimated, from Waterman's seven (the three who fell from the rigging plus four in sick bay) to seaman John Leggett's claim of thirteen. The precise count has never been determined; but the probable number can be calculated from E. A. Wheeler's letter. He mentioned the three who fell to their deaths off Cape Horn, plus five who died in sick bay (presumably including Cleaver, Lessing, and Pawpaw); Wheeler also reported the death of "J.W." on the day of the *Challenge*'s arrival, for a total of nine. And the *Challenge*'s death toll did not cease even after everyone had gone ashore: One more crewman died in the Marine Hospital, bringing the mortality of the *Challenge*'s once-promising maiden voyage to ten.

The *Challenge*'s mutineers were freed. Her officers got off with light sentences. It was the *Challenge* herself and her owners who paid the price. She had been branded a "hellship." Despite the popularity of her next skipper, John Land, the Griswolds' agents could not recruit another crew. Any sailors willing to ship out were superstitious about a vessel with such a bad name; and there were even fewer experienced seamen in San Francisco than in New York. The crimps controlled a sellers' market, and they knew it. The dickering went on for weeks while the *Challenge* sat at her mooring, still undermanned. Violence again erupted on her deck. The new third mate, a man named Sparks, got into a drunken knife fight with one of the recruits, a Sydney Town Duck, and was rushed to a doctor's office with his arm nearly severed below the elbow. Sparks's attacker was in turn attacked by other crewmen led by one George Lewis, who was arrested and fined $25.

Finally, anxious to get the *Challenge* back to sea, Alsop & Co. agreed to pay $200 per man in advance in order to round up 40 sailors. Captain Land looked them over and pronounced "most of them characters of the worst order." But he had little choice. The *Challenge* finally sailed for Shanghai in January. So rebellious was her crew than Captain Land had to cut short her voyage and put into Hong Kong for help. The warship U.S.S. *Vincennes* was in Hong Kong Harbor, and at Land's request the *Vincennes*' Commodore John Aulick sent a squad of Marines aboard the *Challenge* to restore order. Captain Land then took aboard 553 coolies for San Francisco, and at last the *Challenge* proved her promise. She returned to San Francisco in 34 days, one day over the record for the passage.

There is no evidence that Robert Waterman had the slightest twinge of remorse over his treatment of the *Challenge*'s crew. His conviction, instead of making him pause to reconsider, merely confirmed his scornful opinion of the jurors. The brutality aboard the *Challenge*, he was convinced, could be blamed entirely on an incompetent, indolent, and rebellious crew. If he ever regretted signing on "Black Douglass," he did not admit it, despite the testimony of obedient, hardworking sailors that they, too, had frequently been beaten by Douglass. Nor did Waterman consider it inconsistent when, on discovering that one of the men who fell from the mizzen yardam had been married, he wrote to the man's widow expressing his sympathy and enclosing a check for $500.

He turned to his new life ashore, settled down on his ranch, and started to build a house and a barn. Inquiring at the Alsop offices, he found that the steamship *Northerner*, which he had brought out a year ago, was scheduled to leave New York again in a couple of months. He wrote his wife, Cordelia, asking her to take passage on the *Northerner* and dispatched the letter on the next steamer to the Isthmus. She received it in time to board the *Northerner*, bound down the Atlantic and through the Strait of Magellan to California. But by the time the steamer reached Chagres, Cordelia had met two mining engineers named Kerry and Shannon who planned to take the overland shortcut across the Isthmus. It would save her at least a month, they pointed out, and persuaded her to join them.

There is a daguerreotype of Cordelia Waterman at thirty-five that is revealing: the strong, proud profile of a woman with a mind of her own—plus a hairdo of then-fashionable side curls. A woman who could play the submissive charmer to Robert Waterman's machismo and at the same time take charge; a woman who could cry at the launching of her rival the *Sea Witch* but who firmly decided after one voyage to stay home; a woman who waited patiently for her husband but who subtly and surely convinced him that he wanted to retire; in short, a woman in love and in control.

One can imagine Cordelia Waterman's reaction to the confusing reports from San Francisco—the *New York Herald*'s headline "WATERMAN AND FIRST MATE OBLIGED TO FLY FOR THEIR LIVES!," and seaman Wheeler's letter describing a mutiny aboard the *Challenge*. No doubt her husband's letters set her mind somewhat at ease. And the disposition of the final case of *The United States* v. *Robert Waterman*, however painful and seemingly unjust to her mind, must have been a massive relief. The *Challenge* had proved to be as great a rival as the *Sea Witch*. But Cordelia Waterman could not have avoided a flicker of satisfaction that the *Challenge*'s voyage must finally have cured her husband's wanderlust. When Waterman wrote proposing that she book passage on the *Northerner*, she probably was already asking herself why she had not set out for California earlier. So when she was presented with the opportunity to cut a month or more off her time by crossing the Isthmus, she seized the chance. With Kerry and Shannon she debarked at Chagres. They hired two boatmen-guides and set off up the Chagres River toward the jungle trail to Panama City.

The guides were named Ponch and Argo. They obviously had done the forty-two mile river and trail crossing several times. The boat trip up the muddy Chagres went without incident except for melting heat and clouds of ravenous mosquitoes. The two engineers proved to be helpful, gentlemanly traveling companions. At the head of the river the party took to the narrow trail over the ridge and down through the jungle to Panama City. It was during what was supposed to be the last night's encampment that Cordelia Waterman panicked.

Awakened by the mosquitoes, she lay in her tent listening to the night sounds. Nocturnal predators shuffled and sniffed around the clearing. Kerry and Shannon could be heard snoring faintly in the tent near hers. The four pack mules clumped about in their hobbles, chomping at the grass. The guides, rifles in their laps, sat by the embers of the cooking fire, smoking their pipes and talking. Cordelia could hear a phrase now and then; a quick study, she had picked up a bit of Spanish during the trip. And in the suggestive atmosphere of the jungle night, she became convinced that Ponch and Argo were talking about her luggage.

When she had decided to take the Isthmus shortcut she had left most of her belongings aboard the *Northerner*, planning to retrieve them when the steamer reached San Francisco. Traveling light, she had brought along only a few necessities, except for one precious item she had not dared leave aboard the ship: a bag containing her jewelry. Including family heirlooms and rare stones brought home from China by her husband, the jewelry was worth at least $20,000, a fortune in 1852. She had carefully concealed the jewels in a watertight canvas bag secreted in the bottom of a carrying case. Now, in the oppressive jungle darkness, the silhouettes of the guides seemed furtive and menacing. Listening intently and trying to make out what Ponch and Argo were saying, she became convinced that they had somehow found out, or at least that they intended to steal her bags for whatever they contained and slip away into the jungle. She had heard many of the horror stories told aboard the *Northerner* about the Isthmus guides. In her fright she tried to weigh the possibilities. They were supposed to be one day's trek from Panama City. Tomorrow would be the guides' last chance to rob her and her companions, perhaps even murder them and make off with the luggage. She decided to foil the would-be assassins by escaping and pushing on to Panama City on her own.

Watching wakefully, incapable of sleep, she waited until the two guides curled up on the ground. The sky was already lightening. She slipped out of her cot, took only the case containing the jewelry and a blanket for use if she had to spend another night, and padded noiselessly out of the encampment. Striding down the trail toward Panama City, she calculated that she had a few hours' head start.

By midafternoon, fearing that the guides might catch up with her, she turned off the trail into the jungle, An hour or two of trampling through the underbrush was so exhausting that she spread out her blanket for a nap. She awoke in darkness broken by shafts of moonlight through the jungle canopy. Rising and thrashing onward, she continued in what she hoped was the direction of the sea. The trail to Panama City was lost to her by now, and she was afraid to use it anyway. After struggling through the jungle for a few hours, she lay down and slept again, waking in darkness when one large animal, chased by another, thundered past her. At dawn she heard a heart-stopping sound: the guides calling her name. Folding the blanket, she hid it under a bush. With only her carrying case she hurried away from the threatening voices.

By late afternoon the jungle seemed denser than ever; there was no sign of clearing or habitation to suggest that she was nearing Panama City. And the guides' voices still echoed through the trees. She decided that it was useless; she was famished, excruciatingly thirsty, and exhausted. Better the chance of being robbed than sure death in the jungle. Then she heard another sound, a faint, familiar, far-off thunder. She was sure it was surf. Revived by hope and adrenaline, she forced her way through a tangled stand of bamboo and emerged on the edge of a cliff. Below her was the Gulf of Panama, and less than a mile north along the coast was the low skyline of a city.

Later she could not recall how she had found her way down the sandy cliff and along the shore until someone had rescued her. She awoke in a military hospital outside Panama City, to be told by a doctor that she had been ill with yellow fever for three weeks, two of them in delirium. Her carrying case was still beside her bed with its jewelry intact. Shortly Kerry and Shannon called on her. They had continued their trek with no further incident. After searching for her for a day and a night, Ponch and Argo had guided them the rest of the way, accepted their fee, and gone back. The two mining engineers had checked the local hospitals, found her, and waited until they were sure she was recovering. They planned to take the next steamer to San Francisco, where they promised to look up Captain Waterman and tell him that his wife would follow them as soon as she was able to.

Within a few days, still weak but anxious to get to San Francisco, Cordelia inquired about shipping schedules and was told that the clipper ship *Sword Fish* was shortly expected to put into Del Rey Island, off Panama City, for water and provisions en route to San Francisco. She found a fisherman to take her out to the island. As she climbed shakily onto the long Del Rey pier, she was glad to see that the *Sword Fish* had not yet arrived. With luck she could make up for her lost month and still reach San Francisco before the *Northerner* did. She could imagine how her husband would worry if the steamer arrived without her.

Robert Waterman was already worrying. At the Alsop & Co. offices he had been told that a number of passengers, including a woman, had left the *Northerner* to cross the Isthmus. Knowing Cordelia, he guessed that she might well be taking the shortcut. After fretting for a few days, he decided to go to

Panama City to look for her. It took another couple of weeks to find a vessel sailing for New York. Waterman could not persuade her captain to put into Panama City and had to settle for Del Rey Island, where he hoped to find someone to take him across Panama Bay to the city.

As he went ashore on the island, Waterman realized that he was at least three weeks too late to meet a party that had started overland at the time the *Northerner* had put into Chagres. Walking through the big shed at the head of the pier, he noticed a familiar figure at the other end of the building. She was carrying a small bag and wandering about as if lost. It seemed impossible, but he was sure. They met in the center of the big shed in the midst of the swirling crowd. And at the sight of him, Cordelia Waterman fainted.[5]

10

Aftermath

THE CLIPPER SHIP was changing the economy of California, which in turn would change the clipper ship. Huge cargoes brought around Cape Horn by such vessels as the *Flying Cloud* and the *Challenge* relieved the major shortages. But many remained, largely because of the still-growing population. The economy of scarcity in 1849 and 1850 was giving way to one of wild and unpredictable fluctuations. No longer did merchants row out to meet incoming ships, waving bags of nuggets, and offering ridiculous prices for whatever was aboard. No longer did auctions degenerate into shouting matches, except in the now rare instances when a cargo's arrival happened to coincide with a new shortage.

Across the continent in New York there was no way to judge the demand. The shipping merchant who had been confident about selling almost anything now had to gamble that the merchandise he shipped to San Francisco would be in short supply when his vessel got there. A clear sign of the change came when a ship arrived in the early 1850s with a cargo of tacks. Tacks had been in such demand for fastening muslin to partitions in 1849 that they had been literally worth their weight in gold. But so many New York merchants had rushed to take advantage of the high price for tacks that millions of them had been off-loaded in San Francisco. Meanwhile, the city's crude huts had largely given way to more substantial buildings with plastered partitions. So when the latest shipment arrived, no one wanted any more tacks. Moreover, longshoremen's wages were high and warehouse space was scarce and expensive. The unhappy consignee dumped the whole shipload of tacks into San Francisco Bay.

A similarly unfortunate recipient of a cargo of stoves had a more ingenious solution. By chance his shipment arrived shortly after another vessel had unloaded hundreds of stoves; but he still was able to put them to practical use because they arrived during the rainy season. San Francisco's streets were so deep in mud that man and beast sank to their bellies. Town officials tried to fill the mudholes with brush, boxes, and other debris, which promptly sank from sight. Boardwalks on pilings served as sidewalks, and planks were laid across the streets between them. So the merchant dumped his cargo of unwanted stoves into the bog outside his store, where they sank so deep that their lids provided stepping-stones from one boardwalk to the other.

Unable to calculate the demand three or four months hence, New York's merchants turned to more diversified cargoes—and to more clipper ships, on the principle that the only solution was to get there as soon as possible. So even with the California market becoming unpredictable, New York's and Boston's shipping merchants continued to vie with one another to send their merchandise off in the fastest available clipper, and to commission larger clippers for the California trade. Thus Robert Waterman's prediction of the demise of the clipper ship was off by only a couple of years. Although the 1849–51 period had been the time of San Francisco's greatest demand, the merchant shippers in the East did not realize it until too late.

Clipper ships continued to come down the New York and New England ways in increasing numbers. Twenty-four had been launched in 1850 and fifty-four in 1851. There were seventy-five more in 1852 and a record 125 in 1853. Only then, long after most of California's needs were filled, did the headlong momentum slow, with sixty-nine clippers launched in 1854, forty-two in 1855, and forty in 1856. But throughout 1852 and into 1853 the shipyards along New York's East River and Boston Harbor were jammed with huge hulls and busy with workers enjoying salaries nearly double the $1.50 per day of less than a decade earlier.

The clipper's design had reached its perfection in the *Flying*

Cloud and the *Challenge,* none of whose successors had sharper bows or narrower hulls. But the newer clippers were larger. Nonetheless, their greater capacity still was less than that of many of the fatter-bodied nonclippers that continued, in far greater numbers, to be built for the rest of the world's trade. The clipper ship remained an express freighter, and each new model represented a greater gamble. For the time being, the best of them continued to pay off. When Donald McKay attempted in 1852 to surpass his 1,793-ton *Flying Cloud* with the 2,421-ton *Sovereign of the Seas,* he could find no merchant shipper to commission her, so he financed her himself. At first it looked as if he had made a mistake: It was difficult to find cargoes for her. But once she was in service, her great speed paid McKay back in nine months. The merchants continued to finance other clippers despite their rising costs: During one thirty-seven-day period in the autumn of 1852, as many as fifteen clipper ships, an average of one every three days, left for California. And in 1853, eighteen clippers set sail around the Horn in January alone, followed by sixteen more in February.

The racing became even more intense. With some two hundred clippers slashing their way around Cape Horn, they often found themselves in ship-to-ship duels within sight of one another. The most crowded and closely fought sweepstakes of them all occurred a year after the *Challenge* and *Flying Cloud* contest. In a period of a little more than a month during the autumn of 1852, no fewer than fifteen clippers took off around Cape Horn. Historian Carl Cutler described this contest as representing "the very crest of the clipper wave."[1] The overall winner was the *Flying Fish,* which took ninety-two days, four hours for the passage from New York to San Francisco. The average elapsed time of all fifteen clippers in this contest was 112 days.

There was an air of desperation to these clipper races of the early 1850s, as if everyone were trying to overlook the changed situation in California. Clipper fever still ran high in New York and Boston. Those shipping merchants who had begun to worry about the declining and chancy San Francisco market were reinvigorated by the Australian Gold Rush of 1851. It never matched the American stampede to California, but it added further stimulation to New York's clipper fever, especially when British shippers turned to American shipyards to order bigger, faster vessels than their own.

Over the succeeding three years British clients helped make up for the falloff in orders for California clippers. Shipbuilders in New York and Boston continued to produce more and more clippers. The merchant shippers continued to dispatch more of them to San Francisco, and now to London and Liverpool for the Australian passage. Captains raced one another with more daring and determination than ever. But the California clipper cargoes were different. The new clipper *Sweepstakes,* unable to obtain any general merchandise, was loaded with boilers until she rode deep in the water; still she made good time through the deck-washing seas off Cape Horn. Not all the clippers' holds were full. San Francisco's need was for a steady supply of goods for her growing population, and that could be provided by slower, more capacious merchantmen at much lower rates. The clipper ship, sacrificing capacity for speed, had made money by charging express rates as high as $50 and even $60 per ton. By 1853 the rates were falling to $40, some to $35. Yet, paradoxically, the lower rates provided another incentive for the builder of the faster clipper and the driving captain: With express cargo dwindling, the merchants had a wider choice, and they naturally chose the faster ship. So the older clippers waited for cargoes that the newer clippers took away from them. For such reasons the momentum was difficult to halt. Of some three hundred vessels built since 1845 that could truly be called clipper ships, nearly half of them were launched in 1853.

But the pendulum was about to start its backswing. A hint of the trouble on the California passage appeared in the *New York Herald* in the spring of 1853. Donald McKay's magnificent *Sovereign of the Seas* had just returned from her maiden voyage to San Francisco; en route home she had become the first sailing vessel to exceed 400 nautical miles in a 24-hour period. On May 14, McKay's friendly rival William Webb, builder of the *Challenge,* reacted to the *Sovereign's* publicity with a letter to the editor of the *Herald:*

Dear Sir.—My attention having been called to an article in the *Evening Post,* of Thursday last, headed "The

Clipper Ship *Sovereign of the Seas*—A Challenge to the World," I wish to state in reply that I am ready to bet the sum of ten thousand dollars on the ship *Young America,* Captain D. S. Babcock, the last ship of my construction, and now loading at the foot of Dover Street, East River, against the ship *Sovereign of the Seas.*

The trial to be made on the terms proposed, viz., from New York to San Francisco, both ships loaded and to sail together, or within thirty days of each other.

Yours respectfully,
William H. Webb

Donald McKay would have enjoyed nothing more than a race between his newest clipper and Webb's. Instead, four days later, he replied to the *Herald:*

The owner of the *Sovereign of the Seas* begs to state, in answer to the letter from Mr. Webb in Monday's *Herald,* that, though he himself never challenged any ship to a sail against the *Sovereign of the Seas,* he would nevertheless have felt happy to take up the gauntlet, if the present state of the California freight market did not preclude the possibility of laying her on in that direction with any advantage. The *Sovereign of the Seas* will have to make, in all probability, an intermediate trip to England, and the owner can only hope that on her return better feeling for California will enable him to lay her on again for San Francisco—and then, to sail her for the stipulated amount against any clipper which Mr. Webb is willing to match against her.

McKay's *Sovereign of the Seas* never did race the *Young America* around the Horn. And the *Young America* was William Webb's last true clipper ship.

Still the clipper ships raced one another. In the spring of 1853 the *Hornet* and the *Flying Cloud* left Sandy Hook on the same day and arrived in San Francisco 105 days later within 40 minutes of each other.[2] So many clipper ships still sailed for California that as many as three of them sometimes came through the Golden Gate on the same day; in two forty-eight-hour periods San Franciscans watched five of them arrive. But their captains now waited for cargoes instead of sailors. Not until 1860 would California develop a healthy exporting economy. Many clippers returned to New York in ballast. Some followed the old course across the Pacific to China; but here, too, an oversupply of vessels was depressing the freight rates in the tea trade. The Australia run attracted some of the newest clippers, and it was the Australian Gold Rush that induced Donald McKay to build the largest and most ambitious clipper of them all.

McKay designed her for even heavier seas than those on the California run, on the advice of Matthew Maury. The great armchair navigator had become intrigued by the Australia passage and again had proposed a new way to get there sooner. British captains of vessels taking immigrants to Australia and returning with wool had made a habit of touching at Cape Town at the southern tip of Africa. But Maury's study of naval and clipper logs led him to propose a track as much as eight hundred miles to the west in the South Atlantic where there was a band of unusually strong winds to carry the ship down into the Roaring Forties. There, as far south as 48°, Maury promised, the "brave west winds" surging around the globe would send the vessel romping across the bottom of the Indian Ocean to Australia. Returning, Maury advised, the skipper should stay with the strong westerlies, on around the world and up the South and North Atlantic to London, New York, or Boston. Once again Maury proved that the shortest distance for a sailing ship was not necessarily a straight line. His course added more than a thousand miles to the more direct route hugging the Cape of Good Hope; but because of the strong westerlies it cut the time nearly in half.

And because of those gale-force winds, the larger the ship, the better. The seas of the lower forties and fifties, known as the Great Southern Ocean, are moving mountains as high as sixty feet and as long as a thousand feet, rolling around the open ocean with no land to oppose them. It took a large ship with a heavy rudder and stout stern to keep steadily on course. Donald McKay's *Sovereign of the Seas* was 600 tons larger than his *Flying Cloud*. Now he laid down the massive keel for a clipper ship that would be 2,000 tons larger than the *Sovereign*—an unheard-of 4,555 tons. As with the *Sovereign,* no merchant shipper would gamble the $300,000 it would cost to construct the new vessel. So McKay built her himself. His friends tried to warn him; but he pointed out that the *Sovereign of the Seas* had paid him back handsomely, so he expected a much larger clipper to do even better. Here, he obviously felt, was the perfect combination of speed and great carrying capacity.

He decided to name her the *Great Republic.*[3] She was the largest wooden sailing vessel ever built in the United States, 335 feet long, with the usual three square-rigged masts soaring nearly to 300 feet and a fourth mast, which the builder's friends promptly called the "McKay mast"; it carried a fore-and-aft spanker with square-rigged yards above it. The *Great Republic* consumed enough lumber (1½ million feet of pine alone) to build two of the largest U.S. men-of-war. She stretched as long as a city block; she was as wide as a street; her mainmast was more than a yard thick; and her 15,653 yards of cotton duck would have covered a two-lane road for a mile. Her topsails were of the double Forbes rig; otherwise no crew could have been able to handle the monster sails. Her four anchors were so heavy (the largest weighing 8,500 pounds) that she was furnished with an anchor capstan instead of the less efficient windlass; the capstan was an invention of her skipper-to-be, Lauchlan McKay. A 15-horsepower steam engine was stationed on deck to load her cargo and hoist her heavy yards. Even with these mechanical aids, the *Great Republic* required a crew of 100 men and 30 boys, more than twice the crew of the *Challenge.*

Never had so many people attended a ship launching as on October 4, 1853, which was proclaimed a state holiday. More than fifty thousand people came in stagecoaches, carts, sloops, and special trains from all over New England to McKay's East Boston yard. At exactly noon a bottle of water from the new Cochituate reservoir was broken over her bow.[4] A band played "Hail Columbia," church bells pealed, and cannon boomed as the huge hull literally smoked down the ways: Her weight and speed set the oil-soaked timbers afire. Plunging into the harbor, she set all the boats rocking and was barely restrained by two anchors and a tug from crashing into the Chelsea Bridge.

Stepping the *Great Republic*'s tall masts took six weeks, and then she was towed by tug to New York, where she was warped to the deep-water wharf at the foot of Dover Street to load a cargo of grain for Liverpool; there in turn she would take aboard immigrants, argonauts, and supplies for Australia. By Christmas of 1853 she had a full hold and crew and was prepared to sail across the winter Atlantic. On the night of December 26, a fire broke out in the Novelty Baking Company building on Front Street, a block away and upwind.

It was a brisk night, and cinders from the bakery fire were soon showering the *Great Republic*. Her reefed sails caught fire. At Lauchlan McKay's orders men were sent aloft and lines were rigged to haul up buckets of water. But the wind-fanned flames soon enveloped all the sails, driving the men back to the deck. All of the *Great Republic*'s volatile tarred rigging was ablaze by the time the local fire company arrived, and the firemen refused to go aboard because the deck was being showered with burning lines and blocks. The clipper's masts were too tall for the water from the fire hoses to reach the flames. Captain McKay ordered the masts cut down so they would fall into the harbor before they ignited the rest of the ship. Most of them did topple over the side, but the foremast broke and part of it plunged through the deck. Burning rigging littered the cabintops, but the firemen were able to hose down the hull and extinguish the flames. It was morning before the smoking debris was under control. Two other vessels at the wharf, the clipper *White Squall* and the *Joseph Walker,* had been destroyed by the fire. But the *Great Republic* had been saved.

The firemen had just departed when a cloud of smoke bursting through a hatch revealed that the falling topmast had set the grain cargo afire. It was beyond control. Captain McKay reluctantly ordered the clipper scuttled. Holes were hacked through her massive timbers below the waterline and she settled on the bottom; but her 30-foot draft was so deep that her deck and part of her cargo still were above water. For two days she continued to hiss, smoke, and burn to the water's edge, while Donald McKay, who had rushed down from Boston, watched in despair. When the wreckage could be boarded, a cofferdam was built around her and she was pumped out. The water-soaked grain had swelled and strained her timbers. But her hull had not burst. Donald McKay had refused an offer of $280,000 for the *Great Republic* a few days before the fire. He now collected $180,000 in insurance[5] and released her to the underwriters. They in turn sold the dismasted, burned-out hulk to Captain Nathaniel Palmer, who set about restoring her for his employers, A. A. Low & Bros. But the rebuilt *Great Republic* was a much smaller version of Donald McKay's huge clipper ship. Her capacity was reduced by more than 1,500 tons and her rigging was cut down by 25 percent. Still she remained the largest merchant ship afloat, and her draught was so deep that she could not go into many harbors. But her smaller rigging required only half as many crewmen, making her less costly to operate.

Palmer and the Lows were convinced that there was no longer enough business for a clipper the size of the original *Great Republic*. And their cut-down version served them well. She made one record run from New York to the equator in 15 days, 18 hours; and she went to San Francisco in 92 days, one of the fastest passages around the Horn. Still, Donald McKay must have wondered for the rest of his life what records his *Great Republic* might have set while thundering around the bottom of the world before Matthew Maury's "brave west winds" if only that fire at the Novelty Baking Company building had happened a few days later.

By 1854, clipper ship fever was finally abating. Where 145 clippers had sailed for San Francisco in 1853, 111 set out around the Horn the next year. Yet still they raced. No fewer than twenty clippers reached San Francisco in under 110 days in 1854. And it was in 1854 that the *Flying Cloud* bested her maiden voyage record to San Francisco, lowering her 1851 time of 89 days, 21 hours by 13 hours. But by September 1854, New York's piers were crowded with ships awaiting full cargoes. Shipping merchants were postponing plans for new clippers and canceling orders already made. The shipyards' high wages were shortly to plunge back toward the $2 and $1.50 of earlier years. Only six new clippers were launched in 1854 (three of them in Donald McKay's yard). They were the last.

Many clippers, after waiting for weeks in port, were forced

into businesses they had never been designed for, just to keep them sailing. Some went into the old cotton and lumber trades. A few were put to a more sinister use: The handsome clipper *Nightingale,* which had been successful on the China and Australia passages, became a slaver. Other clippers drifted into the no less nefarious coolie trade, their holds lined with shelflike bunks, which were jammed with Chinese being taken to San Francisco, the West Indies, or the guano islands off the western coast of South America. The *Challenge* spent the next few years in this trade. On one of her voyages she reached Havana with 150 of her 900 coolies and seven of her crew near death from disease.

Some clippers that transported coolies to the guano islands also carried guano to the United States and Europe. An era that had started gloriously shipping tea and silks was ending ignominiously hauling slaves and bird droppings. Guano was the cargo of last resort. Most of it came from three of the Chinchas Islands off the coast of Peru, which were covered with hundreds of feet of dried excrement deposited over the centuries by seabirds. The Chinchas in the 1850s were enveloped in a yellow cloud stirred up by the coolies, who dug up the guano and wheeled it in barrows to long canvas chutes at the edges of the islands' rocky cliffs. The sea bottom here drops off so steeply that even a deep-draft clipper could be warped alongside to lower the sleeves of the chutes into her hatches. The yellow guano thundered into the vessel's hold, filling it in a day or two and meanwhile almost smothering everything and everyone aboard with the acrid, ammonia-scented powder.

So popular had this fertilizer become that whole fleets of ships sat an anchor off the Chinchas waiting their turn. As early as the autumn of 1853, one visitor counted half a dozen clippers among the 130 ships waiting off the islands. An American passenger described the scene as "a hell on earth," adding, "with their yards cock-billed, and rolling their royal masts almost against the face of the rock, all covered with guano, you would hardly recognize some of the finest clippers, that before they left New York or Boston were praised in the papers, visited by ladies, and, instead of guano, had their cabins perfumed by champagne."

There was a final irony in 1855. After three years of decline in demand, the U.S. shipbuilding momentum had nonetheless produced a greater tonnage (fifteen million) than ever before. New York and New England sail lofts were turning out some nine million yards of sails. Yet already New York's East River yards were nearly idle. Fewer than 6,500 tons of shipping were under construction, and there were virtually no new commissions. The *Herald* reported, "Experienced shipbuilders pronounce the depression gloom of the past year to be unparalleled." Fewer than a hundred clippers set off for California in 1856; only sixty-eight made the passage in 1857. Freight rates plunged to $10 a ton, one sixth of their peak. Dozens of American clipper ships were sold at a fraction of their original cost, mostly to foreign shipping firms to be converted into ordinary merchantmen. Many of the once-lofty clippers were rerigged with lower masts and smaller sail areas, requiring fewer crew members. Most important, of the record fifteen million American sailing vessels in 1855, a much smaller proportion were true clipper ships. They were fast being replaced by another, more conservative type of clipper.

The lean-hulled clipper ship that had evolved from the old fat-bodied merchantman a decade earlier was now evolving again, into what became known as the medium clipper. Still sharper at the bow than the normal merchant ship, the medium clipper was designed with a rounder, more capacious hull, and she carried a smaller sail area. She was the answer to the shippers' new need: a vessel capable of carrying a larger cargo at a reasonable speed and with a smaller crew. Still, many medium clippers made moderately good time, partly because of their sharp bows and partly because of their size; usually they were larger than their predecessors (which became known as "extreme" clippers),[6] and a larger sailing vessel tended to be a faster sailing vessel. Medium clippers did nearly as well as true clippers in strong winds;[7] but because of their smaller sail area, they were much slower in light airs and accordingly suffered in overall time. In 1852, for example, when some hundred true clippers sailed the San Francisco passage, nineteen made it in 110 or fewer days; in 1859, by contrast, eighty-five vessels called clippers (but mostly medium clippers) went around the Horn, only six of them in 110 days or under.

The medium clippers were in turn replaced by even larger

sailing vessels that came to be known as "down-easters" because most of them were built in Maine. Nearly a thousand
down-easters were launched during the remainder of the nineteenth century. They carried goods to California and brought
out California's new produce—at about $28 a ton, less than half
the clippers' top rates of $60.

The depression of 1857 was felt in seaports all over the
world. In the countinghouses of New York and Boston there
were bankruptcies by the hundreds. With freight rates at $10 a
ton, a shipowner could scarcely afford the necessary wages and
insurance to keep a vessel sailing. Many of New York's once-
busy shipways became ghost yards. In the meantime, the route
around Cape Horn had been eclipsed by the Panama Railroad,
which cut the fastest clippers' three-month time to three weeks.
Then came the Civil War.

Shipping merchants South and North were immediately af-
fected. Union blockaders cut off most of the trade across the
bottom of the cotton triangle; the little cotton that got to England went by blockade-runners, many of them steamers. Unable to keep their vessels in service, Northern and Southern
shipowners sold them abroad; nearly a third of America's
oceangoing merchant marine was snapped up at distress prices
by foreigners. But the coup de grâce was delivered by the Confederate raiders. Powered by steam as well as sails, half a dozen
Confederate raiders put some 150 Northern-owned vessels to
the torch, at least fourteen of them clippers. Insurance rates sky-
rocketed, and foreign shippers picked off much of the American
trade with Europe. By the end of the war, what with the sink-
ings and the panic selling, nearly every one of the few remaining American clippers had gone to foreign owners or to the
bottom of the sea.

In 1865, British shipping exceeded American tonnage once
again, by 1½ million tons. U.S. shipbuilding, which had tripled
in the two decades between 1840 and 1860, now began its long
decline. During the half century to come, while the U.S. population tripled, U.S. shipping would be reduced to a third of its
1860 tonnage. Moreover, the steamer was gradually dominating
ocean trade. The screw propeller, invented in the 1830s, had

revolutionized steamship performance with the introduction of twin screws in the 1860s, vastly increasing a steamer's speed. In America sailing ships would continue to outnumber steamers until the turn of the century. But after the Civil War the sailing ships—the down-easters and the later, even larger windjammers—emphasized carrying capacity; the steamers provided the shorter passages. Steamers, not sailing packets, were crossing the Atlantic in 10 days instead of 15. The tortoise had passed the hare.

The United States was truly no longer the seaboard, maritime-minded country it had been for two centuries, but a continental nation more preoccupied with its land to the West than with its offshore horizons. The rare record set by a medium clipper or steamer appeared in a newspaper's marine columns rather than on the front page. By 1860, rails had spider-webbed across the country for more than thirty thousand miles, probing westward as far as St. Joseph, Missouri. Finally, on May 10, 1869, at 12:20 P.M., two golden spikes were driven home at Promontory Point, Utah, and the Union Pacific and Central Pacific railroad lines were joined. Crossing the once-forbidding three thousand miles of plains and mountains, the railroads provided transportation that spurred production on the farms and in the factories as well as access to coal, iron, and oil, all of which drained off more labor from the shipyards and the ships. With the railroads came the telegraph, linking the towns and cities of the broad continent as the coastal packets and steamers had along the coasts. As Robert Waterman had predicted, the golden spikes of the transcontinental railroad also were spikes in the coffin of the clipper ship.

11

Survivors

THE *Challenge* WAS NOT DESIGNED for longevity; nor was the *Flying Cloud*. Built in a hurry, clipper ships were driven at breakneck speed through the world's most punishing seas; and the combination of radical design and driving captains brought some clippers to an early end. The *Dauntless,* small, beautifully appointed with paneled cabins and stained-glass windows and said to be the most expensive ship built before her launching in 1852, made only one round-trip voyage from Boston to San Francisco; on her second voyage she never appeared on the western side of Cape Horn. And the *Rainbow,* first of John Griffiths' radical new design, was only three years old when she also disappeared rounding Cape Horn. She had been driven mercilessly around the world four times in that short period, with scarcely time for refitting or repairs.

By the end of the clipper ship era, a quarter of these vessels were gone. The pioneer clipper, John Griffiths' *Sea Witch,* lasted only a decade. In 1855, worn and strained by ten years of racing around the world, she sailed from Amoy with a cargo of 500 coolies for Cuba. She almost made it, but struck a reef a dozen miles off the Cuban coast, bilged, and went down. Most of the coolies were rescued, but the *Sea Witch* went to the bottom.[1] A. A. Low & Bros.' *Oriental,* whose lines had been taken off by British designers after her 97-day record run from China to England, was only five years old when the port of Foochow was opened to foreign trade. The *Oriental* was one of the first clippers to navigate the crosscurrents and swirling tides of the

Min River. She made it to the Pagoda Island anchorage, but in February 1854, coasting downriver with $175,000 worth of tea crammed in her hold, she got caught in one of the Min's chow-chow currents, was swept onto the rocks, and holed; she sank in deep water offshore.

Accident more than design brought some clippers to an untimely end. Donald McKay's famous *Sovereign of the Seas* was only seven years old when she piled onto Pyramid Shoal in the Strait of Malacca. In those seven years she had made a name for herself as one of the fastest and most successful American clippers. Spontaneous combustion finished off McKay's first clipper ship, the *Stag Hound,* after eleven years, in 1861. She was en route from London to San Francisco with a cargo of coal and was off the coast of Brazil when the fire was discovered. Evidently it had been smoldering for some time, because the entire cargo erupted when a hatch was opened. Everyone went over the side, and within an hour the conflagration had enveloped the entire ship.[2] She was close enough to the coast, at Pernambuco, so that her boats reached shore next morning.

Yet considering their construction and the way they were driven, a remarkable number of American clipper ships survived to what could be called old age for such vessels. Many that lasted only to middle age probably would have been repaired and continued in service if there still had been a demand for express freight. Those that survived were rerigged, often by their new foreign purchasers, with shorter masts and less sail area to make them more economical. The famous Baltimore clipper *Ann McKim,* whose lines inspired John Griffiths to design the first true clippers, was sold by Howland & Aspinwall to a Chilean shipper who sent her on several runs from Valparaiso to San Francisco during the Gold Rush; she made one return passage in the near-record time of 47 days. By 1852, nineteen years old and worn out from innumerable voyages around the world, the *Ann McKim* finally was broken up. Another preclipper, Nat Palmer's *Houqua,* continued to race to China and back for twenty years until 1864, when she left Yokohama for New York and never arrived, presumably the victim of a typhoon. The *N. B. Palmer,* known as the "gem of the harbor" when Captain Charles Low and his wife had entertained their guests in Hong Kong Harbor, survived her grounding on Broussa Shoal in 1853, was completely overhauled in 1864, and was sold in 1873 to a Norwegian shipping firm. Not until after almost twenty years in the transatlantic trade under her new owners did the wave-battered *Palmer* succumb to the stormy North Atlantic. When she was abandoned at sea on June 10, 1892, she was forty-one years old.[3]

Many of the more famous clippers had respectably long lives. The *Neptune's Car,* her command relinquished in San Francisco by the dying Captain Joshua Patten and his plucky wife, made another voyage around Cape Horn and on to Hong Kong where, like so many others, she waited several months for a cargo of tea. She made two more round-the-world voyages; but as express cargo virtually disappeared, she was sold at auction for $40,000 in Liverpool. Under her British owners the seventeen-year-old clipper still was sailing in 1870 when she disappeared from Lloyd's register. And Donald McKay's ambitious *Great Republic,* with her smaller rig, continued to drive around the world, surviving storms and groundings, carrying everything from general merchandise to guano. In 1866 she was sold to Nova Scotian owners (for $17,000, one twentieth of her original cost), who in turn sold her two years later to a Liverpool shipping firm, which renamed her the *Denmark.* On March 2, 1872, the big clipper was pounding up the North Atlantic from Rio, bound for St. John, New Brunswick, to take on a cargo of lumber, when she ran into a hurricane-force gale, which so loosened her nineteen-year-old timbers that her hull began to fill. When the water level reached 12 feet, all hands went over the side into her boats, and McKay's once-proud masterpiece sank to the bottom off Bermuda.

The less lofty, stronger-built medium clippers set even greater records for staying power. (An exception was the *Andrew Jackson,* contender for the *Flying Cloud*'s New York to San Francisco record, which lasted only thirteen years before being wrecked on a reef in the Gaspar Straits in 1868.) The *Herald of the Morning* survived for thirty-seven years, the *Mary Whitridge* for forty-seven, the *Glory of the Seas* for fifty-four. The ancient mariners of the era were the *Dashing Wave* and the *Syren.* After two decades of sailing to California and around the world, the *Wave* started a long second career as a lumber carrier along the West Coast of the United States, in which she was the fastest of the fleet. She ran aground in the Canton River as well as in New York Harbor; she was dismasted several times but always was repaired and put back into service. She had just been surveyed and declared to be in excellent condition when a tug accidentally towed her onto the mud flats of Alaska's Seymour Narrows, where the heavy seas beat her to pieces. She was sixty-seven years old.

Evidently the Methuselah of them all was the indestructible medium clipper *Syren,* which never set any records but survived a *pampero* that stove in her starboard bow, lightning that set her afire, a Cape Horn gale that washed her deck clean of hatch covers as well as boats, a collision at sea, and grounding on Mile Rock off the Golden Gate that opened such a hole that she just made it to the beach on the harbor's mud flats. By 1888 she was leaking so much that she had to cut short her last voyage around Cape Horn, putting into Rio, where she was condemned. But an Argentine shipper repaired her, renamed her the *Margarida,* and sent her back to sea. When last reported, she was still sailing in 1920, nearing seventy and the last survivor of the American clipper ship era.[4]

The *Flying Cloud* did not match the longevity of the medium clippers, but she had a lengthy, productive life all the same. When she returned home by way of China on her maiden round-the-world voyage in the spring of 1852, she was given a triumphant reception. Her broken top-hamper was taken down and exhibited at the Astor House. Messrs. Grinnell and Minturn, her owners, had copies of her log printed in gold on white silk to be distributed to potential shipping customers. The *Cloud*'s second run to San Francisco, however, must have given Robert Waterman a wry bit of pleasure when the news reached his ranch. Her time on this passage was 115 days, a week longer than the *Challenge* had taken under Waterman. But the *Flying Cloud,* still with Creesy in command and his wife navigating, went on to make a number of fast voyages around the Horn and to China and New York. It was on her fourth run to San Francisco, in

1854, that she lowered her own record to 89 days, eight hours. It also was on the last leg of this round-the-world voyage that the *Cloud* nearly met her end.

She was 19 days out of Whampoa with a cargo of oriental merchandise—which her underwriters described as "a rich and costly cargo of delicate goods"—when in a South China Sea fog she ran onto a coral reef, going so fast that she lurched up onto the bar, rising four feet out of the water. Captain Creesy managed to kedge her off but found that she had been holed to her inner planking. Normally he should have put into the nearest port and had her careened and her planking replaced. But the thrifty Yankee captain realized that a haulout could cost $30,000; men at the pumps cost nothing. Shifting the *Cloud*'s cargo about and making what patches could be managed from inside the hold, Creesy set his course for New York. It took a gang at the pumps during every watch to keep up with the leak; but Creesy brought the *Flying Cloud* home safely, "to the great relief" of her insurers, as Walter R. Jones, president of the Board of Underwriters, attested in a complimentary letter to Creesy that accompanied the gift of a silver service—which the underwriters could well afford, considering what Creesy had saved them.

By 1863, however, the *Flying Cloud*'s years of glamor were over. Badly strained by six breakneck voyages around Cape Horn and four to China, she was sold to James Baines, who had commissioned a number of ships from Donald McKay for his Black Ball Line to Australia. Tightening her seams, Baines put the *Cloud* on his run to Brisbane. Her tall masts were cut back and she carried far less sail than when she had set her records. Yet on one voyage to Australia she reached a speed of 16 knots.

In the 1870s the tired, twenty-year-old *Flying Cloud,* now under another British owner, was put into the transatlantic lumber trade. In 1874, leaving St. John, New Brunswick, with a cargo of timber, she ran into a North Atlantic gale, turned back for port, and bumped onto a bar off Beacon Island. Lighters managed to take off her lumber, but the seas pounding against the bar cracked her hull. She was pumped out and towed ashore for repairs. But in June 1875 she caught fire. Within hours all that remained of the most famous American clipper ship were her copper plates and metal fastenings, which were sold for scrap.[5]

The *Challenge*

The *Challenge* outlived the *Flying Cloud* by a year. Although she made some fast passages from China to England and across the Pacific to California and South America, the *Challenge* never bettered her maiden 108-day run around Cape Horn under Waterman; her next best passage was 114 days. Her last voyage as an American clipper was in 1859, when she sailed from San Francisco for Hong Kong; she was nearing Formosa when a typhoon carried away all her masts. Captain Samuel Fabens managed to jury-rig enough sail to limp into Hong Kong, where the *Challenge* was laid up and neglected until late 1860, when she was sold for one fifteenth of her original cost. A year later she was sold again, to the British shipping firm of Thomas Hunt, which renamed her *Golden City* and put her into the China–India trade.

In 1866 another British shipper, Captain Joseph Wilson, was inspecting a ship at London's East India Dock. He found her tied up alongside another vessel named *Golden City*. "I passed over the deck of this ship," he later recalled, "and observed what a magnificent main deck she had. I was informed by the ship-keeper that she had to be sold by auction. This man had been employed on my own ships and knew me, showed me all over her." Wilson inquired of the *Golden City*'s owners. "All the information I got was 'confounded pick-pocket,' 'weak,' and 'won't sail.' One man said he 'wouldn't be paid to own her.' " Nonetheless, Wilson bought her and had her towed to his own wharf for repairs. "A lot of blocks and other things," he wrote, "were found on overhauling her with the name *Challenge* on them. I looked up Lloyd's and found that the ship had been classed in the book, and after some little bother got all unravelled and proved that this was the same old American clipper *Challenge*."

As it turned out, Wilson was little more pleased than her former owners. "She made very good passages," he wrote, "but in general was not, with me, the very fast ship she had been originally." Part of the reason was her rigging, which Wilson had lowered; without her original sail plan the former *Challenge* was out of trim. But Wilson also had a major complaint that is intriguing in retrospect. "The principal error," he wrote, "was a hollow waterline . . . a sea of three feet was always curling up between the stem and the fore rigging when going fast, and in ballast especially this effectually stopped her from being the very fastest vessel afloat." Wilson claimed that this sidewash was so great that it once swamped a small boat coming along-side when the clipper was going only seven knots. There is no evidence of Waterman or Land, who succeeded him, comment-ing on this drag effect. Waterman did not sail her in ballast, but neither he nor Land was known to complain that the *Challenge*'s bow was too concave. It would have been interesting to hear William Webb's reaction to Captain Wilson's complaint, but apparently the question never was put to him.

Captain Wilson also claimed that the former *Challenge* "rolled with a heavy cargo, but on the whole did her work well." Bad luck continued to dog her, however. On a voyage to Java she smashed into a heavy sea, at 12 knots, that carried away her wheel and the officers' deckhouse, drowning her captain and all of her officers except the third mate (Wilson's nephew), who was crushed by the wreckage but survived. Seven men on deck also were washed overboard; one man at the helm saved him-self by scampering 15 feet up the mizzen rigging. Still the ex-*Challenge* survived and made it to port.

Her last voyage was in 1876, when she was a quarter cen-tury old. Her rudder was wrenched loose off the French coast and she grounded on an island off Ushant. As Wilson described her end, "The crew left her and a French gun-boat got hold of her, and a lot of wooden-shoed and wooden-headed fishermen, and instead of towing the ship stern foremost, took her by the bow, when she took a shear and went on a reef of rocks." The heavy North Atlantic surf rolled her over on her side and pounded her hull to bits. The remains of William Webb's sharpest clipper still lie on the bottom off the western coast of France.[6]

Most of the designers and builders, the shippers and skip-pers outlived the era they had created. John W. Griffiths, the designer of the first clipper ship, continued to write and pro-mote his theories. In 1853 he published his two-volume *Ship-builder's Manual and Nautical Referee*. As editor of *American Ship*[7] he reiterated his arguments for a scientific, engineering ap-proach to shipbuilding instead of the older whittle-the-model method. He continued to delight in attacking conservative designers and shipbuilders, and he put his principles into practice even when he turned to steam. The sharp-bowed steamships he designed in the 1850s were faster than most of their competitors. A man of many talents, Griffiths also produced modern, more effective watertight bulkheads and bilge keels—indeed, everything from a revolutionary new rivet to a triple-screw propeller. He even experimented with a steam-driven lifeboat. Griffiths continued to believe in the superiority of wood over iron for a ship's hull, and in 1870 he perfected a machine to bend the timbers for the hull, thereby saving shipbuilders thousands of man-hours of labor. He was still preaching the gospel of the wooden hull when he died in his Brooklyn home in March 1882.

William H. Webb, builder of the *Challenge,* foresaw the end of the clipper era before most shipbuilders. As early as 1853, while others still were plunging ahead with clipper orders, Webb launched his last clipper, the *Young America,* and converted most of his yard for steamships, while continuing to build some of the fastest transatlantic packets. Within four years Webb had stolen the lead from most of his competitors and had won a government contract for the first steam-powered U.S. revenue vessel.[8] During the Civil War the Union Navy commissioned Webb to build a 7,200-ton ironclad, the *Dunderberg,* the largest of its kind and the fastest, capable of 15 knots despite her heavy armament of 22 large-caliber guns. But the Civil War was over before the *Dunderberg* could be launched, and Webb finally sold her to the French Navy. (The French renamed her the *Rochambeau.*)

By now Webb was one of America's premier builders of steamships, including huge sidewheelers for the transatlantic trade as well as for the passages to the Isthmus and a couple of "floating palaces" that traveled up and down Long Island Sound in the 1860s and 1870s. He continued to build sailing packets; his was the yard that launched in 1869 the last full square-rigged vessel constructed in New York. (She was named the *Charles Marshall,* after the famous captain and owner of the Black Ball Line of transatlantic packets.) Three years later, at fifty-six, Webb retired.

He had been more than a shipbuilder, with financial investments in shipping firms and directorships in a number of U.S. corporations. Three times he had declined formal offers to run for mayor of New York City. He settled down in his mansion, Waldheim, in Tarrytown on the Hudson and devoted the rest of his life to charitable uses of his wealth, mainly in the endowment and construction on thirteen acres in the Bronx of the Webb Academy and Home for Shipbuilders and their families who had been less fortunate than he. Webb died at eighty-three, on October 30, 1899, having seen much of the world's shipping change from sail to steam. His academy, which taught the principles of shipbuilding, survives today, transplanted to Glen Cove, L.I., as the prestigious Webb Institute of Naval Architecture.

William Webb's famous competitor Donald McKay also prospered, but only so long as the clipper era continued. There is a somewhat sentimental legend that the burning of the *Great Republic* was a blow, financial and psychological, from which Donald McKay never recovered. The fact was that insurance covered much of the *Great Republic*'s original cost. And as for the psychological effect, his grandson describes McKay's reaction at the time. On the night of the fire he received the news by telegraph. "He walked the floor until daylight," his grandson recalls, "the telegram in his hand, saying nothing and could not be consoled by his wife or any member of the family." McKay went to New York next day and watched his ambitious clipper ship burn to the water's edge. He promptly returned to Boston, and next day was in his shipyard supervising the finishing touches on the *Lightning,* which was launched a week later. "He was determined not to be idle," his grandson pointed out, "despite the calamity which had befallen him." During the next year alone Donald McKay's East Boston yard launched eight ships and one schooner for a total tonnage of 17,000, the highest rate of production in McKay's career.

After each launching a large party of Boston's elite gathered in McKay's balustraded house on the hill above the shipyard for toasts to the new vessel and an evening of dining and music. Sometimes McKay played his violin; other family members played the piano in the main parlor. Guests on such occasions after 1853 did not consider their host much changed from the years before the fire. The loss of the *Great Republic* did not defeat Donald McKay. What defeated him was the clipper ship itself.

While his competitor William Webb had seen it coming, McKay had refused to accept the end of the clipper ship era. His delusion was abetted by the Australian Gold Rush and by the British shipper James Baines, who commissioned four clippers for his Australian line.[9] Then, as both Australia's and California's demands slackened, came hard times for the McKay yard, made harder because he had stubbornly stuck to his specialty, the clipper ship. By risking his own finances, he managed to keep his shipyard open; usually he maintained hundreds of men on the payroll even when there was nothing for them to do. During 1855, fewer than three thousand tons of shipping were produced in the McKay yard; in 1856 only two medium clippers came down the ways. By 1857, with all the United States in the throes of depression, McKay was at last forced to close his shipyard and lay off his workers. It was estimated at the time that in the dozen years since 1845 he had provided employment for thousands of workmen and infused $7 million into the Massachusetts economy.

McKay was forty-seven. He had no intention of retiring, and in fact he could not afford to retire. A large number of McKays depended on him. His father and mother and most of the rest of his family had come from Nova Scotia to East Boston. Besides Captain Lauchlan McKay, four other brothers—David, John, Hugh, and Nathaniel—had been working in his shipyard. And by now McKay had fifteen children. In 1859 he negotiated a contract to supply New England timber to British shipbuilders, and he went to Europe to drum up more business. Despite his worldwide reputation, he took the precaution of soliciting letters of introduction from Americans with friends in Europe. The one from Matthew Maury to a high-placed Danish acquaintance is typical and not a little poignant:

My Dear Sir,
　　The ships which of late years have won most renown by their performances at sea were built by Mr.

McKay, whom I have the pleasure of introducing to you. He is a famous shipbuilder, and for the purpose of seeking an opportunity still further to display his professional skill, he proposes a visit to Denmark. To that end, I commend him to your favorable consideration.

Respectfully &c

M. F. Maury

But McKay's hat-in-hand tour of Europe produced no new commissions. He decided to attempt a book on naval architecture, devoting some of his time abroad to composing an outline with the ambitious working title of *Prospectus of an Intended Work on the Theory & Practice of Naval Architecture Particularly Illustrating American Ship Building*. The scope of the book was equally promising, including sixty large plates illustrating McKay's ships, with their dimensions and details of their construction. After his return home, the drawings were completed, and McKay wrote the manuscript. But the work never found a publisher.[10]

The major result of McKay's European trip was a change of heart, a belated acceptance of the new age of steam and iron. He returned home arguing that the U.S. Navy should prepare for the inevitable Southern rebellion by modernizing its fleet with ironclad ships like those he had seen in Europe. Simultaneously he reopened his East Boston shipyard and began to convert it to build iron steamships and marine engines. But the Union Navy did not have sufficient funds, so again McKay invested his own financial resources, this time in four modern men-of-war. In 1864 he received contracts for these vessels. But because the Navy insisted on so many alterations during their construction, none was finished in time for extended duty. Adding up his expenses, McKay found that he had been drastically underpaid. At war's end he submitted a bill for his overruns, meanwhile plunging into peacetime work to keep his yard open and his workers employed. He even turned to locomotives, building several for the New England and midwestern railroads that were taking business away from his ships. Again he invested his own money, this time in the medium clipper ship *Glory of the Seas,* a roomy 2,100-tonner launched in November 1869. On her maiden voyage she took 120 days to reach San Francisco from New York, excellent time for a medium clipper. But the call for faster vessels had long since ceased, and the *Glory of the Seas* could command little more than $10 a ton. She did not even finish her maiden round-the-world voyage before McKay was forced to sell her at a sacrifice.[11] The *Glory of the Seas* was his last merchant vessel.

By now his debts amounted to a quarter of a million dollars, and his creditors were closing in on him. At last he was forced to sell his shipyard. For a few more years he built ships on commission, mostly in other yards. His roster of successful ships[12] reads like an honor roll of the clipper era: *Stag Hound, Flying Cloud, Sovereign of the Seas, James Baines Great Republic, Romance of the Seas, Lightning, Champion of the Seas, Glory of the Seas.* Yet unlike his chief competitor William Webb, Donald McKay was virtually impoverished, mainly because of an enduring faith in the clipper ship, which he had backed with his own finances. At sixty-five, suffering from incipient tuberculosis, he moved his family to a farm in Hamilton, Mass., where he attempted to apply modern scientific methods to agriculture. He worked so hard, according to his grandson, that frequently "he dropped down in the fields from sheer exhaustion." His tuberculosis grew worse. In July 1880 he became paralyzed, and on September 20, two weeks after his seventy-first birthday, he died.[13]

He was buried in Oak Hill Cemetery in Newburyport, Mass. Not until the turn of the century did the U.S. Court of Claims rule that the government must settle McKay's overruns on the warships he had built during the Civil War. The settlement came to $300,000, nearly all of which went to the lawyers who had argued McKay's case. There was little left for his widow[14] and children. Donald's youngest brother, Nathaniel, who had spent nearly a dozen years pressing his brother's claim, was the only gainer. In the process he made so many influential friends that he became one of Washington's wealthiest lobbyists.

During the Civil War one of the chief benefactors of the clipper ships was devoting his energies to destroying them. Matthew Fontaine Maury had been born in Virginia and considered himself a Southerner. When in April 1861 Virginia seceded, Maury sent his resignation to President Abraham Lincoln, packed up his family, and moved to Fredericksburg, Va. While he recognized the animosity that had built up between North and South, he was not prepared for the vindictiveness that his resignation stirred north of the Potomac. A few years earlier he had written the first popular book on oceanography, *The Physical Geography of the Sea,* which had become a best seller [15] and had been translated into five different languages. Its sales suddenly dwindled to almost none. The Union government even withdrew his *Wind and Current Charts* and *Sailing Directions,* claiming that they "embrace much which is unsound in philosophy and little that is practically useful." The beneficiaries of Maury's publications, the clipper ship owners and captains, turned against him. A. A. Low & Bros. had named one of their vessels the *Maury* in his honor; its named was changed (evidently with unintentional irony) to *Benefactress.* The Union regarded those Southerners who had resigned their commissions as deserters. A month after Maury had settled in Virginia, he received a copy of the *Boston Evening Traveler* with a page one headline offering a $3,000 reward for the "Head of the Traitor, Lieut. Maury."

Commissioned as a commander in the Confederate Navy, Maury first worked on improving electric torpedoes for use against Union blockaders. In the summer of 1862 he ran the blockade off Charleston, S.C., to Bermuda, Halifax, and Liverpool to join Captain James Bulloch, the Confederate Secret Service chief in England. For the next three years Maury helped Bulloch search out likely British ships to serve as Confederate raiders to sink the same merchantmen and clipper ships whose captains Maury had aided with his *Wind and Current Charts.* In May 1865, Maury completed his tour of duty and set out for home. When his steamer put into Havana for refueling, he was greeted with the news that the Civil War was over.

He also learned that President Lincoln had declared an amnesty that specifically excluded "military or naval officers of the so-called Confederate government," and especially "all those who resigned commissions in the army or navy . . . and afterwards aided the rebellion." Unwilling to risk the noose, Maury booked passage to Mexico. There he attempted to persuade Emperor Maximilian to launch a colonization scheme in which planters from the Southern states could move to Mexico, bringing their newly freed slaves with them as "apprentices." But the plan attracted few Southerners. Maury was a man without a country. He returned to England, sending word to his family to join him there. He opened a torpedo-training school for British naval officers, but it failed. Napoleon III, long an admirer of Maury, offered him a position in France's Meteorological Institute; but because he would have to become a French citizen, Maury declined. A New York publisher took a chance and commissioned him to write a series of geography books for young readers, but they sold poorly because few Northerners would buy a book by a Southern traitor. Maury was on the verge of poverty when in 1867 President Andrew Jackson declared a blanket amnesty and the Virginia Military Institute asked Maury to join its faculty as a professor of physics. By now rheumatism had begun to afflict his crippled knee, forcing him back on crutches. He was still a pariah in the North, and postwar navigators still were denied his *Wind and Current Charts*.[16] But in his declining years he could take some satisfaction in his enduring accomplishments. His example had stimulated captains in nearly a dozen countries to exchange logbook information. The U.S. Naval Academy that he had advocated had been established in 1845 (though the only recognition of his contribution is a Maury Wing in the main building). He had been honored by nearly fifty learned societies and had received medals from half a dozen countries. The transatlantic cable that he and Cyrus Field had persisted in laying despite innumerable difficulties had finally gone into operation in 1866. A pet project remained: a national weather bureau, for which he continued to campaign. While traveling about the South lecturing on the subject, he was taken ill and collapsed in Fredericksburg, not far from where he had been born sixty-seven years earlier. He was brought home to Lexington, where he died on February 1, 1873, unremarked and virtually ignored by the captains and navigators for whom he had helped make the clipper ship era possible.

Considering their dangerous occupation, a remarkably large number of captains survived the clipper era. Captain Philip Dumaresq, who had set an early record to San Francisco with the *Surprise,* tried retirement in Maine. But when his wife and daughter died, he decided to go back to sea, taking command of the medium clipper *Florence* in 1856. He was sixty and still active when he took a steamer from Boston to New York, presumably for a new command. On this brief voyage Philip Dumaresq, who had gone to sea to improve his frail health and had become one of the hardiest clipper captains, fell overboard and drowned. Captain Lauchlan McKay was lured to England by the command of the British ship *Nagasaki*. But instead of taking part in the British clipper ship era, he returned to the United States and formed a shipping company with another captain, Charles B. Dix. Lauchlan McKay did not retire until 1893, when he settled down with his niece and nephew, and died two years later.

Captain Nathaniel Palmer seemed busier in what he called retirement than during his years in the cotton and tea trades.[17] He continued as a consultant to A. A. Low & Bros., meanwhile spending most of his summers racing, buying, and selling yachts; in all he owned fifteen of them, some of which he designed himself. He was one of the founders of the New York Yacht Club. Winters he spent duck hunting along Long Island Sound. He and his wife had no children; and when she died in 1872, Captain Nat turned most of his attention to his nephew and namesake, his brother Alexander's son. Young Nat was a frail child and was found to have tuberculosis. There was still no medical cure for this disease, but Captain Nat decided that the best treatment was an ocean voyage. In 1876 the two sailed to China; but young Nat grew worse. He died one day out of San Francisco on the return passage. Captain Nat arranged for his body to be shipped home, went to a hotel room, and died himself. He was seventy-eight. His body, too, was shipped East, to be buried in Stonington.

Captain Charles Low also kept going to sea, now without his wife, Sarah, who was too busy with growing children. "I am so infatuated with this exciting life," he wrote Sarah from China, "I do not know how I can ever give it up." But by 1863, with Rebel steamers cruising the world looking for Northern-owned ships to seize and burn, A. A. Low & Bros. decided to intern their valuable clipper *N. B. Palmer* in China for the duration.[18] Captain Low tried his hand as a merchant;

but his store failed in the business panic of 1867–68 and he eagerly went back to sea, resuming the *N. B. Palmer*'s quarterdeck on five round-trip passages to China. But cargoes were becoming scarcer every year, and A. A. Low & Bros. finally made the reluctant decision to sell the twenty-one-year-old *N. B. Palmer*. Captain Low admitted that, "as I was tired of being away from my family ten months or a year and at home only some six weeks, I gave up the sea." He persuaded Sarah to go West, and they settled down for his retirement on a hill back of Santa Barbara, Calif., where Captain Low could look out across the Pacific he had crossed so many times. Hearty and toughened by all those years on the quarterdeck, he lived until 1913, and died at eighty-nine.

Captain Josiah Perkins Creesy had the mixed satisfaction of reading his own obituary when in 1852 a rumor spread that he had died aboard the *Flying Cloud* in the Pacific en route to China. In fact, after taking on a cargo of tea, Creesy was heading home when in the Indian Ocean he spoke a merchantman bound for China. Exchanging some fresh provisions for the latest newspapers, he was amused to read: "Captain Creesy of the ship *Flying Cloud* . . . this gallant sailor is no more." The obituary praised Creesy for being "distinguished for the rapidity of his passages" and mentioned that the *Cloud*'s record-breaking maiden voyage to San Francisco "eclipsed the finest and most costly merchant ship in the world," i.e., the *Challenge*. "But now he rests from his toils." Those who knew Creesy well suspected that he had planted the rumor himself, because the mistaken obituary resulted in sparing him a court trial. The mate he had suspended on the *Flying Cloud*'s maiden voyage had found a lawyer and was preparing to sue Creesy; but on reading the obituary the mate shipped out on another vessel and was at sea when his former captain returned.

Age did not mellow or slow Captain Creesy. In 1853, still in command of the *Flying Cloud,* this time racing around the Horn against the clipper *Hornet,* Creesy made the mistake of running too far westward in the Pacific in search of better winds. He encountered one gale that washed the first mate and a foremast hand off the deck to their deaths. But steady winds failed, and the *Flying Cloud* lost her lead. She arrived off the Golden Gate to find the *Hornet* waiting for her tug.[19] Creesy was so angry that he refused to send the abstract log for the last leg of his passage to Matthew Maury, submitting only the section for the voyage to Cape Horn.

Creesy stayed with the *Flying Cloud* for five voyages. As she was being loaded for her sixth, in 1856, he warned her owners, Grinnell, Minturn & Co., that she needed a thorough overhaul. They refused. Creesy decided to retire.[20] He and his navigator wife went home to Salem, Mass., but they were lured back to duty the following year. During a three-month wait for a new cargo, the *Flying Cloud* had had her overhaul in San Francisco, and Grinnell, Minturn asked Creesy to bring her home— which he did in only 91 days.

His second retirement lasted until the Civil War. He volunteered, was appointed an acting lieutenant in August 1861, and was given command of the ten-year-old clipper ship *Ino,* almost half the size of the *Flying Cloud* but a fast little vessel even with her wartime armaments. On his second cruise Creesy went looking for the confederate raider *Sumter,* taking the *Ino* from Boston to Cadiz, Spain, in 12 days, a record. But Creesy characteristically chafed under the rank-consciousness of the Navy. During his search for the *Sumter* he found and arrested two Confederate sailors in Tangier. Ordered by his superior, Commander Craven of the *Tuscarora,* to release his prisoners, the crusty clipper captain replied, "I positively decline to give these men up," and sailed off with them. Commander Craven filed charges against Creesy for "contemptuous disregard" of orders, and Creesy was discharged from the Navy. But he had not had enough of the sea. He took command of the clipper ship *Archer,* which he had beaten on his record Cape Horn voyage in 1854 by 17 days. Creesy took the *Archer* to China twice, finally retiring permanently to Salem. When he died in 1871, he was only fifty-seven.

Robert Waterman was one of the few captains who retired before the clipper ship era ended. Indeed, had he stuck by his initial decision to retire in 1850, he could have avoided the humiliation of the lynch mob and trial for murder.[21] The rich grassland of the Suisun Valley where he now settled down, some fifty miles northeast of San Francisco Bay, bore the promise of a successful farm. The land also lies along the Sacramento River, then a highway for waterborne transport from San Francisco to the gold fields, which were being transformed into huge commercial mines employing thousands of men. Settlers were pouring into the county, and Waterman and Ritchie foresaw a growing demand not only for their produce but eventually for their land as well.

Waterman selected a site alongside a brook and built a house and barn.[22] Off on the horizon the rolling hills of grass resembled the mountainous seas of the Great Southern Ocean. Waterman planted his ranch with hundreds of trees, mostly Smyrna fig, white oak, and black walnut. He seeded the long drive to his house with imported eucalyptus; the tall, spreading trees that grew from the seeds shaded the drive and remain today. The main ranch house was spacious and comfortable, with tall ceilings, imported marble fireplace mantels, and a covered porch from which Waterman could look out on his crops and his pasturelands of cattle and horses. Waterman surrounded the barn, the house, and the cookhouse (separated from the ranch house as a fire hazard) with smaller trees and shrubs, the prize being a rare white Lemark rosebush, which he planted in front of the porch; every year it produced more white flowers, as it continues to do after nearly a century and a half.

Waterman and Ritchie had guessed correctly. Their vegetables and beef brought healthy profits from the start. Waterman soon was able to donate funds to help build a new Methodist church, and when a larger church was needed for the expanding population, he raised much of the necessary money from his neighbors. Clearly he enjoyed playing the role of the local patron. He employed dozens of ranch hands plus a foreman and a young black manservant named Fred Fann, whom he called his "cabin boy"; Waterman's idea of harmless fun was to terrorize Fred by peppering the ground at his heels with a .44 rifle and watching Fred run for cover. Waterman had a favorite horse named Brownie and a favorite spaniel named Spanker. He enjoyed entertaining other sea captains who came to visit the ranch; afternoons and evenings were spent reminiscing in an upstairs room that Waterman furnished to resemble the captain's cabin of the *Sea Witch*—not, significantly, the *Challenge*.[23]

In January 1853 Waterman's partner, Archibald Ritchie, was killed when a herd of deer spooked the horses drawing his wagon. Waterman assumed management of the entire compound and in succeeding years sold off most of the land. Working with surveyors, he laid out a small city that he named Fairfield, after his boyhood hometown in Connecticut. In a local plebiscite in 1858, engineered largely by Waterman's lobbying of the California legislature, Fairfield was chosen as the Solano County seat. Waterman saw to that by promising to donate a sixteen-acre parcel of land for the county courthouse and jail on condition that Fairfield win the election, which it did by 1,730 votes to 625 for nearby Benicia. Waterman celebrated by donating $10,000 toward the cost of the new county buildings; and the central structure became locally known as the "Waterman courthouse."

It was a shrewd investment, enhancing the value of Fairfield's plots and assuring a fortune for Waterman and Ritchie's widow. Besides the fast-growing city of Fairfield, Waterman laid out the plots for a smaller town, to be called Bridgeport; after some cajoling by his wife he renamed it Cordelia. By 1862 Waterman had sold most of the entire area of twelve square miles; he kept two hundred acres for his ranch.

The 1850s and 1860s were a particularly busy period of Waterman's life. The Civil War, virtually a continent away, had little impact on his activities in the Suisun Valley. Besides managing his ranch and surveying and selling plots in Fairfield and Cordelia, he was commuting regularly down the Sacramento River to San Francisco, where he served as the acting West Coast agent for Howland & Aspinwall. He also joined a consortium to develop a steamer line on the Sacramento; he and his colleagues sold the line at a profit. And for nearly two decades he served as San Francisco's Port Warden and Inspector of Hulls. Gone were the days when he was a pariah along the waterfront; instead he had become one of San Francisco's respected businessmen. Seaman E. A. Wheeler, whose letter home had figured in the *Challenge* trials, ran across his former captain in 1855; already, Wheeler reported, Waterman was "about the most popular man on the city front."[24]

With a sharp eye for a profitable deal, Waterman moved quickly onto the scene when in 1854 the new clipper ship *San*

Francisco became a casualty of the strong tides through the Golden Gate. Wreckers swarmed to the scene and were looting the *San Francisco* when a sudden storm swamped their boats and drowned a dozen of them. Waterman promptly called on the *San Francisco*'s agents and bought the salvage rights to the clipper and her cargo, insured for $518,000, at the distress price of $12,000. He hired a salvage crew but could remove only $20,000 worth before the *San Francisco* was broken up by the pounding surf.

A photograph taken when Waterman was sixty-seven, shows an aged man. His hair has turned white and receded, leaving a bald pate. He is still stiffly erect, but his figure is gaunt, his clothes hang loosely on him, and he has a pure-white beard. By now he had relinquished his duties as port warden and shipping agent. The transcontinental railroad, as he had predicted two decades earlier, had displaced not only the clipper ship but also most of the general cargo and passenger traffic around Cape Horn. Only the down-easters regularly sailed out of San Francisco Bay, mostly with the fruit and vegetable produce that was California's major export.

It was in his ranch house, on August 8, 1884, that Waterman died, at seventy-six, of peritonitis, an intestinal infection usually following a burst appendix.[25] His funeral was at the Methodist church that he had helped build in Fairfield, and Cordelia had him buried temporarily in the Pioneer Cemetery in San Francisco until she could return to Bridgeport, Conn., and purchase a cemetery plot for both of them.

The news reached New York by telegraph within the week. Captain Waterman had not been entirely forgotten in the city that had lionized him forty years earlier. But few remembered the *Challenge*. In its obituary, *The New York Times* confused Waterman's last clipper with the *Sea Witch*, referring to him as "commander of the *Challenge*, one of the East India merchant vessels which, under his command made the fastest record of any clipper ship then running, and which records have never been surpassed." A *Times* reporter went out to Sailor's Snug Harbor on Staten Island asking for anyone who remembered Captain Waterman. Of the eight hundred sailors living out their retirement at this haven, the reporter claimed to find two or three who had served under him; they still called him "Bully Waterman" and gave him this epitaph:

Yes, hard a man as he was on shipboard, people who knew Captain Waterman on shore and came in frequent contact with him, declare that he was sound and good at heart. At sea he had no mercy. On shore he was among the first to contribute to the relief of a poor sailor's widow. Once out of sight of land, however, he knew no such sentiment as pity. Sick or well, a man must be at his post. Painful punishment awaited the sailor who failed in even the least of his duties. He paid his men well and fed them well, and in return he expected—and demanded—of them, constant, grinding toil. It was measure for measure all the way.

Cordelia Waterman returned east the following year. She sold the Sterling homestead in Bridgeport and some other real estate left to her by her parents. She bought a lot in the Grove Cemetery and wrote to her nephew in California, Robert Sterling, asking him to send her husband's coffin to Bridgeport. Suddenly taken ill, she died, at seventy-three, on November 29, 1885. She was buried in the new cemetery plot and was joined by her husband a year later. Captain Waterman was accompanied on his last journey home by his nephew. He came by train.

Chapter Notes

1. A few maritime historians have contested the claim that the clipper ship was the ultimate refinement of the sailing vessel. Howard I. Chapelle, for example, argued (in *The History of American Sailing Ships*): "The clipper-ship was not the highest development of the sailing-ship design because of the emphasis placed on speed at the expense of cargo capacity and low operating costs." It is true that the bulkier, slower-sailing ships before, during, and after the clipper ship period carried more cargo at lower rates. But what made the clipper the finest example of the sailing ship, in the opinion of its many advocates, was its combination of speed and beauty, an ability to race around the world faster than had ever been thought possible for a sailing vessel, plus a streamlined hull surmounted by white clouds of canvas. The sight of a clipper ship under full sail was an unforgettable spectacle, in part accounting for the glamour that was somewhat resented by those who favored the practical, plodding sailing vessels left in the clipper's wake. Essentially it was a contrast similar to that between the racing thoroughbred and the more practical truck horse.

2. The name evidently derived from the verb "to clip," or move swiftly, as when one "clips along." The word "clipper' was used in America as early as 1815, sometimes in reference to a fast schooner as a "clipper schooner," before the designation of the "Baltimore clipper." Only with the first of the real clipper ships did the term become accepted to define this special type of vessel.

3. The opening of the American West became a subject of fascination in the Old World as well as the New. Thomas Carlyle wrote to his New England friend Ralph Waldo Emerson, "How beautiful to

think of lean tough Yankee settlers, tough as gutta-percha, with most *occult* unsubduable fire in their belly, steering over the Western Mountains to annihilate the jungle, bring the bacon and corn out of it for the Posterity of Adam—There is no *Myth* of Athens or Herakles to equal this *fact*."

4. "We are the nation of human progress," O'Sullivan wrote in his newspaper, "and who will, what can, set limits to our onward march?" This march westward, O'Sullivan proclaimed, was "by right of our manifest destiny to overspread and to possess the whole of the continent which Providence has given us for the great experiment of liberty."

5. The area had attracted Americans' attention and cupidity ever since John Jacob Astor and other merchant shippers had found the skins of its sea otters a valuable commodity in trade with China. Ownership of the area was in dispute, the United States maintaining that an American, Robert Gray, had laid claim to the land along the Columbia River when he had first sailed up the river in 1792, and that Astor's American Fur Company had founded Astoria, the first permanent settlement. A treaty after the War of 1812 had provided for ten years of joint British-American rights to the Columbia River basin. But by the 1840s American settlers were pouring over the Oregon Trail into the area. Conflicts arose between British and American settlers until another war with Britain was threatened (with the famous battle cry "Fifty-four forty or fight!" advocating a British retreat to latitude 54°40′N). The Oregon Territory created by the Oregon Treaty with Britain in 1848 gave the United States the area extending from 42°N latitude to 49°N. The northern part of the area became Washington Territory in 1853. Oregon became a state in 1859. Washington did not become a state until 1889.

6. Mexico's military dictator Antonio López de Santa Anna attempted to prevent Texas's secession, winning the famous battle at the Alamo but later being lured by the Texans' wily strategist Sam Houston into a trap in which the Texans attacked the Mexicans during their afternoon siesta, captured Santa Anna, and forced him to agree to Texas's independence. By 1836 the United States had annexed Texas, and by 1846 the United States was at war with Mexico; two years later, in the treaty of Guadalupe Hidalgo, Mexico gave up what now are the states of New Mexico, Arizona, and California.

7. It would until the general use of the screw propeller a quarter of a century later.

8. Another reason was that the shipowners who were so ready to wager fortunes on new clippers refused to increase the $10-a-month wages of the crews to man them.

Chapter Notes

1. A small sloop, the 55-ton *Harriet* out of Boston, had sailed for China even earlier than the *Empress,* in 1873. When she encountered some British East Indiamen in Cape Town, the British, fearful of Yankee competition in China, promptly bought the *Harriet's* cargo, paying double its value in Hyson tea that they were bringing to London. The *Harriet* returned home with a tidy profit but without the distinction of being the first American vessel to trade in China. (Her owner claimed that he had planned to sell his cargo in Cape Town all along.)

2. Actually the term "Baltimore clipper" was a partial misnomer. Most of them were built in the Baltimore area, but they were mainly two-masted schooners with fore-and-aft sails or square-rigged brigs. A nineteenth-century fore-and-aft sail was just that: rigged to the mast, supported by a gaff at the top and a boom at the foot, and swinging on a fore-and-aft axis. A square sail was not necessarily square; it was suspended from a yardarm that was set squarely across the mast. Only a three-masted, square-rigged vessel was entitled to be called a ship. All the later clippers were ships.

3. Howard I. Chapelle wryly comments (in *The History of American Sailing Ships*): "It was perhaps fortunate for American designers that there were so many illegal trades being carried out during the years between 1815 and 1845, for it is possible that the fast models of privateer type would otherwise have been quickly forgotten. The fad for fast vessels, that came from the interest in the slaver and pilot-boat type rather than solely from trade requirements, had much influence on the development of the big clipper-ships of the late 40's and early 50's." The pilot boats that raced one another out to meet incoming ships also copied some of the lines of the Baltimore clipper.

4. Beaufoy's beer vat experiments evidently were not the first. There is a manuscript in Cambridge's Pepysian Library in which one Samuel Fortree reports on tests with ship models indicating that a sharp bow and long hull add to a ship's speed. Nor were Beaufoy's findings published until after his death, when his son had them privately printed and sent copies to a number of universities in Europe and America. Apparently it was through a review of the book in a scientific journal that Beaufoy's experiments came to Griffiths' attention.

5. It was true that the sharp bow had proved itself in the pilot boat; but the pilot boat was designed for relatively calm waters, not for the crashing waves of the open ocean.

6. A "knot" is the nautical equivalent of "miles per hour." ("Knots per hour" is a redundancy.) A nautical mile is 6,080 feet, 800 feet longer than a statute mile.

7. Edward K. Collins was a bantam rooster of a man who wore a tall top hat to make up for his short stature. A Cape Codder and the son and nephew of ship captains, Collins had seen service at sea himself, shipping out to the West Indies in his teens; he had survived pirate attacks and two shipwrecks. Now a successful shipowner, he was mercurial, impulsive, and a born gambler. Three years younger than Palmer, he had a high regard for Captain Nat, and he had been impressed by the *Huntsville*'s performance under Palmer's command. So he commissioned four new flat-floored ships for the transatlantic run.

If speed was important in the China trade, it was essential on the North Atlantic. It had been for more than two decades, ever since four New York shipping rivals had joined to launch the Black Ball Line in 1818, promising the first regularly scheduled passages across the Atlantic. Not only did the Black Ballers keep to their schedules, they also cut the usual month to month-and-a-half crossings down to an average of twenty-four days eastward and forty days "uphill" against the Atlantic's westerlies and the Gulf Stream on the return crossing. Shortly two more American packet firms, the Red Star and the Swallowtail Lines, joined in the competition on what became known as "The Railroad Route to Europe." There was plenty of business for all of these vessels. The opening of the Erie Canal in 1825 had helped make New York the major shipping port for most of the inland farms' produce. The transatlantic packets also provided the best possible training for some of the most skillful clipper captains-to-be, including Robert Waterman as well as Nathaniel Palmer. The packets, driven hard by such skippers, enjoyed premium rates for cargoes and for thousands of passengers who appreciated their speed and their dependable schedules. A packet ship that had cost $35,000 to build could pay for itself in three voyages.

8. At least that is the story Captain Nat used to tell. Howard I. Chapelle warns (in *The Search for Speed Under Sail*): "Allegedly [this ship] was modelled by Captain Nathaniel Palmer, but his claim should be accepted only with reservations." In any case, Palmer was a prime mover in the Lows' decision. He also later claimed that the completed vessel was somewhat larger than he had intended.

9. To this day marine architects cannot explain hydrographically why the U-hull should be as fast as the V-hull. One explanation might be connected to Mark Beaufoy's tank test indications that the longer

shape moves faster through the water. Collins' U-shaped transatlantic packets were lengthier than most of their competitors. And perhaps as larger and longer clipper ships were built, the distinction between the V and the U became less significant.

10. Her ratio of length to width was 5.14 to 1; the *Rainbow*'s ratio was 5 to 1. (A contemporary packet's ratio: 4 to 1.) She also had a keel that formed a straight line from bow to stern. The other China traders, including the *Rainbow* and the *Houqua,* had keels that slanted downward to provide a deeper rudder to help the vessel answer the helm. But the Griffiths had noticed during his tank tests that the faster a vessel moved through the water, the more its bow tended to rise, forcing its stern down and increasing the drag. So he broke another rule. The *Ann McKim*'s stern keel, for example, was some five feet deeper in the water than her bow keel. The keel of Griffiths' *Sea Witch* was no deeper at her stern than at her bow.

11. Contemporary newspapers give the date of Robert and Cordelia Waterman's wedding as December 7. But Miss Marion Gorrill, a great-grandniece of Cordelia Waterman, has a gold bracelet that her family has always referred to as a wedding present from the groom to the bride. The bracelet is engraved with the initials "R.H.W. to C.S., Oct. 7, 1846." Perhaps the bracelet was an engagement present, or the wedding date may have been postponed.

12. The time for this passage has often been misreported as 79 days, making the *Sea Witch*'s previous 77-day voyage the record. One reason for the discrepancy is the fact that Waterman brought home the latest issue of the *China Mail* dated January 4, indicating that he had sailed earlier than January 9, the date claimed in the *Sea Witch*'s log (kept by his first mate, George Fraser). Carl Cutler has substantiated the 74-day passage in his *Greyhounds of the Sea* (pp. 138–40) by pointing out, among other arguments, that the *China Mail* of January 11 reported the *Sea Witch* in Hong Kong Harbor on January 8. Presumably Waterman left Whampoa, Canton's anchorage, on January 4, dropped down the Pearl River to Hong Kong, and was delayed there at least through January 8. His departure from Hong Kong, then, must have been on January 9, as noted in the log (Fraser gave the time as 7:30 P.M.). Thus the *Sea Witch* did indeed come home from China in 74½ days, as stated in her logbook. It was not only a record but, as Cutler points out, "the world's first permanent sailing record."

13. The first Navigation Act had been instituted by Oliver Cromwell, largely to shield British colonial trade from the Dutch. Further Navigation Acts had been imposed over the years, and for three centuries the British merchant marine had been protected by re-

strictions limiting most imports to British vessels. (An exception permitting shipping in vessels of the producing country allowed for the American transatlantic packet trade but not for American shipment of Chinese tea to England.) One law, passed after Britain lost the American colonies, had even forbidden Britons from owning foreign vessels. Because of the Navigation Acts, British trade with China—indeed, with all of Asia—had been a British monopoly. As a result, unhindered and unstimulated by any competition, British East Indiamen had been built much more for capacity than for speed.

A fixture of the Asian shipping scene for more than two centuries was Britain's East India Company. Founded in 1600 by Queen Elizabeth, it originally bore the grandiose title "The United Company of Merchant Venturers of England Trading with the East Indies." Charles II promoted the East India Company from a trading group to an autonomous body with the right to establish its own local governments, coin money, and even have an army and a navy. In its heyday it was the world's largest monopoly. By the end of the eighteenth century, the "Honorable John Company," as it was irreverently called, controlled large sections of Asian countries, particularly India, with its own forts, palaces, and courts.

The East India Company had its own quasinavy, prepared—and often forced—to fight off pirates or Dutch warships. Its captains and officers wore elaborate uniforms with gold embroidery, plumed hats, and sidearms. With such "perks" as space in the ships for their own purchases, percentages of the cargo's profit, and high salaries, not to mention "presents" from eastern potentates, an East India Company captain could pocket $50,000 a year. One captain who made a voyage to India, China, and return in 22 months earned $150,000 for that period alone.

The East India Company's network soon spread to China. Its renowned East Indiamen were capacious vessels that moved grandly at speeds of two to three knots (a little slower than the pace of a brisk stride) from Britain to their various Asian ports. These full-bodied "tea waggons," as they were derisively called, furled all their lower sails every night and reefed down at the slightest sign of heavy winds. A normal voyage from China to England could take nearly a year. With no competition there was no hurry, and thus little incentive for advanced ship design. An East Indiaman, as clipper sailors put it, would "beat her head three times against a billow and then fall off and sail around it." Historian Arthur Clark described the long age of the East Indiaman: "It would, of course, be an exaggeration to say that there had been no improvement in British shipping from the reign of Queen

Elizabeth to the Victorian era, but it was so gradual as to be perceptible only when measured by centuries."

CHAPTER 2

1. Many called themselves fandango dancers, and the earliest San Francisco dance halls and brothels were known as fandangos. Because the Chileans were generally the most attractive, the miners referred to all South American women as Chileños. The girls charged as much as $200 a night; and their clients were not put off by their custom of smoking cigars in bed.

2. The fact that New York society snubbed him was of no concern to Bennett. He kept to himself in his Broadway mansion while his wife retreated to Paris with their son, who was to become the spoiled, brilliant editor of the *Herald* on his father's retirement.

3. The *Pacific* made slow time of her passage around the bottom of South America. One boiler sprung a leak; a valve broke and a blowpipe burst—all requiring time-wasting repairs. Captain Cleveland Forbes decided against rounding Cape Horn itself, opting for the Strait of Magellan, a twisting, three-hundred-mile passage just north of the tip of the South American continent. The strait's waves are not so high as those off the Horn and, unlike a sailing ship, a steamer could hold course against the passage's shifting winds. But this narrow, high-sided waterway is frequently bathed in blinding fog, swirls with currents and countercurrents, and is subject to sudden, shrieking squalls that funnel through the cliffs and can knock any vessel onto its beam ends.

Encountering a series of storms, the *Pacific* was almost driven aground. By the time she reached her first Pacific port of call, Valparaiso, the news had preceded her, and scores of Chileans were clamoring to come aboard. Captain Forbes, realizing that hundreds of passengers would be waiting at Panama, refused to take anyone except a relief captain aboard; he had developed lung trouble, and he wanted to have another skipper on board in case he could not continue in command. Captain John Marshall joined him, with Forbes continuing to serve as skipper for the time being. At the next port, Callao, Peru, the steamship line's local agent had sold sixty-nine tickets to San Francisco. When he promised that the Peruvians would sleep on deck for the passage beyond Panama, Captain Forbes reluctantly accepted them.

By the time the *Pacific* reached Panama, on January 17, 1849, Captain Forbes was too ill to continue in command, and Captain Marshall took over, with Forbes electing to stay aboard rather than risk Panama City's yellow fever. When the waiting crowd in Panama saw passengers already aboard the *Pacific,* it was all both captains could do to subdue the understandable pandemonium.

4. He had been named for an ancestor who had fought in the American Revolution, but he spent much of his time denying the legend that he had been named by a whaleman who had found him as a baby floating in a fish box in New Bedford Harbor. He did, however, like to tell an apocryphal story about the officer of a revenue cutter who hailed his vessel one day and demanded:

> "What's the name of that brig?"
> *"Flying Fish."*
> "What's your cargo?"
> "Pickled fish."
> "Who's your captain?"
> "Preserved Fish."

It took an investigation of the brig's papers to convince the cutter captain that he was not the butt of a bad joke.

5. Many New York shipping merchants were also involved in what was known as the "Cotton Triangle." When early in the nineteenth century southern plantationowners adopted Eli Whitney's cotton gin, which mechanically combed the seeds out of harvested cotton, the U.S. South replaced the West Indies, the Mediterranean, and India as the major supplier of cotton to the textile mills of Britain. At first nearly all the American cotton was shipped by the planters from U.S. southern ports directly to Liverpool. It did not take New York's merchants long, however, to spot the profitable prospects of controlling this trade. Shortly New York shipping firms were sending agents south to buy cotton and ship it across the Atlantic. By midcentury most of the cotton shipments were under their control. They accomplished this takeover by using their capital, advancing the price of next season's crop to the plantationowners, who used the money not only for planting but also to expand their estates and purchase more slaves to work the larger fields. The result was that many planters became virtually sharecroppers for the New York shipping firms. Most of the cotton still went to England from New Orleans, Charleston, and Savannah, but the major profits were made by New Yorkers who bought the cotton in the South, shipped it across the Atlantic, and collected large markups from the British purchasers. When the New Yorkers could not buy the cotton, they charged the Southerners premium prices for their fast transatlantic packets. The finished textiles came back to

New York and completed the triangle by being shipped, at more profit, to the stores in the South.

But some of the cannier New Yorkers came up with an even more lucrative trade. They first shipped the cotton to New York, where it was off-loaded from the coastal vessels onto the transatlantic packets for the second leg, to Liverpool. In the course of this procedure half a dozen middlemen—coastal vessel owners and crews, stevedores, insurers, wharfowners, transatlantic packetowners, and crews—as well as the New York merchants, collected their tolls. Although this route added some two hundred miles to the distance from plantation to mill, the New York firms made up for it with their fast coastal ships, such cotton packets as the *Huntsville* and the *Natchez*. And this two-sided triangle made the transatlantic packets a great deal more profitable. By midcentury, with cotton amounting to 60 percent of American exports, Southerners calculated that New Yorkers were pocketing 40 cents out of every $1 paid for it. But with most of the plantationowners perpetually in debt to their New York agents, the Northern monopoly was not broken until just before the Civil War, and in fact was one of the causes of the war.

CHAPTER 3

1. New York's shipyards were nearly as busy with repairs as with building new ships, especially as larger vessels with taller masts returned from Cape Horn with smashed spars and strained hulls. The partners of Smith & Dimon, John Griffiths' employer, divided their responsibilities, William Smith concentrating on shipbuilding and John Dimon handling repairs, which often were more lucrative. "Smith builds the ships," John Dimon once said, "and I make the money."

2. It was used in most British clipper ships a decade later, largely because iron was more plentiful than oak in Britain. The *Challenge* was the first U.S. sailing vessel to have such a construction.

3. On his first voyage across the Atlantic, Christopher Columbus put into the Canary Islands to change the rigging of his caravel *Nina* from fore-and-aft to squared yards like those of the *Pinta* and *Santa Maria* when he realized that the prevailing winds along his route near the equator would not be the westerlies of the North Atlantic but easterlies from astern.

4. By midcentury most sailing ships were using the double topsail, invented by Boston's Robert Bennet Forbes, which divided the topsail into two more maneuverable sails. The double topsail was

popularly known as the "Forbes rig," even after a Brewster, Mass., captain named Frederick Howes perfected a more efficient version in 1853. Most of the later double topsails were Howes's design; yet the term "Howes rig" never became popular.

5. Many years later, in a book about the plans for his vessels, Webb wrote of the *Challenge:* "This ship was originally fitted with too much sail at the dictation of her first commander."

6. The *Challenge* was twice the tonnage of the *Sea Witch*. The American clipper ship had doubled in size in five years.

7. Besides working some seventy hours a week, McKay, like all shipyard apprentices at the time, agreed to serve his "master" faithfully and

> his secrets keep, his lawful commands everywhere readily obey; he shall do no damage to his said master, nor see it done by others without telling or giving notice thereof to his said master; he shall not waste his master's goods, nor lend them unlawfully to any; he shall not contract matrimony within the said term; at cards, dice, or any other unlawful game he shall not play, whereby his said master may have damage; with his own goods nor the goods of others without license from his said master he shall neither buy nor sell; he shall not absent himself day nor night from his master's service without his leave; nor haunt ale-houses, taverns, dance-houses or playhouses; but in all things behave himself as a faithful apprentice ought to do during the said term.

8. As an example of the complex computations involved, the shipbuilding manual in use at the time devoted its first seventy-nine pages to mathematical, geometrical, and trigonometrical equations and formulas.

9. Her construction time has been given variously as sixty days at one extreme (nearly impossible for so large a ship of such new design) to 120 days (Howard I. Chapelle). The figure of 100 days (given by Octavius Howe and Frederick Matthews in *American Clipper Ships*) seems the most likely under the circumstances.

10. Because of this competition, McKay made a canny move. On August 25, 1850, with the *Stag Hound*'s keel being laid down, he announced to the press that he was building a new clipper. Her size, he estimated, would be almost 1,200 tons. Any builder who had been planning the largest clipper presumably relaxed; a 1,200-tonner was large but not the largest. As the *Stag Hound* took shape on her slipway, a sharp-eyed visitor might have begun to suspect that this was

not going to be a 1,200-ton vessel. By that time it was too late. Not until the eve of the *Stag Hound*'s launching did McKay's competitors realize that they had been duped and that his new clipper's tonnage was more than 1,500. Although she was the biggest merchant ship for a short time only, the *Stag Hound* had stolen a march on her competition.

11. George Francis Train referred to Enoch Train as his uncle; actually they were first cousins twice removed: Enoch's and George's fathers were first cousins.

12. While in New York Captain Waterman was increasing the sail plan of the *Challenge*.

13. Colt's canvas was rated by numbers according to strength, ranging from No. 8, the lightest for near-calms, to No. 1, the heaviest. Later there was a No. 0, an even sturdier sail made especially for the winds off Cape Horn.

14. Neither McKay nor Train revealed how much; but based on contemporary shipbuilding costs it should have been about $50,000.

15. His name is more frequently spelled Cressy by historians, but he spelled it Creesy.

16. One ship's reporter was transported into metaphoric archness:

We dined on board yesterday with as fine a "band of brothers" as any man could desire for companions in a *Flying Cloud*. Indeed, so familiar were the voices of many that we could not realize that we had mounted to the nebular regions. Yet all admitted that we actually were inside a *Flying Cloud* whose destination was California, and of which Capt. Cressy, over whose keen eye and intelligent face there was assuredly no mist, had command; and we can only say that more table luxury, more tasteful and costly furniture, more ample ventilation and comfort of every kind, we never knew even in an earth-built packet ship or steamer.

17. An elder in his church, Brewster had been devout and God-fearing to the point that he had refused to buy life insurance because, he explained, "it would show a mistrust in Providence."

CHAPTER 4

1. Another prescient contemporary of Maury's was a fellow midshipman, William B. Whiting, who later recalled, "I encountered some ridicule from my messmates for predicting that Maury would be a

distinguished man." Whiting was impressed by his shipmate's continual inspection of every current along the coast of South America, and described a close call during one of Maury's explorations:

> In a survey of San Lorenzo Island while attached to the *Falmouth* I was an assistant to Maury, and he displayed that perseverance and energy undismayed by difficulty, when he had once determined upon accomplishing a result, which ever marked his career.
>
> He landed on the Labos Rocks to the westward of San Lorenzo to make some astronomical and trigonometrical observations while I remained in the boat. When he landed it was almost a dead calm, and the sea was comparatively smooth; but by the time he had finished his observations a fresh wind had sprung up from the southwards, the tide had risen, and the sea was raging so as to forbid the near approach of the boat, one minute receding from the rock so as to leave a yawning gulf of twenty or thirty feet depth, then rushing up again with an irresistible force.
>
> Calling on me to approach as near as I dared, Maury ascended to the highest point of the rock, took off his jacket, and with a string which he found in his pocket tied in it his watch and sextant, and then threw it with all his might into the sea toward the boat, while the bowman of the boat stood ready to seize it with his boathook before the water had time to penetrate the wrapping. Maury then, watching the culmination of a wave, sprang from the rock himself and, being a good swimmer and possessed of much youthful energy, reached the boat in safety, but it was a fearful leap.

2. No doubt Bowditch remembered with wry amusement that he had written his own *Navigator* after being asked to revise a British volume on navigation used by most Americans and finding that it was full of mistakes.

3. The ingenious method of schematic illustration was Maury's invention; and the illustrator who laboriously drew the thousands of shuttlecocks and arrows, passage routes and temperature recordings on these first charts was Lieutenant William B. Whiting, Maury's old shipmate and assistant aboard the *Falmouth.*

4. It was while compiling the observations for this chart that Maury made an intriguing discovery: Although hundreds of mariners had looked unsuccessfully for the legendary Northwest Passage between the Atlantic and the Pacific, to the extent that some doubted its exis-

tence, the whales had already found it. Sending a set of his charts to Alexander von Humboldt (the explorer for whom the Pacific's Humboldt Current was named), Maury pointed out that some whalemen on the western side of the North American continent had captured whales carrying the rusted harpoon heads of ships from the eastern side—"in other words," Maury asked, "a northwest passage?" His guess was verified five years later when the British Arctic explorer Sir Robert McClure finally traced the Northwest Passage between Baffin Bay, on the North Atlantic side, and the Arctic Ocean.

CHAPTER 5

1. He usually had no medical training except what he picked up by experience. His medicine chest contained a few crude lancets and knives and such nostrums as fever powders, Peruvian bark, and blue vitriol for treating the "proud flesh" of a boil or a sprain. His medical bible was Dr. Abraham Lowe's popular shipboard manual *Sailor's Guide to Health*.

2. Marshall, like Waterman, was the son of a Nantucket whaling captain. A prodigiously successful skipper, he made the then-sizable fortune of $150,000 as a packet captain before purchasing control of the Black Ball Line. He had four brothers who also went to sea; they once estimated that among them they had crossed the Atlantic three hundred times and had amassed nearly a hundred years at sea.

3. Legends, favorable and unfavorable, began to gather around him. One apocryphal story concerned a day when Waterman reported to the Howland & Aspinwall countinghouse to pick up his chronometers and shipping manifest on a sailing day, followed by a sheriff attempting to arrest him at the behest of a disgruntled crewman's lawyer. Supposedly trapped inside the building by the sheriff, Waterman went to the third floor, signaled to his first mate aboard the ship, and rode a bosun's chair across to her deck as her lines were cast off and her tug pulled her away from the pier, leaving the sheriff waiting expectantly in the Howland & Aspinwall reception room. Everyone told the story and it improved in the retelling. But no one ever proved it.

4. Josiah Creesy often is credited with the fast passages made by the tea packet *Oneida*. But there were other Creesys. Carl Cutler mentions two different captains of the *Oneida*: James F. and William A. Creesy.

5. A close rival to Low's memoirs were those of a transatlantic packet captain named Samuel Samuels, who had either one of the liveliest careers in maritime history or one of the most vivid imaginations.

Chapter Notes

If Samuels' memoirs are to be believed, at one time or another he was shipwrecked on the Florida coast, shanghaied aboard a cotton packet, and pursued by Caribbean pirates; he also wrote that in the course of circumnavigating the world he barely escaped from South Seas cannibals, nearly drowned after falling overboard off the Cape of Good Hope, rescued a Swedish lady from a Turkish harem, rejected the offer of an admiral's post in the Turkish Navy, and survived attacks by more pirates off Leghorn and cholera in the port of Hamburg. An officer at seventeen and a captain at twenty one, Samuels became best known as the skipper of the famous Atlantic clipper *Dreadnought,* popularly known as "The Wild Boat of the Atlantic," on seventy-eight of her fastest transatlantic voyages. He came on the scene in the early 1860s too late for the San Francisco trade, in which he surely would have been a standout.

6. A born raconteur, Charles Low recounted a typical incident during the voyage on which he was third mate. Some of the *Houqua's* sailors had bought a Borneo monkey from the sampan salesmen at Anjer. With the clipper at anchor at her destination, Whampoa Reach below Canton, a watch detail was painting her bow. The monkey, tethered to the bowsprit, was able to reach a bucket of black paint and tip it over, sending a broad smear across the white deck as far aft as the mainmast. The enraged second mate, in charge of the paint crew, snatched the monkey from its leash, used it as a mop to swab up the paint, and threw it overboard. The monkey nimbly caught hold of the painters' ladder, climbed back aboard, and led the entire crew on a wild chase, leaving black tracks all over the fresh paint on the bulwarks. All hands were put to the clean-up task, and the monkey's owners had to shave off its paint-smeared fur, producing a disreputable, puzzled simian that was far from an object of pity to the members of the clean-up crew.

7. Low claimed that he did not mind being called "the Old Man" by his crew when he was twenty-nine. But Sarah never got over being called "the Old Woman" at nineteen.

8. There were rumors that Keeler had been paid by the *Car's* competitors to sabotage the ship; but no evidence was found that either of the other clippers' owners (*Intrepid's* Bucklin & Crane of New York, *Romance's* George Upton of Boston) engaged in such tactics.

9. The contemporary accounts described Captain Patten's illness as "brain fever." Consulting a group of doctors, I presented them with the known symptoms. Their diagnosis was tuberculosis, which was endemic in the nineteenth century, especially among seamen, and which in its extreme stage can lead to a progressive, slowly acting,

meningo-encephalitislike brain deterioration resembling Captain Patten's "brain fever."

CHAPTER 6

1. A shipyard carpenter could make as much as $3.50 a day. And even the coastal packets paid seamen up to $18 a month.

2. This loyalty was eloquently expressed by a foremast hand named Robert Steigh, inevitably known to his shipmates as "Bob Stay," who wrote to the *New York Herald* in September 1851 in praise of his clipper *Samuel Russell,* "one of the sweetest crafts that ever danced through old Neptune's dominions." Complaining that a recent *Herald* account of American clippers had omitted mention of the *Russell,* seaman Steigh asked the *Herald* editor to "excuse a wholesome jealousy he feels for the reputation of a craft his heart is somewhat bound up in," and stated the *Russell's* case:

> When I made a voyage to China in that 'ere ship, under command of old Captain Nat. Palmer (a captain, let me tell you, as is a captain), we had an experience of so wonderful a character that it has often been a wonderment to me, that the ship's owners, or some of her relations, did not blow on it through the newspapers. Scores of vessels, on the same tack with ourselves, were overhauled and ran away from. . . . But, lest you consider this only a sailor's yarn, also to give you a more definite idea of her performances on that voyage, allow me to state one fact that may be proved by her log-book. One day, we took a pretty smart breeze upon our starboard quarter, and it continued to blow tolerably steady for the space of ten days. At the end of that time we had skimmed upwards of forty-five degrees, making, as you will perceive, hard on to three thousand two hundred miles in ten days. The handsomest run, in any one day, was three hundred and twenty-eight miles. Now, sir, I humbly submit, is that not a feat to boast of?

3. Captain Arthur Clark seconded Captain Samuels' opinion of the packetarians, pointing out that in the 1840s,

> Those ruffians did not much care for India or China voyages, but preferred to navigate between the dance-halls of Cherry Street and the grog shops of Waterloo Road and Ratcliffe

Highway. As has often been said, they worked like horses at sea and spent their money like asses ashore.

When the California clippers came out, these packet rats, as they came to be called aboard the deep water ships—men who had never before had the slightest idea of crossing the equator if they could help it,—were suddenly possessed with the desire to get to the California gold mines. They, with other adventurers and blacklegs of the vilest sort, who were not sailors but who shipped as able seamen for the same reason, partly composed the crews of the clipper ships. The packet rats were tough, roustabout sailormen and difficult to handle, so that it was sometimes a toss-up whether they or the captain and officers would have charge of ship; yet to see these fellows laying out on an eighty-foot main-yard in a whistling gale off Cape Horn, fisting hold of a big No. 1 Colt's cotton canvas mainsail, heavy and stiff with sleet and snow, bellying, slatting, and thundering in the gear, and then to hear the wild, cheery shouts of these rugged, brawny sailormen, amid the fury of the storm, as inch by inch they fought on till the last double gasket was fast, made it easy to forget their sins in admiration of their splendid courage.

4. The procedure was not called "shanghaiing" until 1855, when Father W. Taylor preached a sermon, "Shanghaiing the Sailor," in front of the El Dorado saloon in San Francisco's Portsmouth Square. The term originated, according to one explanation, because Shanghai was the least visited of the Treaty Ports, so a sailor who shipped out for Shanghai had a difficult time finding another ship; with few volunteers, crewmen for a Shanghai voyage were kidnapped—i.e., "shanghaied." Another explanation for the unpopularity of Shanghai was that most ships heading there from California carried a number of embalmed corpses of Chinese who had died in America and were being returned to their homeland for burial; and superstitious sailors were leery of a dead man aboard a ship.

5. An extreme example of crimping was offered by Herman Melville, who first went to sea aboard a transatlantic packet and described the experience in his semi-autobiographical novel *Redburn*. His ship was about to sail from Liverpool when a crimp delivered an unconscious man who had to be "lowered on board by a rope under his arms and passed forward by the crew," who dumped him in his bunk to sober up. At sea a few hours later the crimps' other victims were up and about their work, however grudgingly. This one remained immobile in the forecastle, which had begun to develop a suspicious smell. The men off watch decided to investigate, and one of them, a

foremast hand named Max, held a lantern over the sallow face of their prostrate shipmate, employing an age-old test of holding a flame near a person's mouth to see if he was breathing.

> "No, he's not dead," he cried, as the yellow flame wav-ered for a moment at the seaman's motionless mouth. But hardly had the words escaped, when, to the silent horror of all, two threads of greenish fire, like a forked tongue, darted out be-tween the lips; and in a moment, the cadaverous face was crawled over by a swarm of worm-like flames.
>
> The lamp dropped from the hand of Max, and went out; while covered all over with spires and sparkles of flame, that faintly crackled in the silence, the uncovered parts of the body burned before us, precisely like phosphorescent shark in a mid-night sea.

Hastily using blankets to snuff out their burning shipmate, the forecastle hands carried him on deck and gave him a quick, uncere-monious burial at sea.

6. The popular sea chantey *Mainsail Haul!* only slightly exagger-ated the polyglot makeup of a clipper ship's forecastle:

> Now, next morning when I 'rived upon the quarterdeck,
> Oh, such a sight you'd never saw before.
> There were sailors there, I'll swear, from every nation;
> There was Rooshian Finns 'n Irish Finns an' Japanese galore. . . .
> Now, when I got down at morning to the fo'csle,
> Oh, such a crew you'd never saw before.
> There wasn't one man that could understand another,
> And I didn't know whether to go ashore. . . .

7. A simple recipe for "sea pie": Chop up equal parts of pork, potatoes, and onions. Cover with dough and cook to a crust. Most cooks cheated on the amount of pork, and some were accused of sub-tituting horsemeat.

Duff (called plum duff if it included dried fruit) was a pudding made in many different ways by different ships' cooks. One sailor gave this recipe for plum duff: "Flour mixed with Salt Water with some *Dried Apples* thrown in it & so is boiled in a Huge Bag tied up tight to Keep it from Swelling. After it is done, it make[s] a very *Solid* food & Sticks to a mans Ribs like wax."

8. The word "scuttlebutt," meaning rumor, came from the gos-sip exchanged around the water container on deck.

9. Few nineteenth-century merchant ships served rations of grog. Not only did most shipowners forbid liquor aboard their vessels (though

it was usually available for the captain and the passengers), but also many of the American insurance companies charged 10 percent less to underwrite a teetotaling ship.

10. China clippers that included a stop in Calcutta attracted a particularly large species of roach. Historian Samuel Eliot Morison exaggerated only slightly when he recorded, "An arrival from Calcutta in Boston was sometimes announced by a pack of terrified dogs running up State Street pursued by an army of Calcutta cockroaches."

11. The derivation of the name may be from the French *chantez,* since most New Orleans blacks spoke a local French patois. The sailors pronounced it "shanty."

12. An ingeniously simple device, the belaying pin in its socket in the pinrail serves as a cleat to hold a line, but can be pulled from its socket for instant release of the line in an emergency.

13. One of the mysteries of the nineteenth-century merchant vessel is the lack of mention of any homosexuality in the forecastle. Considering the situation in modern prisons, it seems surprising that so similar an environment—long absence from female company, enforced intimacy—did not foster similar relationships aboard merchantmen. Herman Melville (in *White Jacket,* which he describes as incorporating his "man-of-war experiences and observations" aboard the frigate *United States*) makes a clear reference to the subject:

> What too many seamen are when ashore is very well known; but what some of them become when completely cut off from shore indulgences can hardly be imagined by landsmen. The sins for which the cities of the plain were overthrown still linger in some of these wooden-walled Gomorrahs of the deep. More than once complaints were made at the mast in the *Neversink,* from which the deck officer would turn away with loathing, refuse to hear them, and command the complainant out of his sight.

If Melville is to be taken at his word, evidently the more notorious practice aboard British men-of-war had spread to the ships of the U.S. Navy. As for the U.S. merchant ship, however, no maritime scholar I have consulted can recall any mention of consenting or forced homosexual activity. Charles R. Schultz, former librarian at the Mystic Seaport Museum in Mystic, Connecticut, currently Archivist at Texas A&M University and the author of numerous studies of shipboard life (see Bibliography), has found a reference similar to Melville's in another work of contemporary fiction but none in any of the countless journals, letters, and memorabilia he has studied. Certainly the moral climate of the mid-nineteenth century was such that homosexuality was regarded contemptuously; Melville considered these "evils in men-of-war" as subjects that "neither bear representing, nor reading, and will hardly bear thinking of." So perhaps homosexuality did occur in the merchantman's forecastle but was unmentionable, as with most sex in Victorian times. Whatever the reason, the most candid memoirs of the period are silent on the subject.

14. William Cullen Bryant, a family friend, persuaded Harper's in New York to publish Dana's journal after a number of other publishers had declined. Harper's offered and Dana was forced to accept a flat fee of $250. *Two Years Before the Mast* made at least $50,000 for Harper's, but Dana never received any royalties.

15. Melville sought out Dana, who had a high regard for his fellow sailor-author, whom he described as "incomparable in dramatic story-telling." But they did not become close friends. Henry David Thoreau was a classmate of Dana's at Harvard, but they did not become friendly either, nor is there evidence that Dana read Thoreau's works.

16. Even before the publication of *Two Years Before the Mast,* while still a law student, he had published in the *American Jurist* in October 1839 an article titled "Cruelty to Seamen," arguing that Boston's eminent Judge Joseph Story (one of Dana's law professors) had unfairly disregarded the testimony of sailors mistreated by their captain and mate and had imposed too lenient a sentence when the officers were found guilty. And one year after the publication of his book, Dana brought out another volume, titled *The Seaman's Friend,* a manual of laws, regulations, and advice for every foremast hand who could read.

17. Dana may have been tempted to sue his former captain for the brutality depicted in *Two Years Before the Mast.* But by the time the *Pilgrim* returned with his witnesses, Captain Thompson (who had come home in the *Alert* with Dana and had not been given another command by Bryant & Sturgis) had shipped out again on a voyage to Sumatra.

18. One of Father Parker's more bizarre soul-saving episodes occurred in July 1847 when, according to one account, New York Harbor was visited by its first Chinese junk, the 300-ton, 160-foot teakwood *Keying,* owned by a British syndicate and crewed by 28 Chinese. Thousands of New Yorkers paid to visit the odd-looking craft (few believed that the top-heavy vessel could have sailed all the way from China), and through one of the visitors the crew members got word to a New York Chinese that they had been kidnapped: The British captain, Charles Kellett, had signed them on only for a trip to Japan; and they had not been paid. Appealed to by the New York Chinese,

Father Parker enlisted the aid of the Seamen's Friends Society, which offered room and board to the 28 Chinese. They were also invited to a service aboard Parker's floating church, where the parishioners were asked to provide clothing for them. Parker and others brought suit against Captain Kellett, who grudgingly paid the back wages (at $6 a month) and found them space on a ship to China. Parker saw them off with presents of warm clothing for the voyage and twenty-eight copies of *The Life of John Newton,* a biography of an English sailor-turned-churchman and composer of "How Sweet the Name of Jesus Sounds"—an odd gift for men who could not read English.

That was one version of the *Keying's* visit. Another, in the *New York Herald,* reported that there were 35 in the Chinese crew; the *Herald* reporter interviewed the *Keying's* cook and made no mention of the crew serving involuntarily. A third version of the story was that most of the crew came ashore and founded New York's first Chinatown. And a fourth version claimed that the whole affair was yet another hoax by P. T. Barnum and that the *Keying* had been built in Hoboken, N.J. (Barnum, however, never mentioned the *Keying* in his memoirs.)

19. The Young Men's Church Missionary Society also set up a Sailors' Home but made the mistake of leasing it to one Henry Smith, who turned it into a crimp's boardinghouse, even competing with other crimps by offering free whiskey. Mrs. Smith, it turned out, was a cardsharp who made a practice of getting her tenants drunk and fleecing them in nightly poker games.

CHAPTER 7

1. A deck hand's primer:
Standing rigging. *Shrouds* are the lines at the sides that hold the masts in place. *Ratlines* are the horizontal lines on the shrouds, used as ladder rungs when climbing the rigging. *Stays* are the diagonal lines supporting the masts fore and aft from the tops to the deck.

Running rigging. *Halyards* hoist and lower the yardarms. *Braces* turn them. *Lifts* tilt them.

2. Like a rudder connected to a straight tiller on a small boat, the nineteenth-century ship's wheel moved the rudder in the opposite direction.

3. The trade winds begin to fade in these bands on both sides of the equator extending as far north and south as 30 degrees. The area evidently got its name when Spanish galleons drifted helplessly until

their food and water supplies got so low that the horses had to be jettisoned.

4. The chronometer is a highly accurate clock adjusted to the precise time for use in the calculations for navigation.

5. The *Challenge*'s recruiting had not been helped when word had spread along the waterfront that merchant Joseph Brewster, checking his shipment aboard the new clipper, had fallen through a belowdecks hatchway, fracturing his skull. A death this soon aboard a ship was enough to scare off many superstitious sailors.

6. Traditionally the captain and second mate were in charge of the starboard watch and the first and third mates in charge of the larboard. The first mate, who had many other duties, thus had some assistance. The second mate, however, rarely called on the captain for help in dealing with his watch.

7. Aboard a clipper the helmsman rang a bell over the compass binnacle every half hour. One bell indicated 12:30 P.M.; two bells indicated 1 P.M.; three bells indicated 1:30 P.M.; and so on to eight bells, indicating 4 P.M., with three sequences in the 12-hour period, six in 24 hours. Today's ship's clock indicates the time in the same sequence.

8. The *Challenge*'s log, unlike that of the *Flying Cloud*, has been lost. What happened during her maiden voyage can be reconstructed in detail mainly from newspaper accounts of a series of trials that were held in San Francisco after the *Challenge*'s arrival, plus some written recollections of Waterman and a couple of others like young Wheeler.

CHAPTER 8

1. It would take a year and a half of heavy traffic before another clipper, Donald McKay's *Flying Fish,* rounded the Horn in seven days. A quarter of a century later, William Webb's *Young America* would cut the time to six days; and not until sixty-three years later would the fast German windjammer *Priwall* set the record for sailing ships: five days, 14 hours.

2. Clipper ship runs were measured by local time, not taking into account the three-hour difference between New York and San Francisco. Thus the *Flying Cloud*'s elapsed time was 89 days, 24 hours, or exactly 90 days, which explained Grinnell, Minturn's reference to her record as "a passage of 90 days." The official time for her maiden voyage, however, remained 89 days, 21 hours.

3. The best system, according to old hands: assume the fetal po-

sition, with knees wedged against the raised edge of the bunk and back against the hull.

CHAPTER 9

1. California's Governor John McDougal issued a statement decrying "the despotic control of a self-constituted association, unknown and acting in defiance of the laws." The committee responded to the charge of secrecy by publishing a list of its membership, which included nearly every prominent businessman in San Francisco. Partly because McDougal was a little-known politician who had just become governor at the death of his predecessor—everyone called McDougal "His Accidency"—few Californians and even fewer San Franciscans paid much attention to his protests.

2. Blundering onto this explosive scene, the Reverend William Taylor and a fellow preacher named S. D. Simonds studied the crowd on the wharf and came to a mistaken conclusion. "Brother Simonds," Taylor mused, "the deck of that ship will be a good place for me to preach tomorrow. If hundreds come to see her in the week, there will be thousands on Sunday, and I'll have an opportunity of preaching the gospel to them."

"Good," said Simonds; "we'll go aboard and get permission of the captain."

The two preachers found no captain aboard. Returning to the wharf, Taylor evidently sensed the mood of the mob. He asked one of them, "What's the matter here?"

"Matter enough," the man responded. "Captain Waterman has killed several of his crew." Another added, "We're after the captain. We'll hang him to the yardarm!"

"The object of our search being so different," Taylor blandly concluded, "we suddenly left."

3. The official transcripts and records of the trial have disappeared, evidently lost in one of San Francisco's many fires. Coverage of the trials by court reporters for three of the city's newspapers provide the major remaining source.

4. His identity remains a puzzle. He claimed to have known Waterman for thirty years (or since Waterman was twelve years old). It is doubtful that Waterman's partner Ritchie had known him that long. Since the letter clearly was written in San Francisco, its author may have been someone at the Alsop office who had come west from Bridgeport or Fairfield, Conn. The *Herald* identified him only as "a gentleman whose views are entitled to consideration."

5. At least that is the way Waterman and his wife later told the story to their friends at the ranch. But some details became confused in retelling. One account gives Captain J. H. Millett as the Good Samaritan who took Waterman to Panama City aboard his clipper *Witchcraft*. The *Witchcraft* was en route from Shanghai to New York at about this time and could have stopped at San Francisco en route; but her captain on this voyage was William C. Rogers. Millett was skipper of the *Witch of the Wave*, which in February 1852 was on her way from Whampoa to London. Nor could Captain David Babcock have had time to bring his clipper *Sword Fish* into Del Rey Island to pick up Cordelia Waterman in February 1852, because he was in a close race to San Francisco with another clipper ship at the time.

CHAPTER 10

1. Cutler lists the ships and their departures:

Wild Pigeon	From New York Oct. 11	
Flying Dutchman	" New York Oct. 15	
Dauntless	" Boston Oct. 15	
Westward Ho	" Boston Oct. 16	
Northern Light	" Boston Oct. 28	
John Gilpin	" New York Oct. 28	
Flying Fish ·	" New York Oct. 31	
Queen of the Seas	" Boston Nov. 3	
Grey Feather	" New York Nov. 9	
Whirlwind	" Boston Nov. 10	
Trade Wind	" New York Nov. 13	
Telegraph	" Boston Nov. 15	
Contest	" New York Nov. 16	
Game Cock	" New York Nov. 16	
Meteor	" Boston Nov. 17	

2. Matthew Maury calculated that someday a clipper ship would cover the "great racecourse" in 85 days; but none did—though Donald McKay must always have wondered whether or not his *Great Republic* could have done it if she had not burned and been cut down. Carl Cutler, however, worked out an intriguing exercise by combining the best runs of six clipper ships to compile the fastest possible time from New York to San Francisco, as follows:

Stag Hound	Boston Light to Cape St. Roque	15 days
Samuel Russell	Cape St. Roque to 50°S in Atlantic	16 "
Young America	50°S in Atlantic to 50°S in Pacific	6 "
Live Yankee	50°S in Pacific to equator	14 "
Mary Sutton	Equator to San	
White Squall	Francisco	16 "
For an ideal composite total of		67 "

3. He had originally intended to call his masterpiece the *King of Clippers,* but while her tall frames were rising in his shipyard he happened to hear the actress Fanny Kemble recite Longfellow's "The Building of the Ship." The poem had of course been inspired by McKay's *Flying Cloud;* but Longfellow, using the vessel to symbolize America's ship of state, called her the *Great Republic.* McKay was so moved by Miss Kemble's dramatic recitation that he decided to switch to *Great Republic.*

4. It was said at the time that McKay had requested water instead of champagne as a gesture to the temperance-minded women of East Boston. But McKay's grandson later revealed that his father (Donald's eldest son) and a few friends had stolen the champagne from the mold loft for a celebration the night before the launching and that its loss had not been discovered until just before the christening, necessitating the substitution of water. When McKay heard that the Boston women took it as a bow to temperance, he wisely did not correct them.

In another gesture to the community, McKay responded to a request from Boston's new Seamen's Society by charging a $1 admission fee to the throngs of people who visited the ship while her masts were being stepped; he collected some $1,000, which financed the opening of the city's new Sailors' Snug Harbor, a home for retired seamen. "This class of men have too long been neglected," McKay wrote the Snug Harbor sponsors; "they do the labor, they sail the clippers of which we boast as a nation; and any little reward that they may be able to collect in this way, will be highly pleasing to me."

5. Plus $275,000 for the cargo, which helped pay back the shippers.

6. Because medium clippers continued to be referred to as "clipper ships," they have been confused with their forerunners, the true, or extreme, clippers, ever since, accounting for the frequent claims by sailors and some skippers of the 1860s and 1870s that they had served

aboard clipper ships. The confusion was not helped by a tendency among owners of medium clippers, and some vessels that were not even medium clippers, to adopt the names of previous true clippers. There was a second *Memnon,* as well as another *Rainbow,* a *Sea Witch,* a *Comet,* and a *Sovereign of the Seas.* Thus many an old-timer at the beginning of the twentieth century maintained that the clipper ships did not have the tall masts and clouds of sails they had been credited with. These men had seen a *Sea Witch* or a *Sovereign of the Seas* but not the real clippers they had been named for.

7. One of the most famous medium clippers precipitated a controversy that has lasted to this day. The *Andrew Jackson* was a big, powerful ship: 1,679 tons and 220 feet long. She was rigged with only one skysail, on her mainmast; her speed came not from a relatively large sail area but because of her sharp bow and her size. In November 1859 there was a scene in New York Harbor that illustrated the decline of the true clipper ship era and the advent of the new medium clipper. The *Andrew Jackson* lay at her wharf at 45 South Street, loading for California, when the eight-year-old *Flying Cloud,* weather-beaten from six voyages around Cape Horn and three around the world, sailed up the East River. The *Cloud* had made her last voyage to San Francisco, and had been laid up in New York for more than two years, awaiting a cargo. The *Jackson* had rounded the Horn three times, and on her upcoming fourth voyage she would make history when her captain, John E. Williams, claimed that he and the *Jackson* had beaten Josiah Creesy's and the *Cloud*'s record from New York to San Francisco.

Captain Williams' log for the voyage has survived, in his flowery handwriting and colorful spelling. By the time the *Jackson* had rounded Cape Horn, Williams was exulting, "I am in hopes Yeat to Do as well as the Flying Clouds time." A week later he was more excited, noting that "we are good for the Flying Cloud Yeat." On March 23, the *Andrew Jackson* raised the Farallon Islands, and Williams wrote in bold script at the foot of her log, "89 Days and 4 houers from New York."

The *Flying Cloud*'s fastest time was officially listed as 89 days, eight hours; apparently the *Andrew Jackson* had beaten her by four hours—a tiny difference after three months of sailing but a new record if true. The merchants of San Francisco seemed to believe that a new record had indeed been set. They presented Captain Williams with a commodore's pennant for the shortest passage and made plans for a parade and a banquet; Williams declined the latter honors. On his return to New York, the *Jackson*'s owners gave him a watch engraved with the ship's time of 89 days, four hours. And ever since then, the proponents of the *Andrew Jackson* and the *Flying Cloud* have argued over which ship deserves the record.

All because of a technicality. The *Flying Cloud*'s time of 89 days, eight hours included entering San Francisco Bay and anchoring, while the record Williams claimed for the *Andrew Jackson* was from Sandy Hook to the waters off San Francisco. On March 23, when he came in sight of the Farallons and the Golden Gate, the wind dropped and he had to wait through the night until there was enough breeze for a pilot boat to come out and meet him. Not until 6 P.M. on the 24th did the *Jackson* drop her anchor, making her anchor-to-anchor passage 90 days, 12 hours, longer than either of the *Cloud*'s passages. (Her 1851 time was 89 days, 21 hours.) *Jackson* supporters point out that the chances of locating a pilot and the time taken to enter the harbor constitute no measure of a ship's speed. But the *Cloud*'s defenders have maintained that there has to be some recognized method of determining when a ship has reached her destination, and the time she dropped anchor, instead of the time she made her landfall, has been generally accepted. How, for example, establish a "finish line" off the Golden Gate, and where? (On her first voyage the *Cloud* sailed back and forth through the night before sighting the Farallons at dawn.) If making a landfall constituted arrival, the *Cloud* certainly sighted the Farallons in under 89 days, four hours (the *Jackson*'s time) on her fastest passage; usually it took more than four hours to work through the Golden Gate, select an anchorage, and drop the hook. Moreover, if the anchor-to-anchor measurement were changed, how to revise all the other records? However unfair it might seem to the *Andrew Jackson,* the *Flying Cloud* officially kept her record: anchor-to-anchor, her best time of 89 days, eight hours was 28 hours shorter than that of the *Andrew Jackson*. And the *Cloud* still holds second place, by seven hours.

CHAPTER I I

1. In 1985 naval architect Melbourne Smith announced plans to build a full-sized replica of the *Sea Witch* under the sponsorship of the American Clipper Trust of Annapolis, Md. Smith, who designed the replicas *Spirit of Massachusetts* and *Pride of Baltimore,* plans to have the new *Sea Witch* sail to Canton and return, after which she would be offered to the U.S. Navy as a training vessel. According to her designer, the modern clipper will have a wooden hull like the original, though probably with stronger laminated framework and watertight compartments. Her masts and spars will be of lighter, more flexible

construction. It will be interesting to see how close she comes to the original *Sea Witch*'s best time (Canton to New York in 74 days) without Robert Waterman on her quarterdeck.

2. Another fire presented a graphic demonstration of the oceans' currents when the fifteen-year-old clipper *Blue Jacket,* off the Falkland Islands in 1869, caught fire. Captain James White, the crew, and passengers abandoned ship; they were barely alive a month later when found by a German vessel. Nearly three years later a charred figurehead washed onto the shore of Rottnest Island off Fremantle, Western Australia. The wooden, blue-jacketed sailor had ridden the east-flowing Great Southern Ocean halfway around the world from the Falklands to Australia.

3. The fast China packet *Natchez,* with which Robert Waterman made his early records, was later converted to a whaler. No clipper could have been adapted to such heavy work, requiring great stability, and the blunt-bowed, flat-bottomed *Natchez* was far from being a true clipper ship. She served as a whaler until 1857 when, more than twenty years old, she was wrecked on a shore of the Okhotsk Sea. Her sister ship, *Huntsville,* which had convinced Captain Nat Palmer that a flat floor meant a faster sailing vessel, also became a whaler in 1844, sailing out of Cold Spring Harbor, N.Y., to the Pacific whaling grounds for fourteen years. She became a merchantman again in 1858; when she disappeared from the sailing registry in 1870, she was thirty-nine years old and still sailing for an owner in San Francisco.

4. In fact, the *Syren* may even have outlived the later down-easters. In 1923 the down-easter *Benjamin F. Packard,* named for her builder and the last square-rigger launched from his yard in Bath, Maine, was given a burial at sea off Eaton's Neck in Long Island Sound. She was fifty-six and the last of the down-easters. There is no record of the *Syren* after 1920, but if she was still sailing in the late 1920s, she had survived not only all American clippers but all of the down-easters as well.

5. In recent years two attempts have been made by yachtsmen to beat the *Flying Cloud*'s time under sail from New York to San Francisco. A large, sturdy trimaran, in a run for charity and named the *Cystic Fibrosis Crusader,* set out from New York in 1983. By December 10, she had rounded Cape Horn, six hours and 55 minutes ahead of the *Cloud*'s time. But two days later she was dismasted off the coast of Chile; her three-man crew was rescued by the Chilean Navy. The following year, Clay Blyth, an adventurous yachtsman who had once crossed the Atlantic in a rowboat, left England in the 65-foot trimaran *Beefeater* (sponsored by the gin makers) to sail to New York for her

Cape Horn passage. She never made it. Blyth was picked up by a passing ship when *Beefeater* sank in mid-Atlantic.

6. Today not one American clipper ship has survived. The largest piece of wreckage lies sprawled under a pier in the harbor of Port Stanley in the Falkland Islands. Only enough is left to identify her as the remains of the *Snow Squall,* built in 1851 by the Alfred Butler yard in Cape Elizabeth, Me. A small clipper with an 800-ton capacity, she made some near-record passages: Amoy to New York in 82 days in 1861, New York to Melbourne in 75 days in 1863. The trim, tough little clipper survived the storms of the China seas, the rolling mountains of the Great Southern Ocean, and even a Rebel raider: Sighting another ship that appeared to be in trouble near the Cape of Good Hope in 1863, Captain James Dillingham took the *Snow Squall* to the rescue, only to find that she was the Confederate sailing cruiser *Tuscaloosa,* whose captain ordered him to heave to. A providential slant of wind filled the *Snow Squall*'s sails at that moment and Captain Dillingham ordered her helm down. With the *Tuscaloosa*'s shells splashing about her, the *Snow Squall* nimbly footed away, clawing upwind more efficiently than her pursuer and leaving her far astern while she fired a frustrated broadside.

But the *Snow Squall*'s nemesis was Cape Horn. On one passage she fought westerly gales for nearly a month, taking 155 days to reach San Francisco, her bowsprit smashed and a jury-rigged rudder replacing the original. On another voyage the Horn's storms ripped off all three of her topmasts, sending her into Montevideo for repairs. Her last voyage, in 1864, ended on the treacherous shoals in the Strait of Le Maire. She limped into Port Stanley leaking so badly that her cargo had to be transferred to another ship. (Captain Dillingham took passage home aboard the bark *Mondamin*—and became a prisoner of the Confederate raider *Florida,* which captured and burned the *Mondamin.*)

Deserted by her owners, the *Snow Squall* was used first as a pierhead, connected to the shore by a dock. During World War II a modern wharf was built over her, its pilings driven through her hull. Not until the 1970s, a century after her abandonment, did maritime historians attempt to salvage America's only clipper relic. In 1976, New York's South Street Seaport Museum sent an expedition to study her. Its members found that the pier that had destroyed part of her hull had also served to hold her in place and partially protect her from tidal surges. Her bow, still defiantly sharp, was visible above water; but her afterbody was a kelp-covered wreck. In 1983, Harvard archaeologist Fred Yalouris and a team of volunteers went to Port Stanley to take measurements of the *Snow Squall*'s remains in hopes of returning as much of her as possible to Maine, where she had been built. They found her bow in such a precarious condition, quivering with each wave, that they immediately went to work salvaging what they could. The team managed to save 19 feet of the clipper's bow, packing up five tons of timbers and iron fittings and shipping this part of the *Snow Squall* home, where the parts were preserved and catalogued. Another expedition is planned, as soon as funds can be raised, to restore enough of the wreckage so that the *Snow Squall* can at least be partially rebuilt at a new museum planned for her in South Portland, Me. A "*Snow Squall* Fund" has been established for the purpose. (Tax-deductible donations can be sent to the fund c/o the Peabody Museum, Harvard University, 11 Divinity Ave., Cambridge, MA 02138.)

The *Snow Squall* can never be restored completely. Thus the only surviving clipper ship is a British version. The tea and wool clipper *Cutty Sark,* sold to a Portuguese shipping firm (for about 12 percent of her building cost), was rescued in the 1920s by a former British sea captain whose widow later presented the clipper to the Cutty Sark Preservation Society, which restored her to her original splendor. Today the *Cutty Sark* sits in her permanent drydock at Greenwich, England, her soaring masts visible for miles up and down the Thames, offering the final testimony to the dramatic days of the clipper ship.

7. With a partner, W. W. Bates, Griffiths also published *The U.S. Nautical Magazine and Naval Journal* from 1853 to 1855, when they renamed it *The Monthly Nautical Magazine and Quarterly Review;* it ceased publication in 1857. In 1875, seven years before his death, Griffiths produced his final work, *The Progressive Shipbuilder.*

8. She was named the *Harriet Lane,* after bachelor President James Buchanan's niece and "lady of the White House."

9. The *Lightning* and the *Champion of the Seas* were two of them; the other two were named respectively for their owner and their builder: the *James Baines* and the *Donald McKay.*

10. The *Prospectus* is now in the Peabody Museum in Salem, Mass.

11. Four years later she made an astonishing Cape Horn passage for a medium clipper: 96 days from New York to San Francisco.

12. From the bewildering number of claimants for the title of fastest American clipper ship, Carl Cutler selected four ships in two categories; all four came from the East River yard of Donald McKay.

Cutler awarded the prize to McKay's *Sovereign of the Seas* on the basis of a claim in the Sydney, Australia, *Empire* that her log (since lost) "proved her to have travelled occasionally at the rate of 22 knots . . ." during a voyage from London to Sydney in 1854. The next fastest burst of speed on record is that of McKay's *James Baines:* 21

knots while en route from Melbourne, Australia, to Liverpool in 1856.

Clipper-ship masters liked to point to a full 24-hour run rather than a short dash as the real measure of a ship's speed. Cutler's choice by that measure was McKay's *Champion of the Seas,* which covered 465 miles in 24 hours in 1854. Second-fastest was his *Lightning,* with 436 miles in 24 hours on her maiden voyage from Boston to Liverpool. Third place also went to the *Lightning,* with a 430-mile run in 24 hours en route to Australia.

Samuel Stratford, the ship's surgeon of the *Flying Scud,* claimed in 1854 that his clipper covered 449 miles in the same period; but Carl Cutler points out that Stratford probably made a miscalculation, pointing to similar mistakes, based on misreading the number of miles in a degree of latitude, made by Stratford during the same voyage.

Most of these records were made on the Great Southern Ocean, running before Matthew Maury's "brave west winds."

13. McKay had saved the lift models of his famous clippers except for that of the *Great Republic,* which he gave to a daughter, and the *Glory of the Seas,* which he gave to a son. After his death his eldest son, Cornelius, discovered that all but one of the remaining models had been burned as firewood during a particularly cold winter; only the model of his first clipper, the *Stag Hound,* was left.

14. Mary Litchfield McKay died in 1923. The same year McKay's last merchant ship, the *Glory of the Seas,* which had spent her declining years as a floating fish storage plant, was towed ashore on a Puget Sound beach near Seattle and burned for her iron fastenings and copper sheathing.

15. It had not been received with the same enthusiasm by the American scientific establishment, partly because of some conclusions that proved false and partly because many scientists were put off by such observations as "the same Almighty hand which decked the lily and cares for the sparrow, fashioned also the pearl and feeds the great whale. Whether of the land or of the sea, the inhabitants are all His creatures, subjects of His laws and agents in His economy." As one scientist put it, "Maury showed his strength by collecting and mapping the normal winds of the ocean; but shows his weakness in speculating on a philosophy of their origin."

16. Ten years after his death they were reissued, with the back-handed acknowledgment: "Founded upon the researches made in the early part of the nineteenth century by Matthew Fontaine Maury."

17. One of his so-called retirement voyages was in command of the steamship *United States,* delivering her from New York to her new owner in Bremen, Germany. When a friend reminded Palmer that he had said he was giving up the sea, the old clipper ship captain replied,

"Well, I don't really know how you can call a trip like this going to sea."

18. En route home Low decided to try a steamer for the first time, and booked passage aboard the *Golden Age,* headed for the Isthmus. He wondered how a steamer would do in heavy weather and told the *Golden Age*'s captain that he hoped for a healthy gale.

The Pacific obliged. Standing on deck with the captain alongside one of the paddlewheels, Low watched as the steamer plunged and crashed into the waves, her engines at full speed but making no headway and gradually slipping sideways into the trough. When a boarding sea smashed part of the deck and the steamer rolled over onto her side, Low shouted above the wind to the captain, "Your vessel is in a dangerous position; you must do something to bring her head to the sea or she will go over and drown us all."

Low had noticed that the *Golden Age* had masts but no sails bent on them. Near the stern, however, were some stout canvas awnings that were used in good weather to shade the afterdeck but were now rolled up. With the steamer captain's permission, Low called for a few crewmen to help him unroll the awnings and lash them to the deck. "It was a hard job," he recalled, "for it was blowing a fierce gale, but the effect on the ship was immediate, for it brought her head to the sea and she was as steady as she could be." Low had in effect "sailed" the steamer into the waves, preventing them from rolling the vessel over. The gale soon abated and the passengers joined in thanking Low for saving the steamer. "As for myself," Low wrote, "I concluded I would rather have a good sailing ship than a steamer, any time."

19. Howe and Matthews, in their *American Clipper Ships,* claim that Creesy in the *Flying Cloud* left New York two days later than William Knapp in the *Hornet,* thereby making the *Cloud* the winner. But most other sources maintain that the two clippers left Sandy Hook on the same day and that both arrived in San Francisco, after 105 days, within 40 minutes of each other.

20. A surveyor pronounced the *Flying Cloud* fit for sea. But shortly after Captain Reynard took her off for San Francisco, he found her bowsprit sprung. Ensuing gales were too much for her weather-beaten rigging, and Reynard had to take her into Rio de Janeiro for a refit before proceeding to California.

21. Evidently his first mate, James Douglass, was forcibly retired when no shipowner would sign him on. His name simply disappeared from the shipping lists.

22. Under his supervision both buildings were constructed like a ship. When 133 years later a San Francisco planning engineer named Gary Odaffer bought the two buildings, he found that despite half a

century of neglect by their last owners, both house and barn still were structurally sound. When Odaffer had the barn moved a hundred yards to a new foundation, it did not even sag.

23. Legend had it that this male hideaway was an addition on the roof of the two-story house. But no sign of it remains in the present structure. Moreover, because the house has a mansard roof, the second-floor walls slant like those of a ship's aftercabin; no doubt the "captain's cabin" of the Waterman ranch was one of the upstairs rooms.

24. Apocryphal stories nonetheless continued to gather around him. One of the least likely accounts claimed that he became a waterfront missionary and that when he tried to organize a prayer meeting aboard one vessel a couple of his former sailors recognized him; he was dumped over the side and held underwater with a boathook, the story went, and nearly drowned before being rescued by the police. Another tale had Waterman as the hero. According to the account, he and Cordelia gave a New Year's Eve party in 1858, at the end of which Hugh Patterson, the former third mate of the *Challenge,* was killed by a rifleman hidden in the bushes near the ranch house. Waterman is said to have pursued Patterson's murderer, supposedly a disaffected *Challenge* sailor named McCorkle, for two years and all the way to England, where he caught up with the man, tricked him into a confession, and turned him over to the British police.

25. Only two years later, Dr. Reginald Fitz of the Harvard Medical School published in the *American Journal of Medical Sciences* a paper entitled *Perforating Inflammation of the Veriform Appendix; with Special Reference to its Early Diagnosis and Treatment.* And a year later Dr. Thomas Morton of Philadelphia performed the first successful appendectomy. Had this operation been available in 1884, Waterman might have survived. Nonetheless, he was seventy-six, a ripe old age in the nineteenth century.

Source Notes

Note: Full details of these sources will be found in the Bibliography.

PROLOGUE

PAGE

16 Philip Hone, mayor of New York: *The Diary of Philip Hone* (A).

16 Alexis de Tocqueville had earlier predicted a major promise of America: Alexis de Tocqueville, *Democracy in America* (A).

19 Three quarters of a century later: Carl Cutler, *Greyhounds of the Sea* (G).

20 One newspaper editorial proclaimed: Carl Cutler, *Greyhounds of the Sea* (G).

20 Historian Samuel Eliot Morison has called it: Samuel Eliot Morison, *The Maritime History of Massachusetts* (C).

CHAPTER I

23 "I have seen many launches": Octavius T. Howe and Frederick C. Matthews, *American Clipper Ships, 1833–1858* (p. 55).

27 He did not endear himself: John W. Griffiths, *A Treatise on Marine and Naval Architecture* (B).

35 Thus started what historian Carl Cutler describes: Carl Cutler, *Greyhounds of the Sea* (G).

CHAPTER 2

41 By day San Francisco was aptly described: Marshall B. Davidson, *Life in America* (A).

42 Another easterner remarked: Marshall B. Davidson, *Life in America* (A).

44 To his partner Ritchie he confided: David A. Weir, *That Fabulous Captain Waterman* (pp. 46–47).

44 Clearly, in Waterman's view: David A. Weir, *That Fabulous Captain Waterman* (p. 70)

46 James Fenimore Cooper occasionally came down: Lloyd Morris, *Incredible New York* (A).

46 Diarist George Templeton Strong: *The Diary of George Templeton Strong* (A).

50 One New York merchant wrote: Walter Barrett, *The Old Merchants of New York City* (A).

52 A New York contemporary provided a glimpse: Walter Barrett, *The Old Merchants of New York City* (A).

CHAPTER 3

64 Carl Cutler called the lift model: Carl Cutler, *Greyhounds of the Sea* (G).

75 "the swift contact of flint and steel": Arthur H. Clark, *The Clipper Ship Era* (p. 55).

76 As George Francis Train remembered it: George Francis Train, *My Life in Many States and in Foreign Lands* (C).

77 When Longfellow returned to his house: Henry Wadsworth Longfellow, "The Building of the Ship."

80 "My speech is rude and uncultivated": Arthur H. Clark, *The Clipper Ship Era* (pp. 256–257).

81 "I never yet built a vessel": From an interview with Donald McKay in the *Boston Daily Advertiser,* October 28, 1864.

81 George Francis Train gave his version: George Francis Train, *My Life in Many States and in Foreign Lands* (C).

CHAPTER 4

94 "The calm belts of the sea": Matthew Fontaine Maury, *The Physical Geography of the Sea* (F).

96 Captain Phinney of the clipper *Gertrude*: Matthew Fontaine Maury, *The Physical Geography of the Sea* (F).

96 Maury was especially gratified: Matthew Fontaine Maury, *The Physical Geography of the Sea* (F).

CHAPTER 5

105 The youngest Low brother: This and other comments on the Palmer brothers are from Captain Charles E. Low, *Some Recollections* (E).

110 But the all-time heroine of the clipper ship era: Most of the material on Mary Patten is from Everett H. Northrup, *Florence Nightingale of the Ocean* (E).

CHAPTER 6

117 Transatlantic packet captain Samuel Samuels: Samuel Samuels, *From the Forecastle to the Cabin* (E).

118 The sort of sailors provided: Charles R. Schultz, *Life on Board American Sailing Ships During the 19th Century* (E).

119 Usually the ingredients were more to blame: Charles R. Schultz, *Life on Board American Clipper Ships* (E).

120 China clippers putting into Anjer: Charles R. Schultz, *Life on Board American Clipper Ships* (E).

120 Hugh Gregory of the *Sea Serpent* complained: Hugh McCulloch Gregory, *The Sea Serpent Journal* (E).

122 One seaman complained that the rats: Charles R. Schultz, *Life on Board American Clipper Ships* (E).

124 Hugh Gregory, again, described a typical episode: Hugh McCulloch Gregory, *The Sea Serpent Journal* (E).

128 After his baptism, Hugh Gregory: Hugh McCulloch Gregory, *The Sea Serpent Journal* (E).

128 Historian-Captain Arthur Clark: Arthur H. Clark, *The Clipper Ship Era* (p. 132).

129 Captain Clark scornfully complained: Arthur H. Clark, *The Clipper Ship Era* (pp. 128–129).

133 Even while suing Boston's shipowners: Charles Francis Adams, *Richard Henry Dana: A Biography* (E).

133 Many sailors, he maintained: Samuel Shapiro, *With Dana Before the Mast* (E).

133 By 1846 he boasted to his father: Samuel Shapiro, *Richard Henry Dana, Jr.* (E).

137 "As a matter of fact," Captain Arthur Clark maintained: Arthur H. Clark, *The Clipper Ship Era* (p. 130).

137 Captain Clark spoke for many of the clipper masters: Arthur H. Clark, *The Clipper Ship Era* (p. 125).

CHAPTERS 7 THROUGH 9

Virtually all quotations in Chapters 7 through 9 are from the *Challenge* trials in San Francisco in the autumn and winter of 1851–1852, as reported in:

The Alta California
The San Francisco Herald
The California Courier

CHAPTER 10

228 An American passenger described the scene: Octavius T. Howe & Frederick C. Matthews, *American Clipper Ships, 1833–1858* (p. 322–333).

CHAPTER 11

238 In 1866 another British shipper: Jacques and Helen LaGrange, *Clipper Ships of America and Great Britain* (B).

242 The one from Matthew Maury: Richard C. McKay, *Some Famous Sailing Ships and Their Builder Donald McKay* (D).

249 Ordered by his superior, Commander Craven: *Dictionary of American Biography*.

Acknowledgments

A third of a century ago, Carl Cutler was simultaneously updating his classic *Greyhounds of the Sea,* researching his *Queens of the Western Ocean,* and carrying out his duties as curator of the Mystic Marine Museum, of which he was a co-founder. Yet he still found time to guide and counsel a neophyte attempting his first book on maritime history. After Cutler's retirement Edouard A. Stackpole, who replaced him as curator, was even more tolerant and patient. Over the years I have found everyone at what is now the Mystic Seaport Museum knowledgeable and helpful, most recently Rodi York in the museum's registrar's office and Douglas L. Stein, Curator of Manuscripts, and Lisa Halttunen and Gerald Morris in the museum's G. W. Blunt White Library.

New York City's South Street Seaport may someday have the research facilities of Mystic; the South Street library is gradually being expanded. Because South Street was at the heart of the clipper era, the seaport has a golden opportunity to become a major center for research material. At present the Peabody Museum and the Essex Institute in Salem, Massachusetts, have the most impressive collections of clipper ship logbooks and memorabilia. Mark Sexton and Kathy Flinn in the museum's picture department have been most helpful. And I am indebted to Philip Chadwick Foster Smith, maritime historian and former head of the maritime collection at the Peabody, especially for his assistance in my vain attempt to track down the log of the *Neptune's Car* on the voyage commanded by nineteen-year-old Mary Patten.

San Francisco's Maritime Museum is fortunate in having Karl Kortum as its curator. His encyclopedic knowledge of maritime history—and his clear perspective on the role of the clipper ship—have helped me enormously. It was through Karl Kortum, with the assistance of James D. Hart, director of the Bancroft Library at the University of California at Berkeley, that my wife and I were able to study the court reporters' detailed, long-buried accounts of the maiden

ACKNOWLEDGMENTS

voyage of the *Challenge*. The New York Public Library's collection of maritime history books and New York newspapers has been invaluable in illuminating the mid-nineteenth-century scene, as has the excellent library of the New-York Historical Society.

Captain Robert Waterman, were he alive, would be pleased to see how authentically and lovingly his ranch house and barn are being restored by their new owner. Waterman might also have a sense of *déjà vu,* because much of his ranch land is being developed, just as he developed the towns of Fairfield and Cordelia a century ago. But the ranch house and barn are being returned to their original by Gary Odaffer, architect, engineer, and man of multitudinous talents, who kindly gave me and my wife a tour of the estate.

So many others have helped me along the way. Gayle Groenendaal led me to Gary Odaffer and the Waterman ranch. Former *Life* photographer Charles E. Steinheimer photographed the ranch and the painting of the young Captain Waterman, which now belongs to the Haley family in Sacramento; Cathy Haley kindly gave me permission to use it. Carolyn Wall Rothery helped me find an essential picture. George Whitmore tipped me off to the death of New York merchant Joseph Brewster, which laid a curse on the *Challenge* in the eyes of superstitious sailors. William Main Doerflinger gave me permission to use a couple of chanteys from his definitive work, *Songs of the Sailor and Lumberman* (see Bibliography). Bruce M. Lane's voluminous studies of Donald McKay (especially Lane's manuscript in the Peabody Museum—see Bibliography) have been most helpful. Melbourne Smith provided the material on his proposed replica of the *Sea Witch,* as did Fred Valouris on his attempt to save the bow of the *Snow Squall,* the last relic of the American clipper ship.

The late John Horace Parry, Gardiner Professor of Oceanic History at Harvard, provided invaluable advice. Charles R. Schultz, Archivist at Texas A&M University and former librarian at the Mystic Seaport Museum, aided me with his inexhaustible knowledge of the life of the nineteenth-century seaman (see Bibliography). Mrs. Cynthia Russell, a descendant of Cordelia Sterling Waterman, helped me search for Sterling and Waterman pictures, as did Henry J. Poett, Jr. Among the other descendants of the Watermans and the Sterlings who helped me, I am especially indebted to Mrs. Catharine Detweiler and Miss Marion Gorrill.

My thanks to them all, and especially to Julian Bach, a good shepherd; to Connie Roosevelt, a perceptive editor; to Ann W. Marr for her help with research on nineteenth-century America; and to my wife Jane who, as always, provided even more research, and her usual wise counsel.

Bibliography

Two books are generally regarded as the bibles of the clipper ship period. Carl Cutler's *Greyhounds of the Sea* was published in 1930; after thirty more years of research (he estimated that in all he studied five thousand ships' logs), Cutler revised and updated the book in 1960. A thorough study of American clippers, *Greyhounds* also provides appendices compiling clipper ship records, measurements, and other data, plus abstracts of the log of the *Flying Cloud* on her maiden voyage and that of the *Andrew Jackson* on the voyage that almost eclipsed the *Cloud*'s. A third edition (Annapolis, Md.: Naval Institute Press) includes *Five Hundred Sailing Records of American Built Ships,* which Cutler compiled for the Marine Historical Association at Mystic, Conn., of which he was a co-founder and curator.

Arthur H. Clark was a captain before he wrote *The Clipper Ship Era* (Riverside, Conn.: Seven C's, 1970; reprint of 1910 edition), so he brings personal reminiscences as well as scholarship to his book, which also contains appendices on most of the clipper ships. But Cutler's work is more comprehensive if only because it had the benefit of half a century of diligent research. (His revised, expanded edition of *Greyhounds* was published fifty years after Clark's *The Clipper Ship Era*.)

There are two other works that are not so popularly recognized but should be ranked with *Greyhounds of the Sea* and *The Clipper Ship Era*. One is William Armstrong Fairburn's *Merchant Sail* (Lovell, Me.: Fairburn Marine Educational Center, Inc.), a monumental six-volume study of the merchant marine, including a thorough account of the clipper ship era. The other is *American Clipper Ships, 1883–1858,* by Octavius T. Howe and Frederick C. Matthews (Salem, 1926; reprinted by Argosy Antiquarian Ltd., New York, 1967), a two-volume alphabetical compilation of extreme and medium clippers that provides a great deal of information not in Cutler's or Clark's books. It also corrects some misinformation in other books about the clipper ship period. And of the recent works on the clipper ship, one of the best is David R. MacGregor's *Clipper Ships* (Watford, England: Argus Books, 1979).

As for the maiden voyage of the *Challenge,* two authors have added to the accounts provided by the major maritime historians. Richard H. Dillon's *Bully Waterman* (San Francisco: The Roxburghe Club, 1956) tends to disparage the captain, as the title implicates. But Dillon turned to a source that had been overlooked by Cutler and Clark. The series of trials held in San Francisco after the *Challenge*'s arrival revealed a detailed picture of the voyage. The log of that passage is lost—though its existence would provide only Captain Waterman's version of the events. So evidently are the court records of the trials, probably burned in one of San Francisco's many fires. But the court reporters of three contemporary newspapers covered the trials at some length, and it is from the microfilmed issues of these newspapers, preserved in the Bancroft Library at the University of California at Berkeley, that Dillon weeded out many of the details of the *Challenge*'s ill-fated voyage.

Another author who delved into these newspaper accounts was Andrew Weir, who also searched out the land records of Solano County to find a great deal of material on Waterman's retirement, which he published in *That Fabulous Captain Waterman* (New York: Comet Press Books, 1957), a book that lionizes his subject even more than Dillon criticizes him.

Both the Dillon and the Weir books have been out of print for many years and are difficult to obtain. (*Bully Waterman* was privately printed.) Following their example, my wife and I have studied the court reporters' accounts of the *Challenge* trials, notably in the *Alta California,* the *San Francisco Herald,* and the *California Courier.* Like Dillon and Weir, we found often-conflicting accounts of the voyage, depending on who was testifying for whom. The contemporary newspapers also tell slightly different stories about the dramatic events following the *Challenge*'s arrival in San Francisco. But by careful co-ordination of the many accounts, it has been possible to re-create what happened both aboard the *Challenge* and after her sailors swarmed ashore accusing Captain Waterman and his first mate of murder.

These revelations cast both the *Challenge* voyage and Robert Waterman in a somewhat different light from that accepted by the maritime historians. Howe and Matthews, for example, concluded, "In the opinion of those best qualified to judge, Captain Waterman was justified in the severe measures he took to suppress and punish the mutiny and the criticisms levelled against him seem to have been based on misconception of the facts." Cutler wrote that it was impossible to find "the slightest suggestion either that Waterman had ever killed a man or that a complaint of any character had even been lodged against him"—despite the fact that he was tried for murder and convicted of cruel treatment of a crewman. Perhaps Clark can be pardoned for defending a fellow captain and a friend who described part of the voyage to him personally (though Clark got many details of the voyage wrong). Brushing off Waterman's accusers as "blatant impostors," Clark praised Waterman as "a humane, conscientious, high-minded man, who never spared himself nor any one else when a duty was to be performed." As the *Challenge* trials revealed, Robert Waterman was a considerably more complicated man.

One of the best published collections of clipper ship plans is in Howard I. Chappelle's *The Search for Speed Under Sail* (New York: Bonanza Books, 1967). Another work, not so easy to find, is William Webb's *Plans of Wooden Ships*. There are large collections of clipper ship plans, including those of Donald McKay, at the Essex Institute in Salem, Mass., and in the Francis Russell Hart Nautical Museum at Pratt Institute of Naval Architecture, Massachusetts Institute of Technology, in Cambridge, Mass.

There are clipper ship logbooks in maritime museums all over the United States, the largest collections being at the G. W. Blunt White Library at the Mystic Seaport Museum in Mystic, Conn. (which has three *Sea Witch* and three *Natchez* logs); Yale's Sterling Memorial Library; the Essex Institute; and the Marine Division of the U.S. Weather Bureau in Washington, D.C., which has most of the logs used by Matthew Fontaine Maury as well as Maury's *Wind and Current Charts* and his *Sailing Directions*.

There is of course a great deal of information on midcentury New York City, including its clipper ship launchings, departures, and arrivals, in the contemporary newspapers, which are preserved on microfilm at the New York Public Library's annex at 521 West 43rd Street. The best source material is in the *Herald,* the *Times,* and the *Tribune.* A periodical that covered the shipping scene in great detail over the years was *Hunt's Merchant's Magazine & Commercial Review,* also available in the New York Public Library annex. The contemporary San Francisco newspapers can be found on microfilm at the Bancroft Library of the University of California at Berkeley.

At least two excellent bibliographies concentrate on or include clipper ships: Charles P. Schultz's *Annotated Bibliography of American and British Clipper Ships* (Mystic, Conn.: Marine Historical Association, 1969) and Robert G. Albion's *Naval and Maritime History* (also the Marine Historical Association at Mystic, 1972).

Here are some other books and articles on the era of the clipper ship:

A. MIDCENTURY AMERICA

Adams, Arthur G. *The Hudson: A Guidebook to the River.* Albany, N.Y.: State University of New York Press, 1981.

Albion, Robert G. *The Rise of New York Port.* New York: Charles Scribner's Sons, 1967.

Barrett, Walter (pseudonym for Joseph A. Scoville). *The Old Merchants of New York City,* 3 vols. New York: Carleton, 1864.

Belson, Ezekiel Porter. *New York, Past, Present and Future.*

Breunig, Charles. *The Age of Revolution and Reaction, 1789–1850.* New York: W. W. Norton, & Company, 1970.

Brooks, Elbridge S. *The Story of New York.* Boston: D. Lothrop & Company, 1888.

Calkins, Carroll C. (ed.). *The Story of America.* New York: Reader's Digest, 1975.

Churchill, Allan. *The Upper Crust: An Informal History of New York's Highest Society.* Englewood Cliffs, N.J.: Prentice-Hall, 1970.

Cornell, James. *The Great International Disaster Book.* New York: Charles Scribner's Sons, 1976.

Crane, Sylvia E. *White Silence: Greenough, Powers and Crawford, American Sculptors in Nineteenth Century Italy.* Miami, Fla.: University of Miami Press, 1972.

Davidson, Marshall B. *Life in America,* 2 vols. Boston: Houghton Mifflin Company, 1950.

Deford, M. A., and Jackson, J. S. *Who Was When: A Dictionary of Contemporaries.* New York: H. W. Wilson Company, 1976.

Dickens, Charles. *American Notes.* London, 1842.

Dodge, William Earl. *A Great Merchant's Recollections of Old New York, 1818–1880.* Valentine's Manual, 1921.

Ellis, Edward Roble. *The Epic of New York City.* New York: Coward-McCann, 1966.

The Encyclopaedia Britannica. London: Encyclopaedia Britannica, 1969.

Flexner, Stuart. *Listening to America.* New York: Simon & Schuster, 1982.

Floyd-Jones, Thomas. *Backward Glances: Reminiscences of an Old New Yorker.* 1914.

Forbes, R. B. *Personal Reminiscences*. Boston, 1878.

Garraty, John A. *The American Nation: A History of the United States*. New York: Harper & Row and American Heritage Publishing Co., 1966.

Gilder, Rodman. *The Battery*. Boston: Houghton Mifflin Company, 1936.

Goetzmann, William H. *Exploration and Empire*. New York: Alfred A. Knopf, 1966.

Goldstone, Herman H. *History Preserved: A Guide to New York City Landmarks and Historic Districts*. New York: Simon & Schuster, 1974.

Gordon, John Steele. *A Thoroughly Unfair Quiz About New York*. New York: The New York Times, August 10, 1985.

Grun, Bernard: *The Timetables of History*. New York: Simon & Schuster, 1975.

Hone, Philip (Allan Nevins, ed.), *The Diary of Philip Hone,* 2 vols. New York: Dodd, Mead & Company, 1927.

Kouwenhoven, John A. *The Columbia Historical Portrait of New York*. Garden City, N.Y.: Doubleday & Company, 1953.

Krout, John A. *United States to 1865*. New York: Barnes & Noble, 1955.

Langer, William L. *An Encyclopedia of World History*. Boston: Houghton Mifflin Company, 1972.

Lavender, David. *Westward Vision*. New York: McGraw-Hill, 1963.

McKay, Richard: *South Street: A Maritime History of New York*. New York: G. P. Putnam's Sons, 1934.

Marcuse, Maxwell F. *This Was New York!.* New York: LIM Press, 1969.

Merk, Frederick. *The History of the Westward Movement*. New York: Alfred A. Knopf, 1978.

Minnigerode, Meade. *The Fabulous Forties*. New York: G. P. Putnam's Sons, 1924.

Morison, Samuel Eliot. *The Growth of the American Republic*. New York: Oxford University Press, 1942.

Morris, Lloyd. *Incredible New York*. New York: Random House, 1951.

Postgate, Raymond. *1848: The Story of a Year*. New York: Oxford University Press, 1956.

Potter, David M. *The Impending Crisis, 1848–1861*. New York: Harper & Row, 1976.

Rosebrock, Ellen Fletcher. *Counting-House Days in South Street*. New York: South Street Seaport Museum, 1978.

Schermerhorn, Gene. *Letters to Phil: Memories of a New York Boyhood, 1848–1856*. New York: New York Bound, 1982.

Schlesinger, Arthur M., Jr. *The Age of Jackson*. Boston: Little, Brown & Company, 1945.

Simon, Kate. *Fifth Avenue: A Very Special Social History*. New York: Harcourt Brace Jovanovich, 1978.

Smith, Page. *The Nation Comes of Age*. New York: McGraw-Hill, 1981.

Stokes, Isaac Newton Phelps. *The Iconography of Manhattan Island* (1915–28).

Strong, George Templeton. *The Diary of George Templeton Strong, 1835–75*, 4 vols. New York: Macmillan, 1952.

Tocqueville, Alexis de. *Democracy in America,* 2 vols. New York: Alfred A. Knopf, 1966.

Trager, James. *The Peoples' Chronology*. New York: Holt, Rinehart & Winston, 1979.

Wetterau, Bruce. *Concise Dictionary of World History*. New York: Macmillan, 1983.

Williams, Neville. *Chronology of the Modern World*. New York: David McKay Co., 1966.

WPA Writers Project. *Maritime History of New York*. New York, 1941.

B. THE SHIPS

Abbey, Charles. *Before the Mast in the Clippers.*

Abbot, Willis J. *American Merchant Ships and Sailors*. New York, 1908.

Albion, Robert G. *Five Centuries of Famous Ships*. New York: McGraw-Hill, 1978.

———. *Square Riggers on Schedule*. 1938.

Bateson, Charles. *Gold Fleet for California, 1849–50*. Auckland, N.Z., 1963.

Bonyun, Bill and Gene. *Full Hold and Splendid Passage*. New York: Alfred A. Knopf, 1969.

Bowen, Frank C. *America Sails the Seas*. New York: Robert M. McBride & Company, 1938.

———. *The Golden Age of Sail*. London, 1925.

Campbell, George F. *China Tea Clippers.* New York: David McKay Company, 1974.

Carse, Robert. *The Moonrakers: The Story of the Clipper Ship Men*. New York; Harper & Brothers, 1961.

———. *The Twilight of Sailing Ships*. New York: Grosset & Dunlap, 1965.

Chapelle, Howard I. *American Sailing Craft*. New York: Kennedy Brothers, 1936.

———. *The Baltimore Clipper*. Tradition Press, 1965.

BIBLIOGRAPHY

————. *The History of American Sailing Ships.* New York: W. W. Norton & Company, 1935.

————. *The Search for Speed Under Sail.* New York: Bonanza Books, 1968.

Chase, Mary Ellen. *Donald McKay and the Clipper Ships.* Boston: Houghton Mifflin Company, 1959.

Coggeshall, George. *History of the American Privateers and Letters-of-Marque During our War with England in the Years 1812, '13 and '14.* New York, 1856.

Cutler, Carl. *Queens of the Western Ocean.* Annapolis, Md.: U.S. Naval Institute Press, 1961.

Daniel, Hawthorne. *The Clipper Ship.* New York: Dodd, Mead & Company, 1928.

Evans, Robert, Jr. *Without Regard for Cost.* Chicago: *Journal of Political Economy,* University of Chicago Press, 1964.

Forbes, Allan. "The Story of Clipper Ship Sailing Cards," *Proceedings of the American Antiquarian Society,* October 19, 1949.

————. *Other Yankee Ship Sailing Cards.* Boston: State Street Trust Co., 1949.

Forbes, R. B. *A New Rig for Ships.* 1849.

————. *Forbes's System of Sails and Their Management.* 1869.

————. *Notes on Ships of the Past.* Boston, 1888.

————. *Personal Reminiscences.* Boston, 1878.

————. *The Story of Clipper Ship Sailing Cards.* Worcester, Mass., 1950.

Green, Fitzhugh. *Our Naval Heritage.* New York, 1925.

Greenhill, Basil, and Stonham, Denis. *Seafaring Under Sail.*

Griffiths, John W. *Treatise on Marine and Naval Architecture.* London, 1850.

Griswold, Frank Gray. *Clipper Ships and Yachts.* New York: E. P. Dutton & Company, 1927.

Harland, John. *Seamanship in the Age of Sail* (Mark Myers, illus.). Annapolis, Md.: Naval Institute Press, 1985.

Heatter, Basil. *Eighty Days to Hong Kong.* New York, 1969.

Holland, Rupert Sargent. *Historic Ships.* Philadelphia: Macrae Smith Company, 1926.

Jennings, John. *Clipper Ship Days.* New York: Random House, 1952.

LaGrange, Jacques and Helen. *Clipper Ships of America and Great Britain, 1833–1869.* New York: G. P. Putnam's Sons, 1936.

Laing, Alexander. *American Sail* (N.Y.: Bonanza Books, 1961)

————. *American Ships.* New York: American Heritage Press, 1971.

————. *Clipper Ships and Their Makers.* New York: G. P. Putnam's Sons, 1966.

————. *Clipper Ship Men.* New York: Duell, Sloan & Pearce, 1944.

LeScal, Yves. *The Great Days of the Cape Horners*. New York: New American Library, 1967.

Lobley, Douglas. *Ships Through the Ages*. London: Octopus Books, 1972.

Lubbock, Basil. *The China Clipper*. Glasgow: Brown, Son, & Ferguson, 1973.

——. *The Opium Clippers*. London: Brown & Ferguson, 1933.

——. *Sail: The Romance of the Clipper Ships*. New York: Macmillan, 1939.

Lyon, Jane D. *Clipper Ships and Captains*. New York: American Heritage Publishing Co., 1962.

MacGregor, David R. *Fast Sailing Ships: Their Design and Construction, 1775–1875*. Lymington, England: Heassner Publishing, 1973.

——. *The Tea Clippers*. London: Percival Marshall & Co., 1952.

Maclay, Edgar S. *A History of American Privateers*. New York, 1899.

Maddocks, Melvin, and the Editors of Time-Life Books. *The Atlantic Crossing*. Alexandria, Va.: Time-Life Books, 1981.

Matthews, Fred C. *American Merchant Ships*, 2 vols. Salem, Mass.: 1930–31.

Men, Ships and the Sea. Washington, D.C.: *National Geographic*, 1962.

Morison, Samuel Eliot. *The Maritime History of Massachusetts, 1783–1860*. Boston: Houghton Mifflin Company, 1941.

——. *Old Ships of New England*. Boston: compiled for Chas. E. Lauriat Co., 1923.

Park, Charles E. *The Development of the Clipper Ship*. American Antiquarian Society, 1929.

Randier, Jean. *Men and Ships Around Cape Horn*. London, 1969.

Reisenberg, Felix. *Cape Horn*. New York, 1939.

—— (ed.). *Clipper Ships*. Currier & Ives prints.

Roscoe, Theodore, and Freeman, Fred. *Picture History of the U.S. Navy*. New York: Charles Scribner's Sons, 1956.

Smith, Melbourne. "The Baltimore Clipper," *Sea History Magazine*, Summer 1979.

Smith, Philip Chadwick Foster. *The Empress of China*. Philadelphia: Philadelphia Maritime Museum, 1984.

Spears, John R. *The Story of the American Merchant Marine*. New York, 1910.

Underhill, Harold. *Deep Water Sail*. 1952.

——. *Sailing Ships and Rigging*. 1956.

Verrill, A. Hyatt. *Smugglers and Smuggling*. New York, 1924.

Villiers, Alan. *The Cutty Sark: Last of a Glorious Era*. London: Hodder & Stoughton, 1953.

———. "The Drive for Speed at Sea," *American Heritage* magazine, October 1955.

Whidden, John D. *Ocean Life in Old Sailing Days.* Boston, 1909.

Whipple, A.B.C. *Tall Ships and Great Captains.* New York: Harper & Brothers, 1960.

——— and the Editors of Time-Life Books. *The Clipper Ships.* Alexandria, Va.: Time-Life Books, 1980.

C. THE MERCHANT SHIPPERS

Adams, Arthur G. *The Hudson: A Guidebook to the River.* Albany, N.Y.: State University of New York Press, 1981.

Albion, Robert G. *The Rise of New York Port.* New York: Charles Scribner's Sons, 1967.

Astor, Brooke. "John Jacob Astor: From the Founder to the Foundation," *Seaport Magazine,* Fall 1983.

Augur, Helen. *Tall Ships to Cathay.* Garden City, N.Y.: Doubleday & Company, 1951. The Low family.

Barrett, Walter (pseudonym of Joseph A. Scoville). *The Old Merchants of New York City,* 3 vols. New York: Carleton, 1864.

Belson, Ezekiel Porter. *New York: Past, Present and Future.*

Bowen, C. W. *Lewis & Arthur Tappan.* New York, 1883.

Brooks, Elbridge S. *The Story of New York.* Boston: D. Lothrop & Company, 1888.

Campbell, George F. *China Tea Clippers.* New York: David McKay Company, 1974.

Churchill, Allen: *The Upper Crust: An Informal History of New York's Highest Society.* Englewood Cliffs, N.J.: Prentice-Hall, 1970.

Dictionary of American Biography.

Dodge, William Earl. *A Great Merchant's Recollections of Old New York, 1818–1880.* Valentine's Manual, 1921.

Ellis, Edward Roble. *The Epic of New York City.* New York: Coward-McCann, 1966.

Evans, Robert, Jr. *Without Regard for Cost.* Chicago: *Journal of Political Economy,* University of Chicago Press, 1964.

Floyd-Jones, Thomas. *Backward Glances: Reminiscences of Old New York.* 1914.

Forbes, Allan. *The Story of Clipper Ship Sailing Cards.* Worcester, Mass., 1950.

Forbes, R. B. *Personal Reminiscences.* Boston, 1878.

Gilder, Rodman. *The Battery*. Boston: Houghton Mifflin Company, 1936.

Goldstone, Herman H. *History Preserved: A Guide to New York City Landmarks and Historic Districts*. New York: Simon & Schuster, 1974.

Griswold, Frank Gray. *Clipper Ships and Yachts*. New York: E. P. Dutton & Company, 1927.

————. *House Flags of Merchants of New York City*. New York, 1926.

Heatter, Basil. *Eighty Days to Hong Kong*. New York, 1969.

Hone, Philip (Allan Nevins, ed.). *The Diary of Philip Hone*, 2 vols. New York: Dodd, Mead & Co., 1927.

Kouwenhoven, John A. *The Columbia Historical Portrait of New York*. Garden City, N.Y.: Doubleday & Company, 1953.

Laing, Alexander. *American Sail*. New York: Bonanza Books, 1961.

Low, William Gilman. *A. A. Low & Brothers' Fleet of Clipper Ships*. New York, 1922.

McCullough, David. *The Path Between the Seas*. New York: Simon & Schuster, 1977.

MacGregor, David R. *The Tea Clippers*. London: Percival Marshall & Company, 1952.

McKay, Richard. *South Street: A Maritime History of New York*. New York: G. P. Putnam's Sons, 1934.

Maddocks, Melvin, and the Editors of Time-Life Books. *The Atlantic Crossing*. Alexandria, Va.: Time-Life Books, 1981.

Minnigerode, Meade. *The Fabulous Forties*. New York: G. P. Putnam's Sons, 1924.

Morison, Samuel Eliot. *The Maritime History of Massachusetts, 1783–1860*. Boston: Houghton Mifflin Company, 1941.

Morris, Lloyd. *Incredible New York*. New York: Random House, 1951.

Rosebrock, Ellen Fletcher. *Counting-House Days in South Street*. New York: South Street Seaport Museum, 1978.

Schermerhorn, Gene. *Letters to Phil: Memories of a New York Boyhood, 1848–1856*. New York: New York Bound, 1982.

Simon, Kate. *Fifth Avenue: A Very Social History*. New York: Harcourt Brace Jovanovich, 1978.

Smith, Arthur Douglas Howden. *Commodore Vanderbilt*. 1927.

————. *John Jacob Astor*. 1929.

Smith, Rev. Asa D. *The Guileless Israelite*. New York: Anson D.F. Randolph, 1854. A sermon on the death of Joseph Brewster.

Somerville, Col. Duncan S. *The Aspinwall Empire*. Mystic, Conn.: Mystic Seaport Museum, 1983.

Spears, John R. *The Story of the American Merchant Marine*. New York, 1910.

Stokes, Isaac Newton Phelps. *The Iconography of Manhattan Island, 1915–28.*

Strong, George Templeton. *The Diary of George Templeton Strong, 1835–75,* 4 vols. New York: Macmillan, 1952.

Tappan, Lewis. *Life of Arthur Tappan.* New York: Hurd & Houghton, 1870.

Train, George Francis. *My Life in Many States and in Foreign Lands.* New York: D. Appleton, 1902.

Whitmore, George. "The Old Merchants House," *Seaport Magazine,* Winter 1983.

WPA Writers Project. *Maritime History of New York.* New York: 1941.

D. THE SHIPBUILDERS

Abbot, Willis J. *American Merchant Ships and Sailors.* New York, 1908.

Albion, Robert G. *The Rise of New York Port.* New York: Charles Scribner's Sons, 1967.

"The Builders of the Ship," *Harper's* magazine. Vol. XVIV.

Bradlee, Francis B.C. *The Ship 'Great Republic' and Donald McKay Her Builder.* Salem, Mass.: History Collection, Essex Institute, 1927.

Brouwer, Norman. "William H. Webb's East River Shipyard, and the Warship Built for the Czar," *Seaport Magazine,* Winter–Spring 1983.

Campbell, George F. *China Tea Clippers.* New York: David McKay Company, 1974.

Chapelle, Howard I. *American Sailing Craft.* New York: Kennedy Brothers, 1936.

———. *The History of American Sailing Ships.* New York: W. W. Norton & Company, 1935.

———. *The Search for Speed Under Sail, 1700–1855.* New York: Bonanza Books, 1968.

Chase, Mary Ellen. *Donald McKay and the Clipper Ships.* Boston: Houghton Mifflin Company, 1959.

Daniel, Hawthorne. *The Clipper Ship.* New York: Dodd, Mead & Company, 1928.

Dictionary of American Biography.

Fassett, F. G. (ed.). *The Shipbuilding Business in the U.S. of A.,* 2 vols. 1948.

Forbes, R. B. *A New Rig for Ships.* Boston, 1849.

———. *Forbes's System of Sails and Their Management.* Boston, 1869.

———. *Notes on Ships of the Past.* Boston, 1888.

Griffiths, John W. *Treatise on Marine and Naval Architecture*. London, 1850.

———. *The Shipbuilder's Manual and Nautical Referee,* 2 vols. 1855.

Jennings, John. *Clipper Ship Days*. New York: Random House, 1952.

LaGrange, Jacques and Helen. *Clipper Ships of America and Great Britain, 1833–1869*. New York: G. P. Putnam's Sons, 1936.

Laing, Alexander. *American Ships*. New York: American Heritage Press, 1971.

———. *Clipper Ships and Their Makers*. New York: G. P. Putnam's Sons, 1966.

Lane, Bruce M. and Lane, Gardner. "New Information on Ships Built by Donald McKay," *The American Neptune,* Vol. XLII, No. 2, 1982.

———. "The Flying Cloud," manuscript in Peabody Museum, Salem, Mass. An in-depth study of the clipper's construction.

LeScal, Yves. *The Great Days of the Cape Horners*. New York: New American Library, 1967.

MacGregor, David R. *Fast Sailing Ships: Their Design and Construction, 1775–1875*. Lymington, England: Heassner Publishing, 1973.

———. *The Tea Clippers*. London: Percival Marshall & Company, 1952.

McKay, Lauchlan. *The Practical Shipbuilder*. 1839.

McKay, Richard. *Some Famous Sailing Ships and Their Builder Donald McKay*. New York: G. P. Putnam's Sons, 1931. Richard McKay was Donald McKay's grandson.

———. *Donald McKay and the Ships He Built*. Boston: Charles E. Lauriat Company, 1925.

———. *South Street: A Maritime History of New York*. New York: G. P. Putnam's Sons, 1934.

Morison, Samuel Eliot. *The Maritime History of Massachusetts, 1783–1860*. Boston: Houghton Mifflin Company, 1941.

Morrison, John H. *History of New York Shipyards*. New York: William F. Sametz, 1909.

Park, Charles E. *The Development of the Clipper Ship*. American Antiquarian Society, 1929.

Sheldon, G. W. "The Old Shipbuilders of New York," *Harper's* magazine, Vol. LXV, 1882.

Smith, Melbourne. "The Baltimore Clipper," *Sea History,* Summer 1979.

Spears, John R. *The Story of the American Merchant Marine*. New York, 1910.

Underhill, Harold. *Deep Water Sail*. 1952.

————. *Sailing Ship Rigging*. 1956.

WPA Writers Project. *A Maritime History of New York*. New York, 1941.

E. THE SKIPPERS AND CREWS

Abbey, Charles. *Before the Mast in the Clippers*.

Adams, Charles Francis. *Richard Henry Dana: A Biography*, 2 vols. Boston: Houghton Mifflin Company, 1890.

Augur, Helen. *Tall Ships to Cathay*. Garden City, N.Y.: Doubleday & Company, 1951.

Bonyun, Bill and Gene. *Full Hold and Splendid Passage*. New York: Alfred A. Knopf, 1969.

Bowen, Frank C. *Sea Slang*. London, 1920.

Brouwer, Norman. "American Schoolships: Nineteenth Century Beginnings," *Sea History*, Spring 1984.

Buckley, Christopher. *Steaming to Bamboola*. New York: Congdon & Lattès, 1982. The merchant seaman then and now.

Carse, Robert. *The Moonrakers: The Story of the Clipper Ship Men*. New York: Harper & Brothers, 1961.

————. *The Twilight of the Sailing Ships*. New York: Grosset & Dunlap, 1965.

Clark, Joseph C. *Lights and Shadows of Sailor Life*. Boston: 1848.

Colcord, Johanna C. *Roll and Go*. Indianapolis, Ind.: Bobbs-Merrill Company, 1924. Chanteys and sailors' songs.

Copeland, Peter. "A Seaman Remembers South Street," *Sea History*, Summer 1983.

Creighton, Margaret S. *Dogwatch & Liberty Days*. Salem, Mass.: Peabody Museum, 1982.

Dana, Richard Henry, Jr. *Cruelty to Seamen*. 1837.

————. *Speeches in Stirring Times*. Boston: Houghton Mifflin Company, 1910.

————. *The Seaman's Friend*. Boston: Little, Brown & Company, 1844.

————. *Two Years Before the Mast*, Harvard Classics Edition. New York: P. Collier & Son, 1909.

Dictionary of American Biography.

Dillon, Richard H. *Embarcadero: Being a Chronicle of True Sea Adventures from the Port of San Francisco*. 1959.

————. *Shanghaiing Days*. New York: Coward-McCann, 1961.

Doerflinger, William Main. *Songs of the Sailor and Lumberman*. New York: Macmillan, 1951; revised edition, 1972.

BIBLIOGRAPHY

Gale, Robert Lee. *Richard Henry Dana, Jr.* 1969.

Gifford, Ann, and Greenhill, Basil. *Women Under Sail.* Newton Abbot, David & Charles, 1970.

Gosnell, Harper A. *Before the Mast in the Clipper.* New York, 1937.

Grant, Linda. *Seafaring Women.* Boston: Houghton Mifflin Company, 1982.

Greenhill, Basil, and Stonham, Denis. *Seafaring Under Sail.*

Gregory, Hugh McCulloch. *The Sea Serpent Journal.* Charlottesville, Va.: University Press of Virginia for The Mariner's Museum, Newport News, Va., 1975.

Harland, John. *Seamanship in the Age of Sail.* Annapolis, Md.: U.S. Naval Institute Press, 1984.

Hart, James David. "The Education of Richard Henry Dana, Jr.," *New England Quarterly,* March 1936.

Healey, James C. *Foc's'l & Glory Hole.* New York, 1936.

Hugill, Stan. *Sailortown.* New York: E. P. Dutton & Company, 1967.

Laing, Alexander. *American Sail.* New York: Bonanza Books, 1961.

———. *Clipper Ship Men.* New York: Duell, Sloan & Pearce, 1944.

Low, Captain Charles P. *Some Recollections.* Boston: George H. Ellis Co., 1905. One of the best of the captains' memoirs.

Lyon, Jane D. *Clipper Ships and Captains.* New York: American Heritage Press, 1962.

McCabe, J. D. *Secrets of the Great City,* 1865. Including sailors' boardinghouses.

Maddocks, Melvin, and the Editors of Time-Life Books. *The Atlantic Crossing.* Alexandria, Va.: Time-Life Books, 1981.

Men, Ships and the Sea. Washington, D.C.: National Geographic, 1962.

Mjelde, Michael Jay. *Glory of the Seas.* Middletown, Conn.: Wesleyan University Press for the Mystic Marine Historical Association, 1970.

Northrop, Lieutenant Everett H., U.S.M.S. *Florence Nightingale of the Ocean.* Kings Point, N.Y.: U.S. Merchant Marine Academy, 1959. An account of Mary Ann Patten.

Randier, Jean. *Men and Ships Around Cape Horn.* London, 1969.

Reisenberg, Felix. *Cape Horn.* New York, 1939.

Samuels, Samuel. *From the Forecastle to the Cabin.* New York: Harper & Brothers, 1887. The redoubtable skipper of the *Dreadnought,* the "Wild Boat of the Atlantic."

Schultz, Charles R. *Life on Board American Clipper Ships.* College Station, Tex.: Texas A&M University Press, 1983.

———. *Life on Board American Sailing Ships During the 19th Century.* College Station, Tex.: Texas A&M University Press, 1977.

Shapiro, Samuel. *Richard Henry Dana, Jr., 1815–1882*. East Lansing: Michigan State University Press, 1961.

———. "With Dana Before the Mast," *American Heritage* magazine, October 1960.

Spears, J. R. *Captain Nathaniel Brown Palmer*. 1922.

Tocqueville, Alexis de: *Democracy in America*, 2 vols. New York: Alfred A. Knopf, 1966.

Uhl, Robert. "They Got It All And They Ain't Too Holy," *Seaport Magazine*, Fall 1984. The Seamen's Church Institute, the floating chapels, etc.

Whidden, John D. *Ocean Life in Old Sailing Days*. Boston, 1909.

F. MATTHEW FONTAINE MAURY

Corbin, Diane Fontaine Maury. *A Life of Matthew Fontaine Maury*. London, 1888. Mrs. Corbin was one of Maury's daughters.

Hawthorne, Hildegarde. *Matthew Fontaine Maury: Trail Maker of the Seas*. New York: Longmans, Green & Company, 1943.

Lewis, Charles Lee. *Matthew Fontaine Maury, the Pathfinder of the Seas*. Annapolis, Md.: 1927.

Maury, Matthew Fontaine. *Explanations and Sailing Directions to Accompany the Wind and Current Charts*, 6th ed. E. C. & J. Biddle, 1854.

———. *The Physical Geography of the Sea*, 2nd ed. New York: Harper & Brothers, 1850.

Stein, Douglas. "Paths Through the Sea: Matthew Fontaine Maury and His Wind and Current Charts," *The Log of Mystic Seaport*, Fall 1980.

Weyland, John W. *The Pathfinder of the Seas*. Garrett & Massie, 1930.

Williams, Frances Leigh. *Matthew Fontaine Maury, Scientist of the Sea*. New Brunswick, N.J.: Rutgers University Press, 1963.

G. THE VOYAGE: *Flying Cloud* vs. *Challenge* (BESIDES CONTEMPORARY NEWSPAPER ACCOUNTS)

Boswell, Charles. *The America*. New York: David McKay Company, 1967.

BIBLIOGRAPHY

Cutler, Carl. *Greyhounds of the Sea,* 3rd ed. Annapolis, Md.: U.S. Naval Institute Press, 1984. Appendix 5 is an abstract of the *Cloud*'s log on her record-breaking maiden voyage.

Randier, Jean. *Men and Ships Around Cape Horn.* London, 1969.

Reisenberg, Felix. *Cape Horn.* New York, 1939.

H. CALIFORNIA AND THE GOLD RUSH

Asbury, Herbert. *The Barbary Coast.* New York: Alfred A. Knopf, 1933.

Bancroft, Hubert Howe. *History of California,* 6 vols. San Francisco: The History Company, 1887.

Bateson, Charles. *Gold Fleet for California, 1849–50.* Auckland, New Zealand, 1963.

Chidsey, Donald Barr. *The California Gold Rush.* New York: Crown, 1968.

Dillon, Richard H. *Embarcadero: Being A Chronicle of True Sea Adventures from the Port of San Francisco.* San Francisco, 1959.

Griswold, C. D. *The Isthmus of Panama and What I Saw There.* New York, 1852.

Howe, Octavius T. *Argonauts of '49.* Cambridge, Mass.: Harvard University Press, 1923.

Jackson, Donald Dale. *Gold Dust.* New York: Alfred A. Knopf, 1980.

Lewis, Oscar. *Sea Routes to the Gold Fields.* New York: Alfred A. Knopf, 1949.

———. *This Was San Francisco.* New York: David McKay Company, 1962.

McCullough, David. *The Path Between the Seas.* New York: Simon & Schuster, 1977.

McGlain, John B. *San Francisco: The Story of a City.* San Francisco: Presidio Press.

Rasmussen, Louis J. *San Francisco Ship Passenger Lists.* Colma, 1965–70.

Reisenberg, Felix. *Golden Gate.* New York, 1940.

Schott, Joseph L. *Rails Across Panama.* Indianapolis, Ind.: Bobbs-Merrill Company, 1967.

Taylor, Rev. William. *California Life.* London: Jackson, Walford, and Hodder.

Wright, Benjamin C. *San Francisco's Ocean Trade.* San Francisco, 1911.

BIBLIOGRAPHY

I. AFTERMATH

Duncan, Fred B. *Deepwater Family*. New York: Pantheon Books, 1969. The Afterword by Karl Kortum is especially good on the downeasters and other postclipper vessels.

History of Solano County. East Oakland, Calif.: Wood, Alley & Company, 1879.

Throckmorton, Peter. "The American Heritage in the Falklands," *Sea History*, July 1976.

Index

Able-Bodied seamen (A.B.'s), 140, 148
Adams, John Quincy, 92
Allen, T. H., 195, 196–197
Allison, Joseph, 44
Alsop & Company, 195, 212
Amelia Paquet, 176–177
America, 177
American Atlantic and Pacific Ship Canal Company, 54
American Revolution, 24
American Seamen's Friends Society, 341
American Ship, 239–240
America's Cup, 177
Andrew Jackson, 235
Andrews, Mrs. Thomas, 110
Ann McKim, 25–26, 27, 29, 30, 234
Archer, 249
Aspinwall, William, 21, 25
  Panama Railroad and, 53–54
  see also Howland & Aspinwall
Astor House, 45
Audubon, John James, 47
Aulick, John, 212
Australian Gold Rush, 221–222, 224, 242
Australian passage, 222, 224

Babcock, Charlotte, 110
Babcock, David, 109–110, 223
Baines, James, 237, 242
Baltimore clippers, 15, 25–26, 29
Beaufoy, Mark, 28
Bell, Jacob, 74

Benham, Calhoun, 203, 205
Bennett, James Gordon, 48
Birds of America (Audubon), 47
Birkenshaw, Fred, 152
  disciplinary action against, 188–189
  Douglass attacked by, 160, 161, 162
  injuries to, 189, 191, 206
  testimony by, 206, 211
  trial of, 201, 202–205
Black Ball Line, 101, 102, 237, 240
Bluff, Harry, 90
  see also Maury, Matthew Fontaine
Bolívar, Simón, 105
Boole, John, 73
bow design, 30
Bowditch, Nathaniel, 86, 88, 140
Brandywine, 86
Brenham, Charles, 194, 199–200
Brewster, Joseph, 84
Brown, John, 185, 201, 203, 211
Brown, Mrs. Charles, 110
brutality, acts of:
  on *Challenge* maiden voyage, 158, 159, 163, 184–186, 187, 189
  Challenge officers tried for, 201, 205–207, 210–211
  legal recourse against, 129–130, 132–133
  in *Two Years Before the Mast,* 131–132
Building of the Ship, The (Longfellow), 82–83
Bulloch, James, 244

California Courier, 198–199, 207
California Gold Rush, *see* Gold
    Rush, California
Cape de São Roque, Brazil, 94–95
Cape Horn passage, 56, 174
    by *Challenge,* 178–187
    by *Flying Cloud,* 173–175
    Maury and, 87–88
    Patten and, 111–112
captains:
    American vs. European, 97
    careers of, 100–108
    discipline by, 128–130, 131–132,
        137–138
    duties of, 98–99
    elitism of, 99–100
    wives of, 108–114
cargo:
    on *Challenge,* 149, 195–196
    express rates for, 222
    fluctuating demands for, 219–220
    see also tea trade
Carnes, Frank, 55–56
Carnes, Nathaniel, 55–56
casting the log, 154–155
Challenge:
    building of, 21, 22, 61, 64–69
    cargo of, 149, 195–196
    crew quarters of, 155–156
    design of, 24, 65, 221, 233
    Flying Cloud rivalry with, 149–
        150, 195
    Griswold brothers and, 51, 103
    launching of, 23, 84
    main cabin of, 162
    rigging of, 22, 34, 61, 69–72, 156
    size of, 70–71, 156–157
    subsequent voyages of, 212, 228,
        238–239
Challenge, maiden voyage of:
    Atlantic leg of, 151, 154, 158,
        159, 164, 178–179
    Cape Horn passage on, 178–187
    crew fatalities on, 211–212
    crew recruited for, 138, 148–149,
        152–153
    New York departure of, 147–148
    Pacific leg of, 187–190
    San Francisco arrival of, 190–195
    watch detail on, 152–154
chanteys, 125–127, 137
Charles Marshall, 240

China, immigration from, 41
China trade, 24–25, 37–38, 55–57
Chinchas Islands, 228
Christian missions, 133–135
circadian rhythms, 154
Civil War, U.S., 230, 244–245, 249
Clark, Arthur, 75, 119, 128–130,
    137–138
Cleaver, Richard, 159, 211
Cleaver, Thomas, 201
clipper ships, 14–15, 18–22
    captains of, 97–100
    costs of, 72, 81–82, 225, 227
    decline of, 227–231
    design of, 220–221
    medium, 229–230
    production of, 220, 222
    races of, 221–223
    rigging of, 69–70
    see also specific ships
Coghill, Alexander:
    alleged brutality of, 185, 201,
        203, 205, 211
    mutiny plot and, 161, 164, 189,
        201, 203, 205
    as second mate, 150, 152, 154,
        162, 180–181, 185
Collins, E. K., 33
Committee of Vigilance, 39, 193–
    194, 199–200
composite construction, 67
Condry, Dennis, 74–75
coolie trade, 228, 233
Cooper, James Fenimore, 46, 47
countinghouses, 49
Crane, James M., 198
Craven, Commander, 249
Creesy, Eleanor:
    Flying Cloud navigated by, 21, 84,
        109, 144, 173–175, 177
    navigational aids used by, 85, 96,
        140
Creesy, Josiah Perkins, 21, 81, 84,
    85
    background of, 83, 103–104
    crew's relations with, 104, 138,
        140, 146, 176, 248
    Flying Cloud maiden voyage and,
        109, 140, 143–147, 173–177
    later voyages by, 236–237, 248–
        249
    retirement of, 249

INDEX

crew(s):
  on *Challenge* maiden voyage, 138,
    148–149, 152, 153, 155–156,
    211–212
  discipline of, 128–130, 137–138
  on *Flying Cloud* maiden voyage,
    109, 138, 140, 148
  foreign sailors in, 118–119, 137
  illnesses of, 122, 125, 134–135,
    137, 184
  land activities of, 134–137
  legal advocacy for, 129–130, 132–
    133
  leisure activities of, 127–128
  living conditions of, 119–123
  recruitment of, 117–119, 137, 212
  working conditions of, 115–116,
    123–127
crimps, 118, 127, 134
Currier, Nathaniel, 44, 47
Currier, William, 74
Cutler, Carl, 19, 35, 64, 221

Daily Alta California, 195, 207–209
Daily Evening Picayune, 194
Dana, Richard Henry, Jr., 40, 130–
    133, 134, 202
Dana, Sarah Watson, 133
dance halls, 136
Dashing Wave, 235–236
Dauntless, 233
Dead Horse Day, 127
deck work, 124–125
Delano, Warren, 57
Democracy in America (Tocqueville),
    96
design, *see* ship design
dismastings, 143
Dix, Charles B., 247
Douglass, James:
  attack on, 160–162, 189
  Birkenshaw found by, 188
  brutality of, 151, 158, 159, 162–
    164, 184–186
  Cape Horn passage and, 180–181
  capture of, 200–201
  charges against, 197–198, 201,
    202
  hiring of, 150–151
  newspapers on, 207, 208
  San Francisco arrival of, 191, 195,
    196, 197
  self-protection by, 163–164
  testimony on, 203, 204–205, 206,
    211, 213
  watch detail of, 152–154, 159
  as witness, 204, 207
down-easters, 230, 231, 252
driftbolts, 67
dry rot, 66, 78
Ducks, 192, 193, 194
Dumaresq, Philip, 59–60, 246–247
Dunderberg, 240

Emerson, Ralph Waldo, 47
Empress of China, 24–25
Erie Canal, 17

Fabens, Samuel, 238
Fairfield, Calif., 251
Falmouth, 87–88
Fann, Fred, 250
Fell, Father, 134
Field, Cyrus, 246
Fillmore, Millard, 202
Fish, Preserved, 55
Flanders, Charles, 205
Floating Church of Our Savior, 134
floating jail, 193
flogging, 133, 162
Flying Cloud:
  building of, 60–61, 76–79, 81
  Challenge rivalry with, 21, 149–
    150, 190, 195
  design of, 20, 78–79
  dismasting of, 143
  launching of, 82–84
  sailing records of, 223, 227, 235
  size of, 221, 224
  subsequent voyages of, 190, 193,
    236–237, 248–249
Flying Cloud, maiden voyage of:
  Atlantic leg of, 143–147
  Cape Horn passage of, 173–175
  crew for, 109, 138, 140, 148
  New York departure of, 139–140
  Pacific leg of, 175–177
Flying Fish, 220
food supplies, 119–121, 179
Forbes, Robert Bennet, 78
forecastles, 122–123
Fraser, George, 36, 58
freight rates, 222, 229, 230
Fulton, Robert, 20

Gallagher, Michael, 152, 201, 211
"Gallus Meg," 136
gambling, 42
gangs, 192–194
George, 98
Glory of the Seas, 235, 243–244
Goin, Thomas, 119
Golden City, 238
Gold Rush (Australia), 221–222,
    224
Gold Rush (California), 18, 38
    population explosion from, 40–41
    San Francisco's inflation and, 41–
        42
    shipping trade influenced by, 56–
        57, 58–59
Goofty, Oofty, 135
Gordon, George, 57
Great Britain, shipping industry of,
    16–17, 37, 230, 247
Great Republic, 225–227, 235, 241
Great Southern Ocean, 224
Greeley, Horace, 48
Gregory, Hugh, 120–121, 123, 124,
    128
Griffiths, John Willis:
    background of, 26–27
    design theories of, 21, 27–29, 32,
        59, 61, 74, 239–240
    McKay influenced by, 73, 78–79
    Memnon designed by, 57
    Rainbow designed by, 30–31, 65
    Sea Witch designed by, 33–34, 36,
        65
Grinnell, Joseph, 55
Grinnell, Minturn & Co.:
    Flying Cloud owned by, 60, 61,
        81–82, 249
    formation of, 54–55
Griswold, Charles, 13, 22, 195, 199
Griswold, George, 50–51, 70, 103
Griswold, Nathaniel L., 50–51
Griswold, N. L. & G.:
    Challenge owned by, 22, 64, 72,
        138, 195
    history of, 49–51
guano, 228

Hall, Samuel, 59
hawsehole skippers, 104
Hayes, Jack, 200–201

Hayes, William, 37
Herald of the Morning, 235
Hill, George, 186, 203
Hoffman, Ogden, 201–202, 205,
    209–210, 211
holystoning, 124–125, 187
Hone, Philip, 16
Hornet, 223, 248–249
Hounds, 192, 193, 194
Houqua:
    captains of, 57, 105–107
    design of, 33–34, 105
    voyages of, 58, 234
Howland, William, 107
Howland & Aspinwall:
    Griffith's designs for, 26, 27–32
    Sea Witch of, 35, 37, 58
    steamship line of, 52–53
    Waterman hired by, 25, 251
hull construction, 67
Huntsville, 33
hurricanes, 158

immigration in California, 40–41
inflation, 41–42
Ino, 249
Intrepid, 110, 112
Ives, James Merritt, 44, 47

Jackson, Andrew, 246
Jackson, Captain, 93–95
"Jimmy Ducks," 120, 123
Jones, Cynthia, 102
Jones, Samuel, 102
Jones, Walter R., 237
Joshua Bates, 74, 75
juries for *Challenge* trials:
    press influence on, 209–210
    selection of, 202, 203, 205–206
    verdicts by, 210–211

keels, 66–67
keelsons, 67

Lafayette, Marquis de, 86
Laing, Alexander, 30
Land, John, 13, 31, 37, 199–200,
    212
launchings, 82–84, 225
lawyers, 129–130, 132–133
Leggett, John, 152, 205, 206, 211

Lessing, George (The Dancing
 Master), 153
 death of, 184–185, 211
 trial for murder of, 201, 202, 210
Lewis, George, 212
Lick, James, 42–43
lift models, 64–65
Lightning, 20, 241
Lincoln, Abraham, 244–245
living quarters, 122, 155–156
logbooks, 91
Longfellow, Henry Wadsworth,
 77–79, 82–83
Low, Abiel, 33, 52, 56, 59
Low, Ann, 33
Low, Charles:
 background of, 106, 109
 as captain, 57–58, 106–107, 109,
 234–235, 247–248
 on Palmer, 105
Low, Sarah Tucker, 109, 247, 248
Low, Seth, 52
Low, William, 33
Low, A. A., & Bros., 52
 Palmer and, 105, 227, 247
 Pook's ship design for, 59
 ships owned by, 233, 247–248
lumber, 62, 66
lynch mob, 199–200

McCartney, James, 201
McKay, Albenia Boole, 73, 80
McKay, Donald:
 background of, 63–64, 72–75, 80
 financial decline of, 241–244
 Flying Cloud built by, 60–61, 77–
 81
 Great Republic built by, 224–227,
 235
 ships built by, 21, 110, 143, 221,
 237
 Sovereign of the Seas built by, 221,
 222–223, 234
 Train's backing of, 74–77
McKay, Hugh, 107, 242
McKay, Lauchlan:
 background of, 72, 107–108, 242
 ships commanded by, 225, 226,
 247
McKay, Mary Cressy Litchfield, 80
McKay, Nathaniel, 242, 244

McKim, Isaac, 25, 26
Marine Hospital, 134–135
Marshall, Charles, 101
Marshall, James, 42
Mary Whitridge, 120, 235
Masten, William, 159–160, 161,
 162, 185, 204
Maury, Ann Herndon, 88
Maury, Matthew Fontaine (Harry
 Bluff):
 on Australian passage, 224
 on Cape Horn passage, 87–88,
 174, 184
 Civil War and, 244–246
 family life of, 85, 88–89
 logbook information collated by,
 90–93
 McKay recommended by, 242–
 243
 navigational writings by, 21, 84,
 85, 88–89, 93–96, 140, 144
 postwar career of, 245–246
 sea duty of, 86–88, 89–90
 U.S. Navy criticized by, 90
Maximilian, emperor of Mexico,
 245
Mechanics' Bell, 63
medium clippers, 229–230
Melville, Herman, 47, 130
Memnon, 57
millionaires, 51
Minturn, Robert, 55
Moby Dick (Melville), 47
models, 64–65
Monell, "One-Arm Charley," 136
Morison, Samuel Eliot, 11, 20
Morse, Richard, 162
mutineers:
 plot by, 163
 trial of, 201, 203–205

Napoleon III, emperor of France,
 41, 246
Natchez:
 rigging design of, 34
 sailing record of, 35, 36
 Waterman as captain of, 25, 26,
 31, 32, 102, 103
Nautical and Hydraulic Experiments
 (Beaufoy), 28
Naval Academy, U.S., 246

Naval Observatory, U.S., 92
navigation, 85–96, 140
Navigation Acts, 37
Navy, U.S.:
  Confederate vs., 245
  Creesy and, 249
  McKay and, 243
  Maury and, 88, 90–91, 93
  N. B. Palmer, 109, 234–235, 247–
    248
Neptune, rites of, 128
Neptune's Car, 110–113, 235
New American Practical Navigator
    (Bowditch), 86, 88
New England Society, 52
newspapers:
  Challenge trials covered by, 207–
    210
  in New York, 47–48
New Theoretical and Practical Treatise
    on Navigation, A (Maury),
    88–89
Newton, Isaac, 28
New York, N.Y.:
  as maritime center, 15, 44–45
  nineteenth-century culture in, 47–
    48
  saloons in, 135–136
  San Francisco vs., 39
  shipyards of, 61–63
  wealth of, 45–47
New York Herald, 48, 208–209
New York Journeymen Shipwrights'
    and Caulkers' Benevolent
    Society (NYJSCBS), 62–63
Nicoll, Alex, 201, 210–211
Nightingale, 228
Nisrop, John, 153
Northerner, 213, 214, 216, 217

oak, live, 66
Ocean Monarch, 76
Oriental, 37, 233–234
Oriental imports, 24
O'Sullivan, John L., 17–18
Ottinger, Captain, 191, 206

packet rats, 117
Palmer, Alexander, 105–106
Palmer, Nathaniel Brown:
  background of, 104–105, 109

Great Republic rebuilt by, 227
retirement of, 247
ship design by, 21, 32–34, 105,
    234
wife of, 109, 247
Palmer, Theodore, 105
pamperos, 144–145, 179
Panama, 50
Panama Railroad, 53–54, 230
Parker, Benjamin, 134
Patten, Joshua, 110–114, 235
Patten, Mary Ann, 110–115
Patterson, Hugh, 152
Paul Jones, 33
Pawpaw (Challenge crewman), 153,
    185–186, 201, 203, 211
Peabody, Joseph, 98
Pearson, Charles, 152–153, 159,
    201, 205
Physical Geography of the Sea, The
    (Maury), 245
Pickett, William, 74
Pilgrim, 130–131, 133
planking, 67–68
Polk, James, 53
Pook, Samuel Hartt, 59, 60
porcelain trade, 25
Practical Shipbuilder, The (McKay),
    107
prostitution, 42, 136

races, 221–223
railroads, 17, 21–22, 53, 54, 231,
    252
Rainbow:
  construction of, 30, 33
  design of, 30–31, 32, 34, 65
  disappearance of, 36–37, 233
  records set by, 31–32
Rapid, 111
Raymond, Henry J., 47–48
real estate, San Francisco, 42–44
rigging design, 22, 34, 61, 69–72,
    156
Ritchie, Archibald, 44, 103, 209,
    250, 251
Romance of the Seas, 110, 112–113

Sailing Directions (Maury), 84, 93–
    96, 144, 245
sailors, see crew(s)

Sailor's Guide to Health (Lowe), 112
sails, setting of, 141, 157
saloons, 135
Samuel Russell, 37, 57–58
Samuels, Samuel, 117
San Francisco, 251–252
San Francisco, Calif.:
  fluctuating markets in, 219–220
  Gold Rush influences on, 40–42
  lawlessness in, 192–194
  New York vs., 39
  real estate investments in, 42–44
  saloons in, 135
San Francisco Bay, deserted vessels
  in, 196–197
San Francisco Daily Herald, 197, 207,
  209
schooners, 69
screw propellers, 230–231
seamen, *see* crew(s)
Sea Serpent, 107, 120–121, 123, 124
Sea Witch:
  design of, 22, 34–35, 36, 65, 78–
    79
  sailing records set by, 21, 35–36,
    37, 58, 60
  sinking of, 233
  Waterman's command of, 35–36,
    103, 213, 250
sheer plan, 65
*Shipbuilder's Manual and Nautical
  Reference* (Griffiths), 239
shipbuilding:
  Longfellow on, 77–79
  process of, 64–69
  wood used in, 62, 66–67
ship design, 220–221
  Griffiths on, 27–30
  rounded vs. V-shaped hull in,
    33–34
  tea trade and, 24–25
  see also specific ships
shipping merchants, 51–56
shipyards, 61–63
Silliman, Benjamin, 88
Smith, George, 160–161, 162–163,
  204
Smith, Ralph, 163, 201
Smith, William, 30
Smiti, Jon, 153, 187, 201, 210, 211
"So Handy," 126

South Street (New York), 48
Sovereign of the Seas:
  construction of, 221
  design of, 20, 224–225
  sailing records of, 108, 222
  shipwreck of, 234
  Webb's challenge to, 222–223
Sparks (*Challenge* crewman), 212
speed, measurement of, 154–155
square-riggers, 69–70, 141–142, 240
Stag Hound, 76, 79, 81, 82, 234
steamships, 20, 21, 52–53, 230–231
Sterling, Cornelius, 159–160, 162,
  189
Sterling, John, 101, 103
Sterling, Robert, 253
sterns, design of, 29
Stevens (*Challenge* crewman), 201,
  203
Stewart, A. T., 46
stoves, shipment of, 220
Strait of Le Maire, 173
Strong, George Templeton, 46
studdingsails, 157
Surprise, 59–60, 177, 246
Sweepstakes, 222
Sword Fish, 216
Sydney Town, San Francisco, 192
Syren, 236

tacking, 141–143
tacks, shipment of, 219–220
tank tests, 28–29
tars, 119
Taylor, Edward Thompson, 133–
  134
tea trade, 24–25, 37–38, 52, 55, 56–
  57
Telegraph, 195
thievery, waterfront, 136–137
Thompson, Francis A., 130–132
Thoreau, Henry David, 16, 47
Tocqueville, Alexis de, 16, 97
trade routes, 25, 37–38, 222, 224
Train, Enoch, 74–75, 76–77, 82, 83
Train, George Francis, 76–77, 81–
  82
transatlantic voyages, 98
*Treatise on Marine and Naval Archi-
  tecture, A* (Griffiths), 78
treenails, 68

trial(s):
conflicting testimony in, 202–203, 206
for cruelty to the crew, 201, 205–207, 210–211
for mutiny, 201, 203–205
newspaper coverage of, 207–210
Two Years Before the Mast (Dana), 40, 130–132

unions, 62–63
United States:
maritime supremacy of, 16–17, 230–231
westward expansion of, 17–18

Vanderbilt, Cornelius, 54
Very, Samuel, 109
Vincennes, 86, 212

Wakeman, Edgar, 110
Wakeman, Mary, 110
watches, 152–154
Waterman, Cordelia Sterling:
husband's career and, 36, 108–109
last years of, 252, 253
marriage of, 35, 102–103
town named for, 251
westward journey by, 213–217
Waterman, Eliza, 100
Waterman, Robert H.:
bad temper of, 149, 155, 158
on *Challenge* brutality incidents, 212–213
Challenge captaincy assumed by, 22, 50, 103
charges against, 197–198, 201
on clipper ships, 21–22, 220, 231
crew selection and, 138, 150–151
crew's relations with, 151–152, 158–159, 164
death of, 252–253
disciplinary actions by, 101, 160, 161, 162–163, 178, 184–185, 186, 187
early career of, 100–102
mob evaded by, 13, 194–195, 199, 200
Natchez commanded by, 25, 26, 31, 32, 102, 103

newspapers on, 207–210
New York departure of, 147–148
personal background of, 100, 102–103
physical appearance of, 102, 147
real estate investments by, 43–44, 56, 250–251
rigging supervised by, 22, 34, 61, 69–72, 156
sailing tactics of, 157, 179–180, 184, 186
Sea Witch commanded by, 21, 35–36, 58, 103, 250
shore life of, 213, 249–252
testimony on, 204–205, 206, 211
as trial witness, 203–204, 206–207
wife rejoined by, 216–217
Waterman, Thaddeus, 100
water supplies, 121
Webb, Isaac, 63–64, 72–73, 107
Webb, William:
background of, 63–64, 73, 74
Challenge built by, 22, 23, 61, 64–69, 70, 72, 182
retirement of, 241
ships built by, 21, 81, 110
steamship production by, 240
Young America built by, 222–223, 240
Weldon, Charles, 186, 188
Wetmore, Mrs. William, 46
Wheeler, E. A.:
on deaths at sea, 182, 191, 211–212
published letter by, 208–209
on Waterman, 208, 251
on weather at sea, 154, 208
White, Thomas W., 90
Wilson, Joseph, 238–239
Wind and Current Charts (Maury), 84, 85, 93–96, 144, 245, 246
Winsor, Phineas, 111
wood for shipbuilding, 62, 66–67

Yerba Buena, 40
Yorkshire, 64
Young America, 223, 240
Young Men's Christian Missionary Society (YMCMS), 134

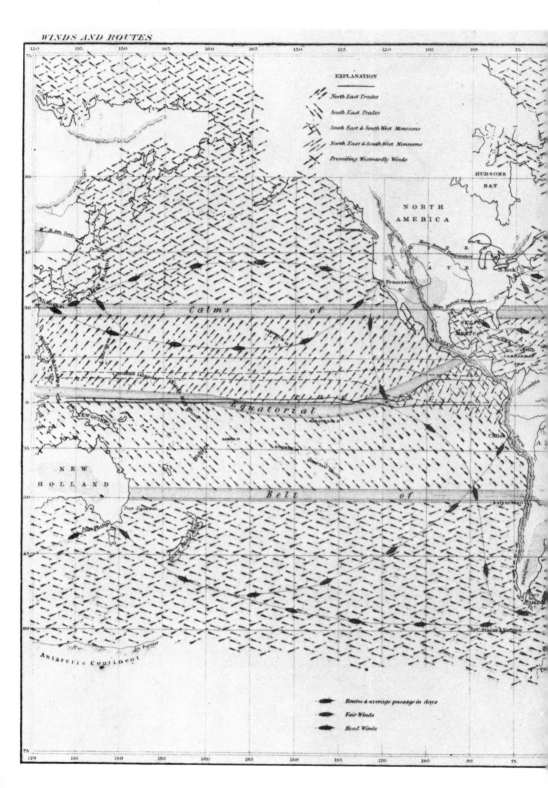